Organization CHARTS

Highlights

The second edition of *Organization Charts* contains the corporate structures of 200 companies and associations from around the world, including:

- Aerospace Corp.
- Beth Israel Hospital
- Credit Suisse
- Green Bay Packers
- Harrah's Entertainment, Inc.
- La-Z-Boy Chair Co.
- Nestlé S.A.
- North Limited
- PPG Industries, Inc.
- Sony Corp.
- Woodward-Clyde Companies

Companies are listed in alphabetical order, along with the source and date of the chart.

Companies of all types and sizes are represented, as well as corporations listed in various rankings (*Business Week, Forbes, Fortune*, etc.).

Features:

- Appendix containing company contact information
- Alphabetical index of companies and their affiliates and subsidiaries
- Standard Industrial Classification (SIC) Table
- Standard Industrial Classification (SIC) index
- List of companies in *Organization Charts*, first edition, 1992

Organization CHARTS

2nd Edition

Structures of 200 businesses and nonprofit organizations

Edited by John G. Maurer,
Judith M. Nixon and Terrance W. Peck

GALE

DETROIT · NEW YORK · TORONTO · LONDON

John G. Maurer, Judith M. Nixon, and Terrance W. Peck, *Editors*
Robert W. Beller, *Advisor*

Gale Research Staff:

Donna Craft, Jane A. Malonis, *Contributing Editors*

Carol T. Gaffke, Scott Heil, and Camille Pippen, *Associate Editors*

Donald P. Boyden, *Managing Editor*

Mary Beth Trimper, *Production Director*
Shanna Heilveil, *Production Assistant*
C.J. Jonik, *Desktop Publisher*
Assistance provided by: Marilyn Jackman

Gwen Tucker, *Data Entry Supervisor*
Beverly Jendrowski, Nancy Sheridan, Constance Wells, *Data Entry Associates*

Library of Congress Cataloguing-in-Publication Data
Organization charts : structures of more than 200 businesses and non
-profit organizations / edited by John G. Maurer, Judith M. Nixon,
Terrance W. Peck ; with a foreword by John G. Maurer.
  p. cm.
  Includes indexes.
  ISBN 0-8103-6446-8 (alk. paper)
  1. Industrial organization--Charts, diagrams, etc.
  2. Organanization charts. 3. Business enterprises--Charts, diagrams,
etc. 4. Nonprofit organizations--Charts, diagrams, etc.
  I. Maurer, John G. II. Nixon, Judith M. III. Peck, Terrance W.
  HD38.0738 1996   96-8231
  658.4'02--dc20   CIP

The paper used in this publication meets the minimum requirements of American National Standard for Information Sciences—Permanence Paper for Printed Library Materials, ANSI Z39.478-1984.

ISBN 0-8103-6446-8
Printed in the United States of America

10 9 8 7 6 5 4 3 2 1

Contents

Preface

Users of the second edition of *Organization Charts* have at their fingertips, in one easy-to-use source, 200 actual organization charts for active companies throughout the world. A wide variety of groups are included in this publication: for- and nonprofit, global and local, public and private, small and large.

Business professionals, corporate librarians, students, faculty, and researchers will find *Organization Charts* a useful tool when comparing companies within and across industries, when identifying key positions within an organization, when analyzing the span of control in corporations, when studying how competitive companies organize their activities, and when remodeling their own corporate structure after successful companies.

Compilation

Printed corporate organizational structures are difficult to obtain as many groups consider such information proprietary and will not authorize its release. The vast majority of the charts in the second edition came from the companies themselves. The editors contacted all of the companies on the following lists: *Business Week* 1000: America's Most Valuable Companies, *Forbes* 500: Largest Private Companies in the U.S., *Fortune* 500, *Fortune* Global 500, *Inc.* 500: The Fastest-Growing Private Companies in America. Many of the companies cited in these lists are included in this edition. (*Business Week* 1000: BellSouth Corp., General Electric Co., Exxon Corp., Hewlett-Packard Co. *Forbes* 500: Battelle Memorial Institute Corp., Sheetz, Inc., Long John Silver's, Inc. *Fortune* 500: Chrysler Corp., General Motors Corp., Xerox Corp. *Fortune* Global 500: Mitsubishi Corp., Mitsui Co. Ltd., Taiwan Power Co. *Inc.* 500: K.P.R. Sports International, Inc., Paria Group, Inc., ProMark One Marketing Services Inc.)

Additionally, companies representing a variety of industries and listed in *Ward's Business Directory* were contacted; and charts were pulled from annual reports at the Purdue University Library and through internet searches.

This edition includes 47 Japanese companies, reflecting the fact that Japanese companies comprised 30% of the *Fortune* Global 500.

All charts show some type of reporting relationship among position holders and/or divisions. This publication's primary intention is not to represent inclusive and up-to-date subsidiary and affiliate relationships.

Presentation

Using graphics software, editorial staff formatted charts to assist users in corporate structure comparison. Each chart lists the name of the company, the group's location if other than the United States, and the source and date of the chart. Some of the charts contain annotations to aid the reader in understanding what is represented.

Because *Organization Charts* is not intended as a source book for names of current position holders, and because names of such holders change frequently, only position titles have been listed. For some organizations, not all of the information provided could be included because of the extent of detail; in these cases, the editorial staff reproduced the charts as given up to a certain line of authority. Except for these changes, the collected charts reproduce as closely as possible the originals.

User's Guide

Arrangement. Charts are arranged alphabetically by company or association name.

Foreword. An essay by John G. Maurer, professor of business at Wayne State University, Detroit, discusses changes in the field of organization theory, the use and importance of organization charts, and analyzes specific charts listed in this edition.

Appendix. Includes contact information (address, phone, fax, etc.) for each company.

List of companies in the first edition of *Organization Charts*. A separate list of all companies whose charts were in the first edition. Those companies marked with an asterisk (about 30) are represented in the second edition.

Standard Industrial Classification (SIC) Table. The complete list of four-digit codes established and maintained by the U.S. government's Office of Management and Budget.

Standard Industrial Classification (SIC) Index. Contains the four-digit SIC codes and descriptors for each company. Aids the user in quickly identifying groups in specific industries and in comparing industries by type.

General index. An alphabetical list of all companies cited in the main body, including parent organizations and subsidiaries.

Comments Are Welcome

The editors welcome any comments regarding this publication. Please address correspondence to: Editor, Organization Charts, Gale Research, 835 Penobscot Bldg., 645 Griswold St., Detroit, MI 48226; or call, toll-free, 1-800-347-GALE.

Foreword

Organization charts depict, in a two-dimensional manner, how individual positions (jobs) are specialized and coordinated within a company or organization. The horizontal dimension describes "who does what," that is, the nature and degree of job specialization. The vertical dimension depicts how specialized positions are coordinated through authority relationships. Organization charts pictorially represent the essence of an organization's structure, namely, the specialization and coordination of jobs.

Brief History

David C. McCallum constructed the first U.S. organization chart in 1854 when he was appointed General Superintendent of the New York and Erie Railroad. McCallum's chart resembled a tree with roots (Board of Directors and President), branches (the five operating divisions and the freight and passenger departments), and leaves (e.g., ticket and freight agents, crews, and foremen). By 1910, organization charts were widely implemented by U.S. businesses, with DuPont and General Motors prominent among early adopters (Chandler, pp. 156-157).

Caplow notes that while organization charts are relatively new, the basic concept is very old. He traces the concept back to the Ts'in and Han dynasties in China, the Roman republic, the Prussian civil service, and the Venetian constitution (Caplow, pp. 50-55). Shafritz and Ott (pp. 11-28) provide an interesting chronology of organization theory from the fifteenth century B.C. to the present day. In 1491 B.C., Jethro advised Moses to delegate authority along hierarchical lines (Exodus xviii: 14-22). In 500 B.C., Sun Tzu's *The Art of War* emphasized the importance of hierarchical organization. In 1377 A.D., the Muslim scholar Ibn Khaldun introduced the concepts of formal and informal organization in *The Muqaddimah: An Introduction to History*.

The Horizontal Dimension

Specialization (also often referred to as division of labor or functionalization) divides each organization's primary task into smaller activities or components. Each box on the organization chart represents a position assigned to undertake a unique, detailed portion of the organization's overall mission. The organization chart of AlliedSignal Aerospace (p. 8) indicates that their overall task has been initially divided into fifteen different positions, represented by the boxes, which report directly to the President & CEO.

One way to understand specialization is to examine the chart of an organization as it grows from a one-person to a larger more complex organization (Scott and Mitchell, p. 38). See exhibit 1.

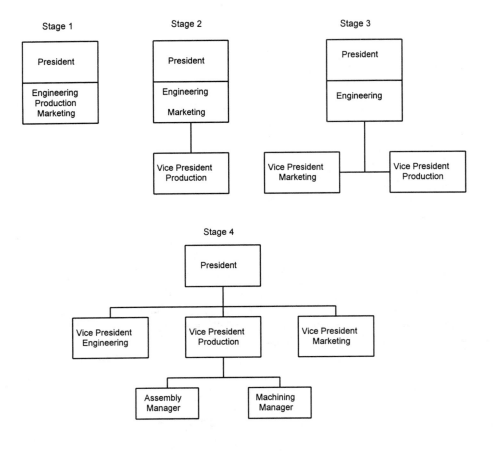

Exhibit 1

In Stage 1 of Exhibit 1, the President performs all of the organization's tasks, including engineering, production, and marketing activities. In Stage 2, as the sales and net income of the organization grow, the President hires more employees and begins to divide up the work. While continuing to perform engineering and marketing activities, the president specializes the production activity and places a Vice President in charge of it. In Stage 3, further division of labor occurs. Stage 4 depicts additional specialization with the creation of a third vice-president position. Notice how specialization results in the addition of organization levels. As we will see in the discussion of the vertical dimension, the President's job changes from primarily "doing" (Stage 1) to primarily "managing" (Stage 4), which includes the task of directing and coordinating the jobs of the three Vice Presidents (Stage 4). Note that in Stage 4 a third organizational level is created with the positions of Machining Manager and Assembly Manager reporting to the Vice President of Production. Job specialization, the horizontal dimension of organization design, also involves the grouping or departmentalization of positions. Positions can be grouped on a functional, self-contained unit, hybrid, or matrix basis.

FUNCTIONAL

The functional method of departmentalization groups similar positions necessary to produce and sell a product or service. For example, in a manufacturing firm the functions of Research and Development, Engineering, Manufacturing, and Marketing would each be placed in four separate departments, each department headed by a manager (perhaps a Vice President in a larger firm) who reports to the President. All of the positions associated with the manufacturing process would be placed under the control of the Manufacturing Manager. Stage 4 of Exhibit 1 depicts a functional structure.

Functional structures are typically used for smaller organizations employing simpler technology and operating in a more stable, less complicated environment (Daft, p. 204). Their major advantage is efficiency and the economies of scale which result from the grouping of specialists within each function who can then attain in-depth skill development (Duncan, p. 65). The major disadvantage of functional structures is the difficulty of achieving cross-department communication, cooperation, and coordination. There is a decided tendency for specialists within a functional department to focus on the pursuit of departmental goals rather than to cooperate with other functional departments in the pursuit of organizational goals (Robey, p. 186). These coordination difficulties may increase the organization's response time to environmental threats and opportunities, since problems or opportunities must first rise to a higher level in the organization where a position occupant has authority over two or more functional departments, which takes time. But even when the problem finds this "cross-over" point, the coordinating position occupant may be too distant from the problem to be of much help (Mintzberg, p. 59).

SELF-CONTAINED UNIT

As an organization becomes larger (more employees or participants) and more complex in terms of the number and/or types of products produced and markets served, there is a tendency for the organization to change from a functional structure to a self-contained unit structure. These self-contained departmentalization groups combines under a single manager, positions whose occupants are performing dissimilar functions, but who are focusing on: 1) a specific product or group of products; 2) a specific customer or customer/client group; or, 3) a particular geographic area (Schermerhorn, pp. 221-222). The Dana Corporation chart (p. 59) depicts a self-contained unit structure organized by five product groups. Structuring an organization by the use of self-contained units can be thought of as the disassembly of a large organization with a functional structure into a number of smaller "companies" (e.g., product groups or product divisions), each of which incorporates its own set of functional activities like manufacturing, marketing, etc.

Organization by self-contained units is typically used by larger organizations which employ more complex technology and operate in a more unstable and complex environment (Daft, pp. 206-209). Its major advantages are better coordination between and among functions within the self-contained unit and more intense focus on the product or service (i.e., a customer/client orientation) rather than primary focus on the processes involved in creating the product or service (Duncan, pp. 65-68). This improved coordination and product/market focus is associated with faster response time to environmental threats and opportunities. The major disadvantages of a self-contained unit structure lie within the reduction of the benefits in specialization provided by the functional structure, and the difficulties in achieving coordination across the self-contained units (Daft, p. 208).

HYBRID

A hybrid organization structure incorporates organization by self-contained units but also contains functional departments that are centralized and located at corporate headquarters (Daft pp. 209-213). Potlatch Corporation (p. 168) uses this type of structure. In this chart there are four self-contained product divisions (Wood Products, Northwest Paper, Pulp and Paperboard, and Consumer Products) as well as organization by function at the corporate level (finance, legal, public affairs, employee relations, planning and business development, and industrial relations).

A hybrid organization structure is typically employed by a large organization facing an uncertain external environment. A major strength of this structural type is that it retains the focus and coordination benefits of the self-contained unit structure and incorporates the benefits of specialization for certain functional areas, e.g., Research and Development, at the top of the organization. A major weakness is that the probability of conflict increases between managers in charge of self-contained units and those functional managers at the top of the organization (corporate level) whose role it is to advise and provide services to self-contained unit managers and their subordinates.

MATRIX

This type of departmentalization represents the simultaneous use or blending of both a functional structure and a self-contained unit structure. One feature of this structure is that some individuals may report to more than one supervisor. In Exhibit 2, engineers in cell 1, who are working on a certain project or product, will have a functional supervisor (engineering) and a self-contained unit supervisor (Product A Manager). Functional supervisors "are responsible for developing and deploying, in the form of skilled personnel, a technical resource. Project managers are responsible for project completion" (Bedeian, p. 209). The intent of this complicated structure is to achieve a balance of authority between product and functional managers, rather than permit either group dominance over the other. If the functional manager dominated, the product may be technologically superior, but may not meet the client's needs (delivery date, price, product features). If the product manager dominates, the customer's needs may be met, but the product may be technologically inferior, e.g., lower quality. The matrix is designed to force collaboration between product and functional managers. Note in Exhibit 2 that the Product A manager must work with three different functional managers, and that each functional manager must work with three different product managers.

Function ⟍ Product	FUNCTIONAL MANAGERS		
	Engineering Manager	Manufacturing Manager	Marketing Manager
Product A Manager	1	2	3
Product B Manager	4	5	6
Product C Manager	7	8	9

Adopted from Gibson *et al.*, p. 451

Exhibit 2

Three conditions cause an organization to consider using a matrix structure (Davis and Lawrence, pp. 11-24):

1.   Strong outside pressure exists for a dual focus on technology (functional groupings) and product (self-contained units). For example, to be effective in the aerospace industry, a firm must "focus intensive attention both on complex technical issues and on the unique project requirements of the customer."

2.   Pressure exits for high information-processing capacity. The matrix structure is designed to cope with information overload caused by rapidly changing and relatively unpredictable environmental demands. Reasonable responses to these complex demands requires the interaction of a large number of different individuals.

3.   Pressures exist for shared resources. The need for economies of scale in functional areas causes the firm to wish to retain the functional structure, while it adds a product structure. Functional specialists can be shared across self-contained units.

The major disadvantages of the matrix structure "lie in the confusion it creates, its propensity to foster power struggles, and the stress it places on individuals" (Robbins, p. 337). Confusion results from the dual command structure, while power struggles occur as functional and product managers wrestle for dominance.

The Vertical Dimension

The solid vertical lines which connect the boxes on an organization chart depict authority relationships. The occupant of the higher position has the authority to direct and control the activities of the occupant of the lower position. A major role of the vertical lines of authority on the organization chart is to depict the way in which specialized positions are coordinated. The Hewlett-Packard Company chart (p. 94) shows that the Computer Systems Senior Vice President has the authority to direct and coordinate seven General Manager positions. Authority flows in an unbroken line (the chain of command) from the President at the top of the organization to the first-line supervisor at the bottom of the organization. This chain of command also depicts the formal conduit through which formal information and communication flows. As a first approximation, directives flow from the top to the bottom of the organization; information about results flows from the bottom to the top.

Four major decisions must be made regarding authority:

1.   Management must insure that the occupants of positions who are being held accountable for the performance of certain duties have sufficient authority to accomplish them.

2.   Because there is a limit on the number of positions which one manager can supervise, management must decide the number of positions which should report to a single managerial position. This is referred to as the span of control or span of management. The Chrysler Corporation chart (p. 50) shows that the span of control of the Chairman and CEO is six, while the span of control of the President and COO is nine. A low average span of management will cause more levels of management to exist in the hierarchy. As the number of employees increases in the organization, the choice between increasing levels of management or increasing spans of management must be made (Child, p. 60).

3.   Counting from the top of the organization to the bottom, how many levels of arrangement will exist? The Bob Evans, Inc. charts (p. 35) show eight levels of management. Downsizing the organization through the removal of management positions will flatten the organization. This delayering will also result in less specialization (the managers who remain will have additional and different activities to perform) and their spans of control will increase (Gibson et al., p.445).

4.   How shall authority be distributed? Decentralization of authority refers to the systematic delegation of more authority to managers at lower levels in the organization. A self-contained unit structure provides the opportunity to delegate authority by granting product division managers considerable authority over their "smaller businesses" and holding them accountable for "bottom-line" results.

Line-Staff Structure and Conflict

Line authority refers to that authority which exists along the chain of command and which is dedicated to the achievement of the organization's primary objective. Staff positions provide information, advice, and services to line positions, and, in some cases, engage in control activities such as monitoring a line manager's compliance with the company's personnel policies and procedures. There are two types of staff: personal and specialized. Personal staff exists to support a single line manager. Representative titles of personal staff include Executive Assistant, Assistant to, and Administrative Assistant. The Executive Secretary to the Chairman in the Bethlehem Steel Corporation chart (p. 33) is an example of personal staff. Specialized staff supports all positions (both line and staff) which require its assistance (Gerloff, p.253). The seven positions depicted on level two of the Campbell Soup Company chart (p. 42) provide advice and services to the seven positions on level three of the chart.

Varying degrees of line-staff conflict may occur depending on whether the staff specialist has: 1) advisory responsibility (staff advises when requested; line managers may accept or reject advice); 2) compulsory staff advice (line manager must obtain staff advice, but need not accept it); 3) concurring staff authority (the line manager and the staff specialist must agree on the decision); or 4) functional authority (prior to making a decision in the staff specialist's area of expertise, the line manager must seek out and accept the advice of the staff specialist) (Gerloff, p. 253). In types 3 and 4, the line manager may receive "advice" from the staff specialist that not only may conflict with her/his personal judgement, but may also conflict with the directives of his/her immediate line superior and/or with the "advice" of other staff specialists. Attempts to minimize line-staff ambiguity and conflict take the form of using dotted lines on the organization chart to denote staff relationships, labeling staff positions on the chart (White, p. 37), and explicating the nature of the relationship in policy manuals which may accompany the chart (Famularo, p. 331; p. 351).

International Organization Structure

The international organization structure adds the issues of geography and cultural difference to the horizontal and vertical dimensions of organization structure described above. Phatak (pp.135-161) proposes that there are five stages in the evolution of the organization structure of international business firms.

Stage 1. Creation of an Export Department. If the company's product line is narrow, the export department manager typically reports to the marketing manager. If the product line is broad, she/he reports to the president.

Stage 2. The establishment of foreign subsidiaries. Manufacturing plants or service operations are located within the foreign country. Each foreign subsidiary manager reports to the president.

Stage 3. The formation of an International Division Staff. The International Division is headed by a senior executive who reports to the President. This position typically appears on the organization chart on the same horizontal plane on which domestic product division senior executives appear. The subsidiary managers report to the International Division's senior executive.

Stage 4. Departmentalization of the International Division. The International Division is departmentalized by product or geographic area. Product or geographic area managers report to the head of the International Division. Subsidiary Managers report to either the product managers or the geographic area managers.

Stage 5. The Global Structure. The emergence of a global structure parallels the change from viewing international operations as an appendage of the company to a view of the company as an integrated world-wide competitor. There are four possible global structures:

1.   The global product division structure: each of the previous <u>domestic</u> product division managers is given <u>world-wide</u> authority for his/her specific product group. Each product manager has line authority over all functional activities (e.g., finance, marketing) concerning her/his product division regardless of the country in which they are occurring (Daft, pp. 246-248).

2.   The global geographic division structure: the global market is divided into geographic regions or countries. The regional or country manager is granted authority over all functional activities for all products within his/her geographic area.

3.   The global functional division structure: each functional vice president, e.g., vice president of manufacturing, is given authority for her/his speciality across all domestic and foreign operations. As Phatak notes (p. 152), this structure is not commonly used by international firms because of coordination difficulties between and among functions in a given geographic area.

4.   The global matrix structure: operates two organization design variables simultaneously, namely, product and area. It has been adopted in order to solve problems that are caused by the unidimensional structures described immediately above. For example, in the global product division structure, two or more product managers will be operating independently of each other in the same country. While the global geographic division structure coordinates products within countries. In order to reduce the disadvantages of these two types, the global matrix structure is used. As Exhibit 3 shows, it blends location with product. This blending causes a dual authority structure to exist, e.g., the foreign subsidiary manager receives directives from two superiors: the Product 1 Manager and the Country A Manager.

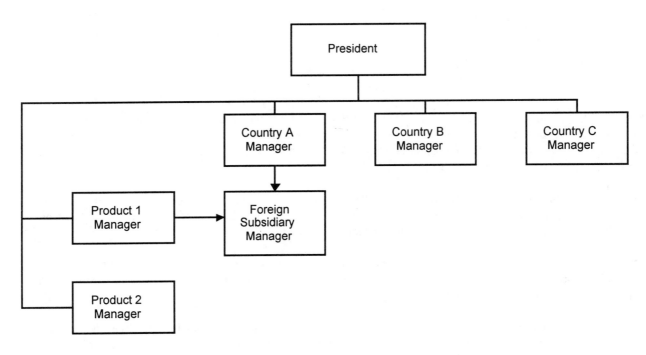

Exhibit 3

Contributions of Organization Charts

Since organizations are created to achieve specific objectives, it is important to identify which positions within an organization are responsible for which activities, and also to clarify relationships among those positions: who has authority over whom, and who has the authority to direct and coordinate which activities. Organization charts perform these functions. The major contributions of organization charts are as follows:

1.   They explain how the work of a position, department, or division connects with the work of other organizational subunits (Gibson *et al.*, p. 436), i.e., how the parts fit into the "big picture." The organization chart can be used to orient new employees or current employees in a reorganization, as well as explain the organization to outsiders (Albanese, p. 281). Some companies publish their organization charts in company magazines and in annual reports.

2.   They explain where the occupant of one position goes to solve a problem (Bedeian, p. 258).

3.   They depict the type of positions that exist in an organization, the number of management levels, the span of control, the bases for departmentalization, and the flow of authority, through the solid lines connecting the shapes.

4.   Engaging in the process of constructing the organization chart may be more valuable than the ultimate product. The process of drawing the organization chart may cause managers both to perceive and then to resolve latent division of labor and coordination problems, as well as to spot "potential sources of conflict or areas where unnecessary duplication exists." (Stoner and Freeman, p. 266). Excessive levels of management and problems in span of control may also be identified.

5.   Organization charts may serve very specific functions. Financial institution regulators may expect to see an organization chart that depicts the relationship of an institutions's compliance activity to other units of the institution. Organization charts are often required as part of a company's loan proposal or business plan.

Disadvantages of Organization Charts

Very rational managerial actions often result in unintended consequences. The design and use of an organization chart is no exception. Robert Townsend, the former president of Avis Rent-A-Car and the author of *Up the Organization* and *Further Up the Organization*, believes that organization charts are demoralizing to the organization because they tend to imply that higher positions are more important than lower positions in achieving the organization's mission. Some executives argue that organization charts tend to reduce teamwork, give individuals "occupying a rectangle" too strong a feeling of ownership, and make it more difficult to change the organization's structure (Koontz *et al.*, p. 259).

Among the major disadvantages of organization charts are:

1. They do not depict the informal organization. The formal organization is pre-planned and prescribes tasks and relationships of authority. Dalton (p. 18) refers to the organization chart as an optimistic chart of expectations about relationships. The informal organization is an emergent phenomenon. It arises "spontaneously as people associate with one another" (Davis and Newstrom, p. 308). Because organization designers are neither clairvoyant nor omniscient, they cannot construct in advance an organization structure that can anticipate all future contingencies, especially for an organization coping with an unstable and unpredictable external environment. The emergence of an informal organization, consisting of vertical, horizontal, and diagonal interactions and communications outside the formal lines of authority, is essential to the effective functioning of the organization. Also, organizational charts do not capture informal power arrangements, such as the development of dominant coalitions of top-level managers who coalesce to set the agenda of the organization (Hall, pp. 112-129). Nor do they depict the formulation and operation of middle-level management informal cliques (Dalton, pp. 52-65).

2. They do not reflect the operation of officially-prescribed horizontal linkages such as: direct contact between managers across departmental boundaries; liaison roles; task forces; committees; and, full-time integrators (Daft, pp. 195-200). While a task force tends to be a temporary lateral linkage, "the standarding committee is a more permanent interdepartmental grouping, one that meets regularly to discuss issues of common interest" (Mintzberg, p.83). Organization charts may identify the members of standing committees by placing asterisks in various rectangles, with the title of the committee footnoted on the bottom of the page on which the chart appears. Effective horizontal linkages are vital for an organization that is characterized by a high degree of job specialization.

3. They may cause the reader to make faulty inferences about the amount of formal authority or the amount of influence a given position occupant possesses. In the former case, one may incorrectly infer the amount of formal authority a position occupant possesses by the distance of his/her "rectangle" from the President's (Gary and Smeltzer, p. 345). In the latter case, the rectangles of two position occupants may be the same distance from the President's (i.e., they may lie on the same horizontal plane) and they may, in fact, enjoy roughly equivalent amounts of formal authority, but one position occupant may be considerably more influential than the other. This may occur because she/he possesses greater power. This power may result from better conceptual, administrative, or social skills (including charisma).

4. They may cause managers to adopt an overly narrow view of the required duties and interactions of their positions. Managers may be reluctant to engage in creative or proactive activities and interactions which are not sanctioned by the formal cain of command (Gibson *et al.*, p. 437).

5.   Organization charts may supply competitors with strategic information by providing some indication about the relative status of the various functional areas and the coordination and emphasis that are deemed strategically important. For example, if the sales department is headed by a senior vice-president who reports directly to the president, it is an indication that sales is more influential than manufacturing, if manufacturing is headed by a director who reports to the senior vice-president for administration (Porter, p. 52 and p. 55).

6.   Many organization charts become outdated while they are being reproduced and distributed. This is especially true for organizations adapting to high rates of technological and environmental change.

The Pyramid and Other Shapes

Organization charts tend to be depicted as pyramidical in shape with authority delegated from the top position down the hierarchy to the first-line supervisor. If organizations were perfectly pyramidical, the drawing of a horizontal line across the organization chart at any level would result in a larger number of positions below the line than above the line. Few organizations are perfectly pyramidical. For example, some are diamond-shaped, with more of the positions concentrated at the middle levels (Caplow, pp. 58-59).

Some organizations choose to depict the organizational pyramid sideways on the page. See the All Nippon Airways, Co., Ltd. (Japan) chart on page 4. There appear to be three reasons for this. First, this represents an attempt to reduce symbolically the emphasis on top-down authority relationships depicted in the traditional chart. Second, the rank or status differences between and among positions are more obscured. Third, if the use of rectangles is eliminated in favor of a title only, a more complete picture of a complex organization can be captured on a single page.

Some organizations invert the pyramid to emphasize the primary importance of the workers' contributions to the success of the organization. Placing managers below the workers on the chart is designed to signal the manager's primary role of support for those who are performing the work of the organization. Some inverted-pyramid charts place the customer at the very top in order to symbolically underscore the importance of an organization-wide marketing orientation. See the Invetech Company chart on page 97. A few organizations reject the pyramidical shape in favor of a circular or concentric chart (see Atmosphere Processing, Inc. on page 12). As with the "sideways pyramid," this chart seeks to obscure rank or status differences and to de-emphasize top-down authority relationships. In addition, it appears designed to evoke a systems view of the organization, i.e., that an effective organization relies heavily on horizontal relationships between and among positions, in addition to the vertical authority relationships depicted on the more traditional pyramidical organization chart. In some charts the perimeter positions are connected in order to emphasize these horizontal linkages.

Are Organization Charts Obsolete?

The increased attention given to new developments in structuring organizations may lead one to think that traditional organization charts are passé. These new and important developments include delayering, decentralization, re-engineering, teams, horizontal linkages, the boundary-less organization, virtual or modular organizations, empowerment, networking, etc. Mills' (1991) cluster organization with its concentric, tangential, and interlocking circles and Quinn's (1992) spider's-web organization are representative of the new organizational pictograms. Both models embody a reduced emphasis on authority-based relationships and increased emphasis on horizontal relationships.

While a myriad of complex and innovative relationships such as cross-functional teams, are occurring in the white space of conventional organization charts, it is doubtful whether their depiction will replace the traditional chart. Many managers, when asked to describe their organizations, still produce organization charts. Those in organizations with no formal charts are able to draw them rather easily. The box-and-line charts continue to serve the dual functions of depicting "who does what" and "who reports to whom."

Schoonhoven and Jelinek (1990) provide empirical support for the chart's viability. In their seven-year study of five large and highly innovative U.S. electronic firms (Intel, National Semiconductor, Texas Instruments, Hewlett-Packard and Motorola Semiconductor), they found that all "...had explicit organizational charts readily available and formalized from the top to the bottom of their companies." These charts depicted well-articulated organization structures, definite and explicit reporting relationships, and clear job titles and responsibilities. At the same time, the researchers found that these progressive companies engaged in frequent reorganization and used "quasi-formal structures" like committees, task forces, and teams.

The publication of some of these innovative, structural relationships in a very small number of company magazines and annual reports may signal the potential emergence of these new pictograms as supplements to rather than replacements for the traditional organization chart.

Conclusion

Because there is no one best way to design an organization structure, there can be no one best organization chart. Contemporary managers take a contingency approach to the design of organization structures. This means that their task is to design an organization structure that is congruent with the organization's contextual dimensions, namely size, technology, environment, goals, strategy, and culture (Daft, pp. 15-25). There are numerous organizational life cycle models which analyze the types of structural changes that must occur over time as changes occur in these six contextual dimensions (Scott, pp. 177-178). Finally, because organization charts provide only a skeletal depiction of an organization's structure, they should be used in conjunction with written job descriptions and formal policy and procedure statements. These additional documents can identify potential structural problems as well as provide guidelines for their solution, e.g., line-staff relationships (Famularo, pp. 187-194 and 315-361).

References

Albanese, Robert. *Management* (Cincinnati, Ohio: South-Western, 1988).

Bedeian, Arthur G. *Management* (New York: The Dryden Press, 1989).

Caplow, Theodore. *Principles of Organization* (New York: Harcourt, Brace & World, 1964).

Chandler, Jr., Alfred D. "Origins of the Organization Chart" *Harvard Business Review*, 66, March-April, 1988, pp. 156-157.

Chermerhorn, Jr., John R. *Management* (New York: Wiley, 1996).

Child, John. *Organization: A Guide to Problems and Practice* (London: Harper & Row, 1984).

Daft, Richard L. *Organization Theory and Design* (St. Paul, MN: West Publishing, 1995).

Dalton, Melville. *Men Who Manage* (New York: Wiley, 1959).

Davis, Keith, and Newstrom, J. *Human Behavior at Work* (New York: McGraw-Hill, 1985).

Davis, Stanley M., and Lawrence, Paul R. *Matrix* (Reading, Mass.: Addison-Wesley Publishing, 1977).

Duncan, Robert. "What is the Right Organization Structure?" *Organization Dynamics*, Winter, 1979, pp. 59-80.

Famulro, Joseph J. *Organization Planning Manual* (New York: Amacom, 1979).

Gerloff, Edwin A. *Organization Theory and Design* (New York: McGraw-Hill, 1985).

Gibson, James L., Ivancevich, John M., and Donnelly, Jr., James H. *Organizations* (Homewood, IL: Irwin, 1991).

Gray, Edmund R., and Smeltzer, Larry R. *Management: The Competitive Edge* (New York: MacMillan, 1989).

Hall, Richard H. *Organizations* (Englewood Cliffs, N.J.: Prentice Hall, 1996).

Koontz, Harold, O'Donnell, Cyril, and Weihrich, Heinz. *Essentials of Management* (New York: McGraw-Hill, 1986).

Mills, D. Quinn. *Rebirth of the Corporation* (New York: Wiley, 1991).

Mintzberg, Henry. *Structure in Fives: Designing Effective Organizations* (Englewood Cliffs, NJ.: Prentice-Hall, 1993).

Phatak, Arvind V. *International Dimensions of Management* (Boston: PWS-Kent, 1992).

Porter, Michael E. *Competitive Strategy* (New York: The Free Press, 1980).

Quinn, James B. *Intelligent Enterprise* (New York: The Free Press, 1992).

Robey, Daniel and Sales, Carol A. *Designing Organizations* (Homewood, IL: Irwin, 1994).

Robbins, Stephen P. *Organization Theory* (Englewood Cliffs, N.J.: Prentice Hall, 1990).

Schoonhoven, Claudia B., and Jelinek, Mariann. "Dynamic Tension in Innovative, High Technology Firms: Making Rapid Change Through Organization Structure" in *Managing Complexity in High Technology Organizations*, edited by M.A. Von Glinow and S.A. Mohrman, pp. 90-118 (New York: Oxford University Press, 1990).

Scott, W. Richard. *Organizations* (Englewood Cliffs, N.J.: Prentice-Hall, 1992).

Scott, William G., and Mitchell, Terence R. *Organization Theory* (Homewood, IL: Irwin-Dorsey, 1972).

Shafritz, Jay M. And Ott, J. Steven. *Classics of Organization Theory* (Pacific Grove, CA: Brooks/Cole, 1996).

Toner, James A.F., and Freeman, R. Edward. *Management* (Englewood Cliffs, N.J.: Prentice-Hall, 1989).

White, K.K. *Understanding the Company Organization Chart* (New York: American Management Association, 1963).

Professor John G. Maurer
School of Business Administration
Wayne State University
Detroit, Michigan

Organization CHARTS

ABB Asea Brown Boveri Ltd. (Switzerland)
Source: ABB Asea Brown Boveri Ltd., 1996

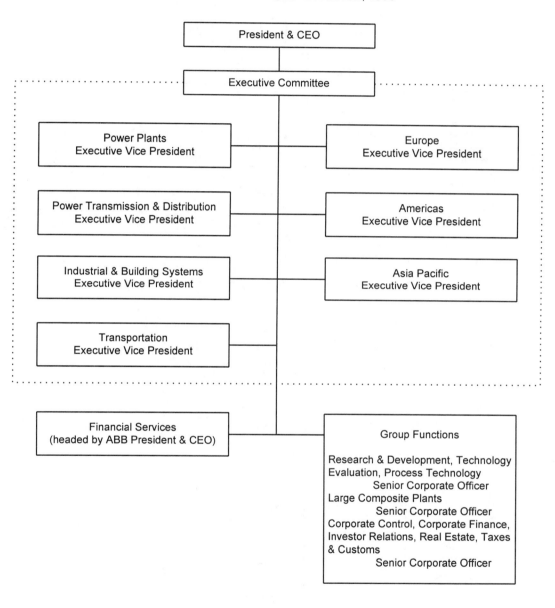

Adventist Health System - West

Source: Adventist Health System West, 1996

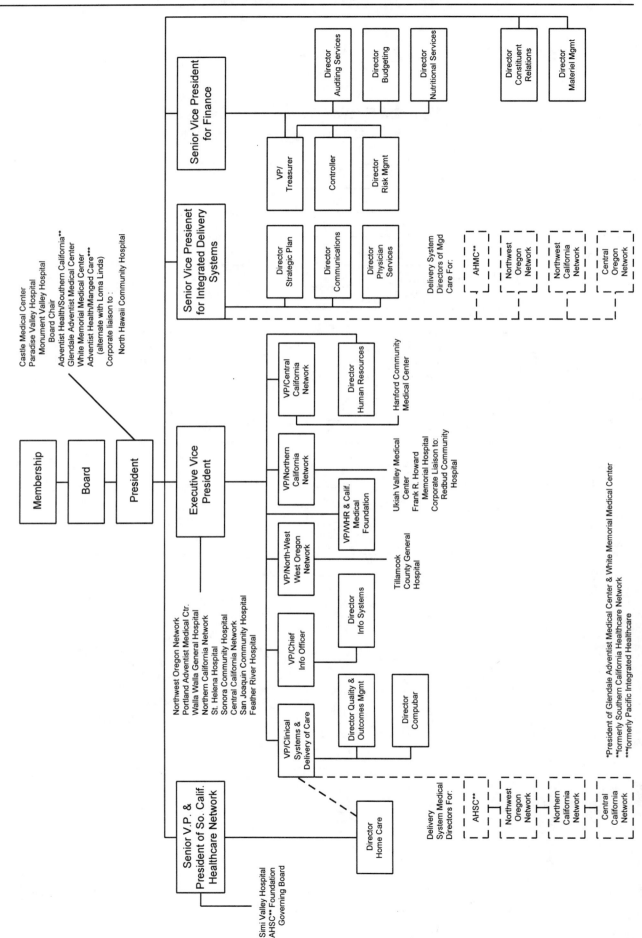

The Aerospace Corporation

Source: The Aerospace Corporation, 1996

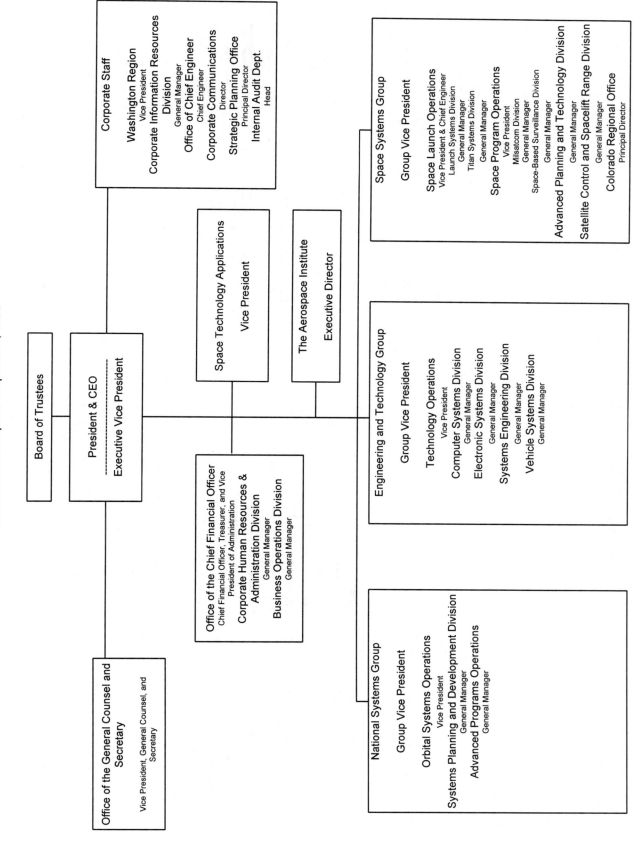

Board of Trustees

President & CEO
Executive Vice President

Office of the General Counsel and Secretary
Vice President, General Counsel, and Secretary

Corporate Staff

Washington Region
Vice President
Corporate Information Resources Division
General Manager
Office of Chief Engineer
Chief Engineer
Corporate Communications
Director
Strategic Planning Office
Principal Director
Internal Audit Dept.
Head

Space Technology Applications
Vice President

The Aerospace Institute
Executive Director

Office of the Chief Financial Officer
Chief Financial Officer, Treasurer, and Vice President of Administration
Corporate Human Resources & Administration Division
General Manager
Business Operations Division
General Manager

Space Systems Group
Group Vice President

Space Launch Operations
Vice President & Chief Engineer
Launch Systems Division
General Manager
Titan Systems Division
General Manager
Space Program Operations
Vice President
Milsatcom Division
General Manager
Space-Based Surveillance Division
General Manager
Advanced Planning and Technology Division
General Manager
Satellite Control and Spacelift Range Division
General Manager
Colorado Regional Office
Principal Director

Engineering and Technology Group
Group Vice President

Technology Operations
Vice President
Computer Systems Division
General Manager
Electronic Systems Division
General Manager
Systems Engineering Division
General Manager
Vehicle Systems Division
General Manager

National Systems Group
Group Vice President

Orbital Systems Operations
Vice President
Systems Planning and Development Division
General Manager
Advanced Programs Operations
General Manager

All Nippon Airways Co., Ltd. (Japan)
General Administration

Source: All Nippon Airways Co., Ltd., 1996

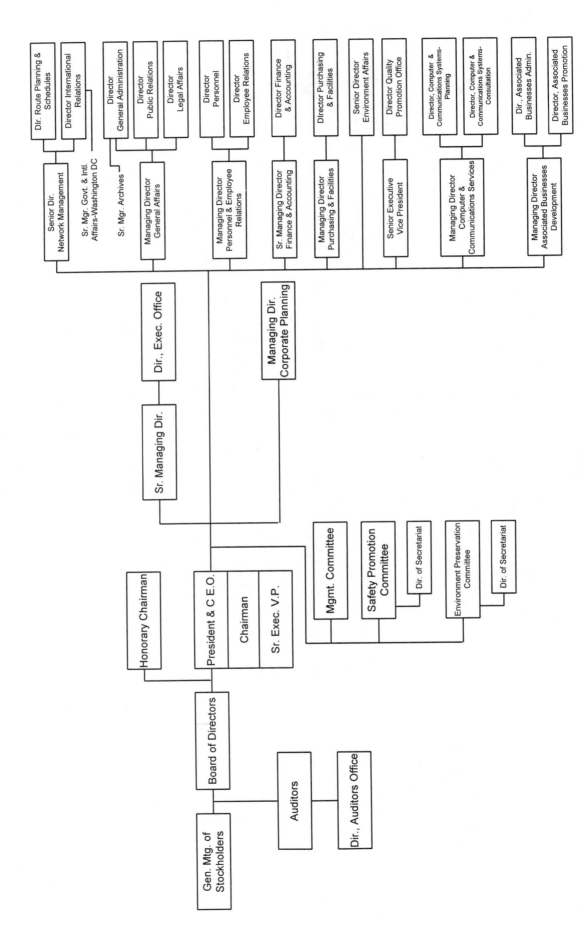

All Nippon Airways Co., Ltd. (Japan)
Tokyo Office

Source: All Nippon Airways Co., Ltd., 1996

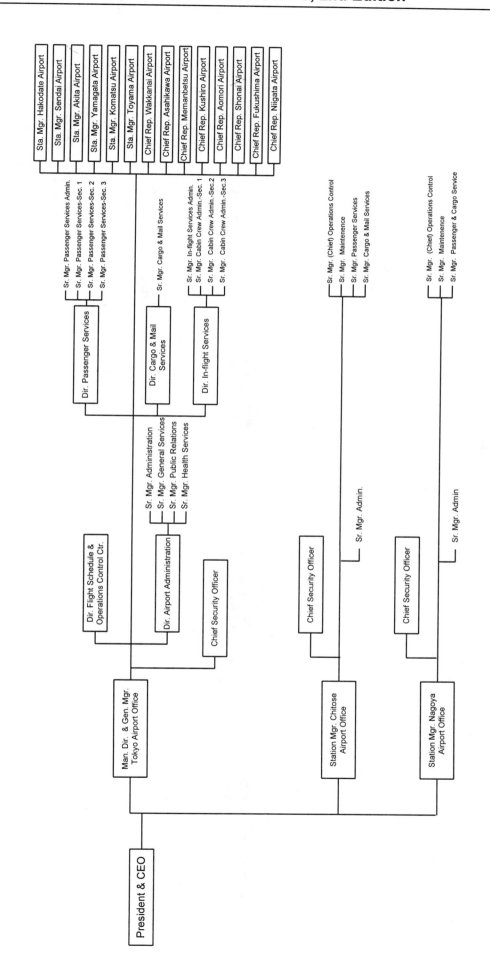

Alliant Health System

Source: Alliant Health System, 1996

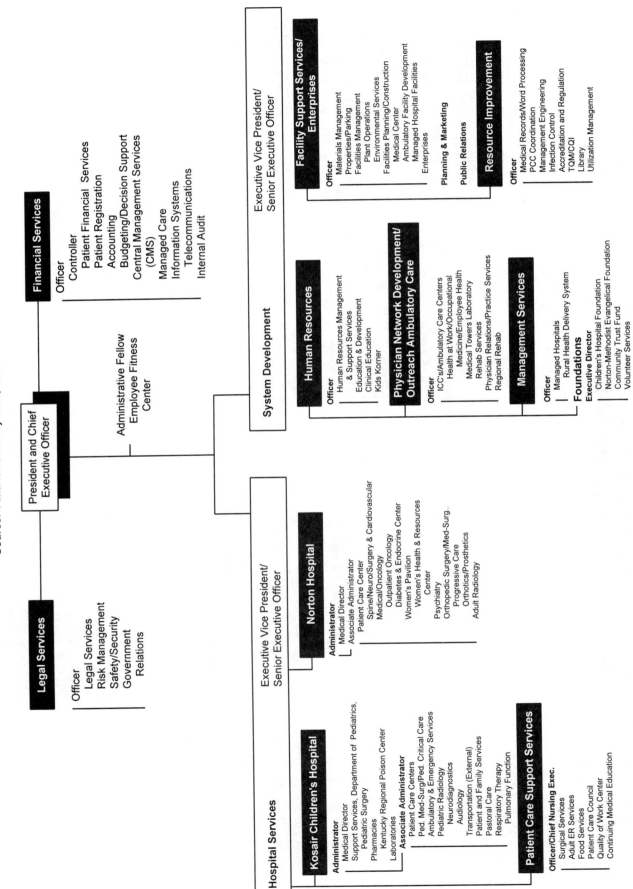

President and Chief Executive Officer

Administrative Fellow
Employee Fitness Center

Legal Services

Officer
Legal Services
Risk Management
Safety/Security
Government Relations

Financial Services

Officer
Controller
Patient Financial Services
Patient Registration
Accounting
Budgeting/Decision Support
Central Management Services (CMS)
Managed Care
Information Systems
Telecommunications
Internal Audit

Executive Vice President/ Senior Executive Officer

Facility Support Services/ Enterprises

Officer
Materials Management
Properties/Parking
Facilities Management
Plant Operations
Environmental Services
Facilities Planning/Construction
Medical Center
Ambulatory Facility Development
Managed Hospital Facilities
Enterprises

Planning & Marketing

Public Relations

Resource Improvement

Officer
Medical Records/Word Processing
PCC Coordination
Management Engineering
Infection Control
Accreditation and Regulation
TQM/CQI
Library
Utilization Management

System Development

Human Resources

Officer
Human Resources Management & Support Services
Education & Development
Clinical Education
Kids Korner

Physician Network Development/ Outreach Ambulatory Care

Officer
ICC's/Ambulatory Care Centers
Health at Work/Occupational
Medicine/Employee Health
Medical Towers Laboratory
Rehab Services
Physician Relations/Practice Services
Regional Rehab

Management Services

Officer
Managed Hospitals
Rural Health Delivery System

Foundations

Executive Director
Children's Hospital Foundation
Norton-Methodist Evangelical Foundation
Community Trust Fund
Volunteer Services

Executive Vice President/ Senior Executive Officer

Hospital Services

Norton Hospital

Administrator
Medical Director
Associate Administrator
Patient Care Center
Spine/Neuro/Surgery & Cardiovascular
Medical/Oncology
Outpatient Oncology
Diabetes & Endocrine Center
Women's Pavilion
Women's Health & Resources Center
Psychiatry
Orthopedic Surgery/Med-Surg.
Progressive Care
Orthotics/Prosthetics
Adult Radiology

Kosair Children's Hospital

Administrator
Medical Director
Support Services, Department of Pediatrics,
Pediatric Surgery
Pharmacies
Kentucky Regional Poison Center
Laboratories

Associate Administrator
Patient Care Centers
Ped. Med-Surg/Ped. Critical Care
Ambulatory & Emergency Services
Pediatric Radiology
Neurodiagnostics
Audiology
Transportation (External)
Patient and Family Services
Pastoral Care
Respiratory Therapy
Pulmonary Function

Patient Care Support Services

Officer/Chief Nursing Exec.
Surgical Services
Adult ER Services
Food Services
Patient Care Council
Quality of Work Center
Continuing Medical Education

Allianz AG Holdings (Germany)

Source: Allianz AG Holdings, 1996

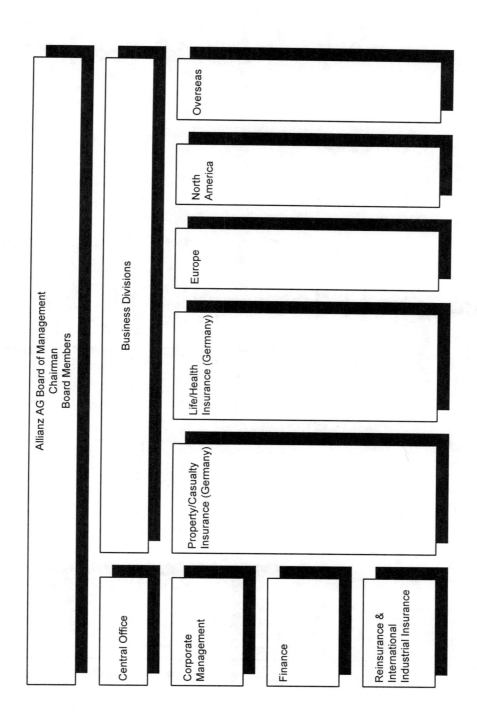

Allianz AG Board of Management
Chairman
Board Members

Business Divisions

Overseas

North America

Europe

Life/Health Insurance (Germany)

Property/Casualty Insurance (Germany)

Central Office

Corporate Management

Finance

Reinsurance & International Industrial Insurance

Each board member is responsible for one or more central offices/business divisions. The chairman serves as "first among equals."

AlliedSignal Aerospace

Source: AlliedSignal Aerospace, 1996

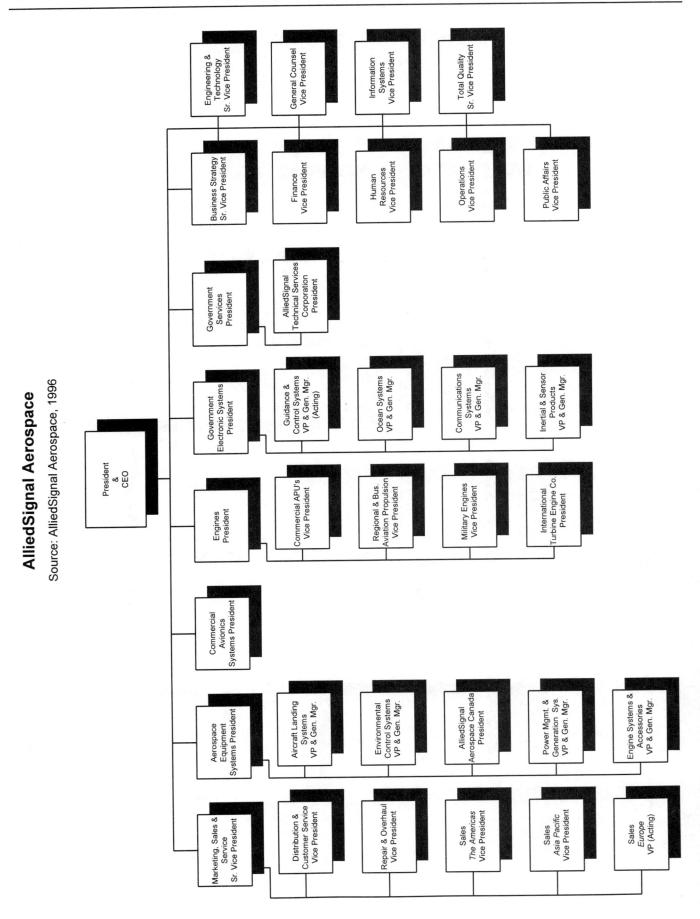

Asahi Chemical Industry Co., Ltd. (Japan)

Source: Annual report, 1995

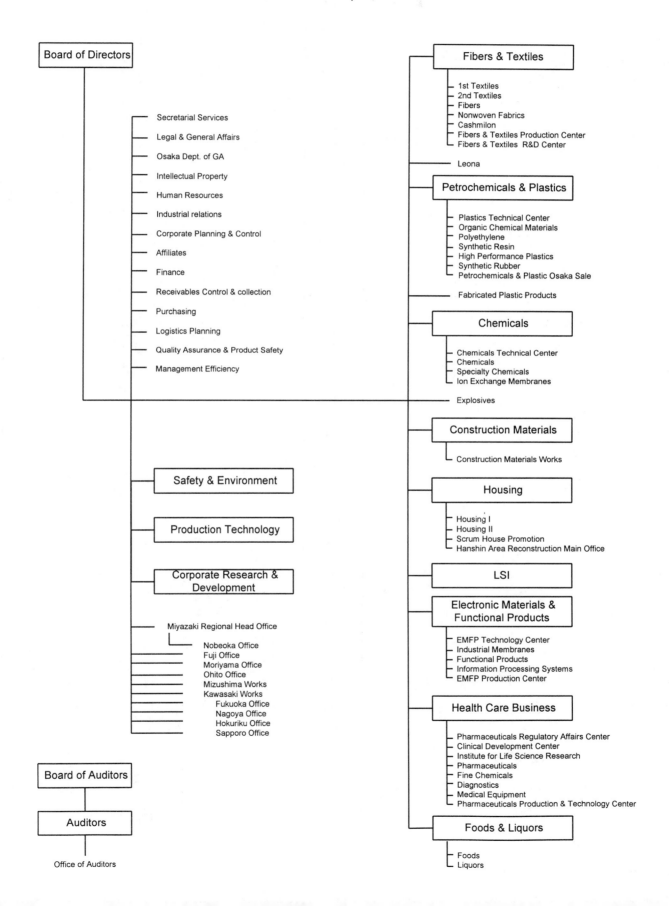

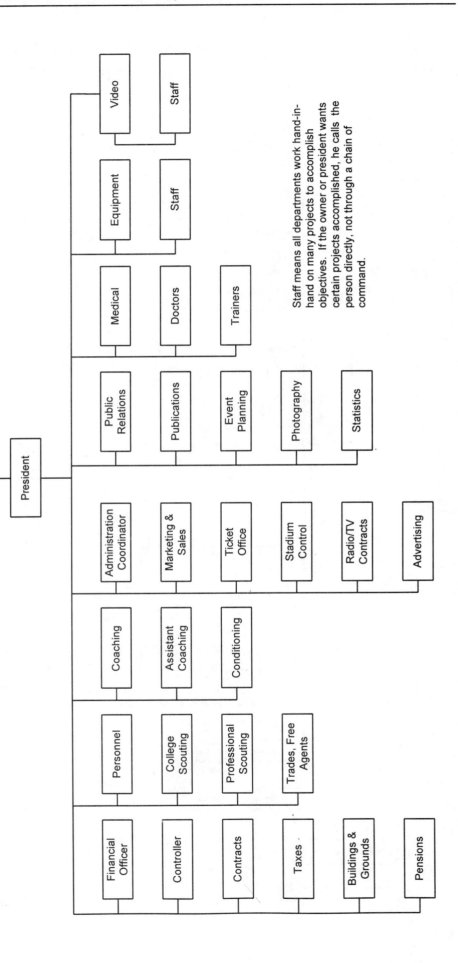

Atlanta Falcons

Source: Atlanta Falcons, 1996

Staff means all departments work hand-in-hand on many projects to accomplish objectives. If the owner or president wants certain projects accomplished, he calls the person directly, not through a chain of command.

Atlanta Gas Light Company

Source: Annual report, 1995

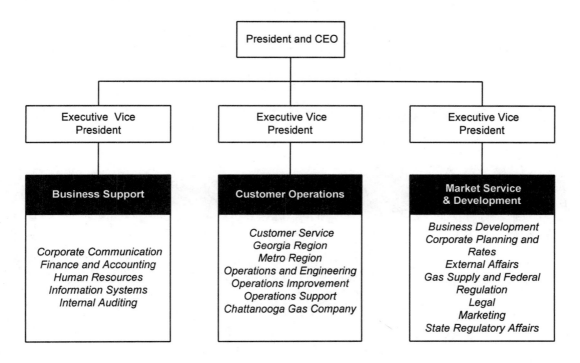

Company Structure
on September 30, 1995

During fiscal 1995, Atlanta Gas Light Company completed comprehensive
organizational changes that will help the Company achieve its vision of
becoming America's leading natural gas and energy services company.
Three business units were created to focus on meeting the needs of
customers, shareholders and employees.

Atmosphere Processing, Inc.

Source: Atmosphere Processing, Inc., 1996

Austrian Postal & Telegraph Administration (Austria)
Postal Division

Source: Austrian Postal & Telegraph Administration, 1996

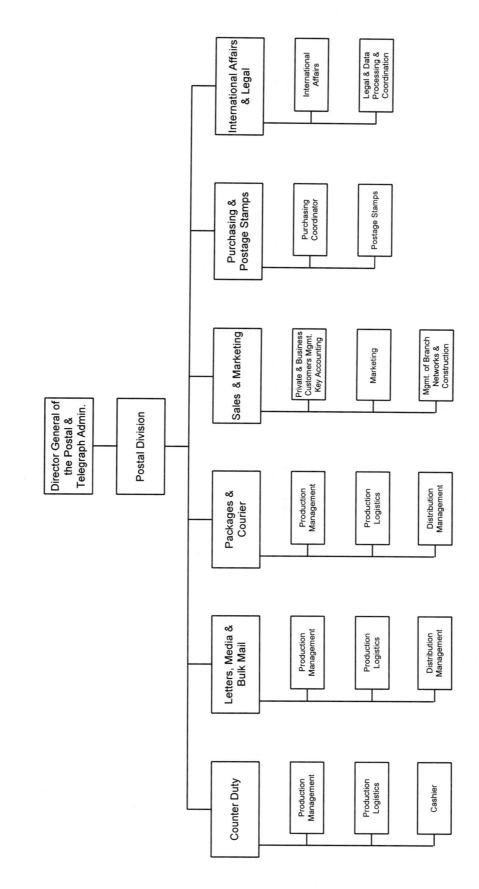

Austrian Postal & Telegraph Administration (Austria)
Postauto Division

Source: Austrian Postal & Telegraph Administration, 1996

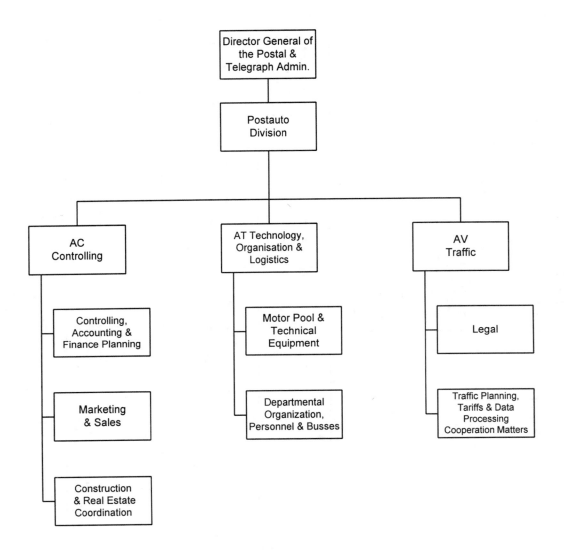

Austrian Postal & Telegraph Administration (Austria) Telecommunications Group

Source: Austrian Postal & Telegraph Administration, 1996

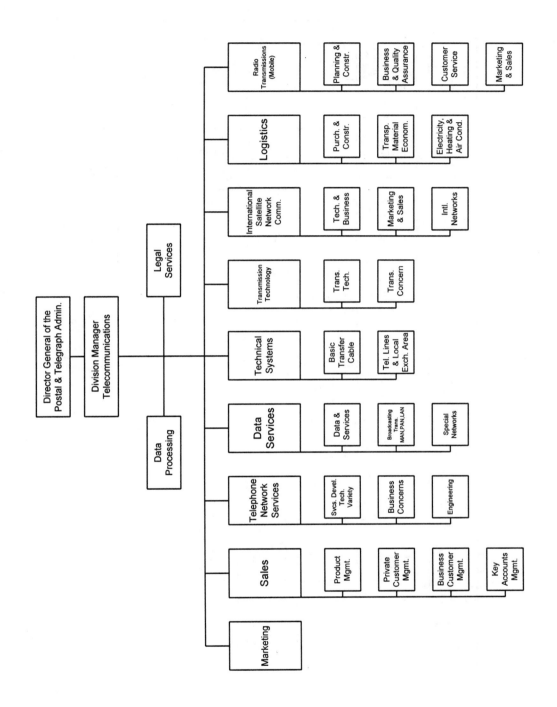

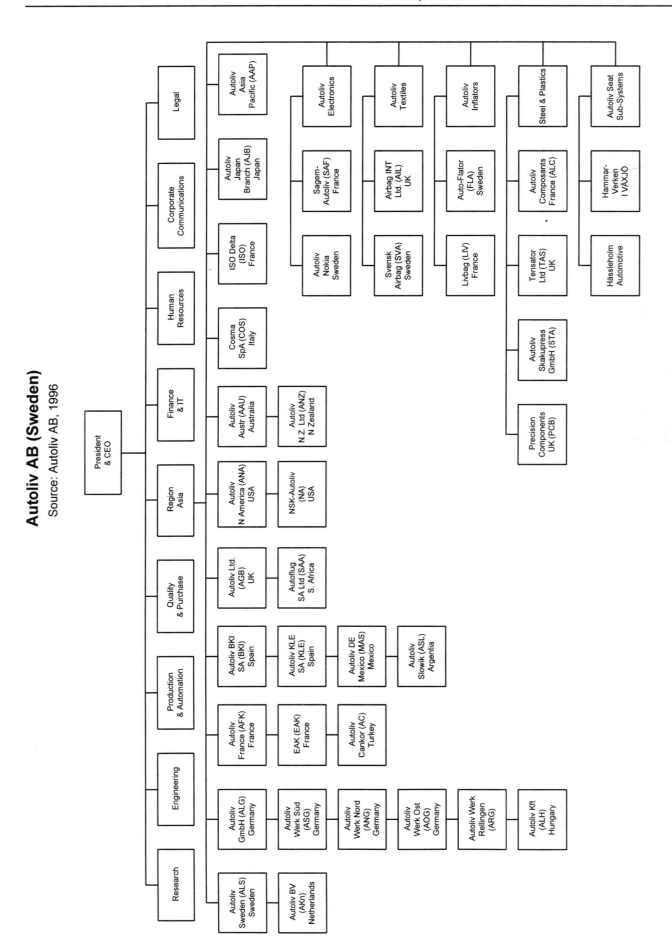

Autoliv AB (Sweden)

Source: Autoliv AB, 1996

Continued on next page

Autoliv AB

Continued from previous page

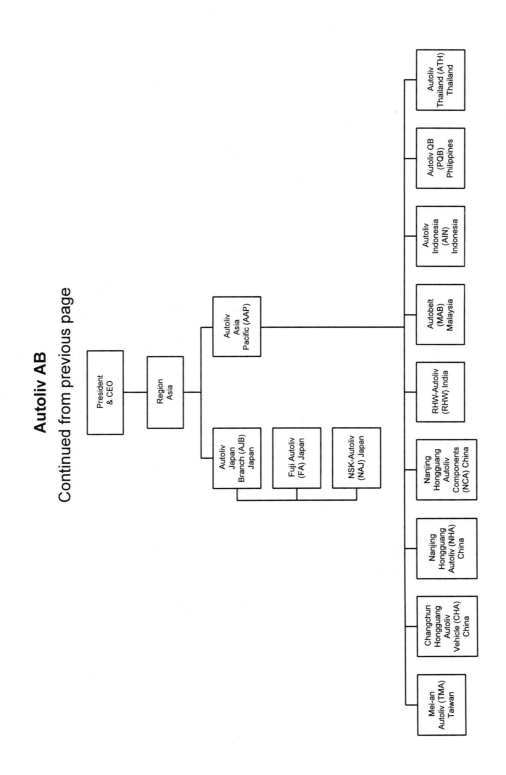

Avalon Natural Cosmetics, Inc.

Source: Avalon Natural Cosmetics, Inc., 1996

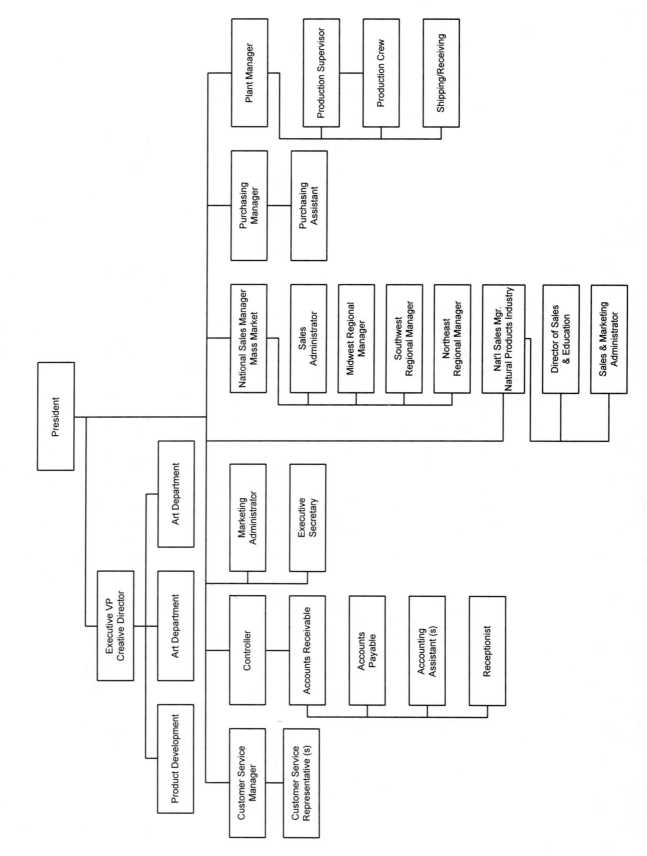

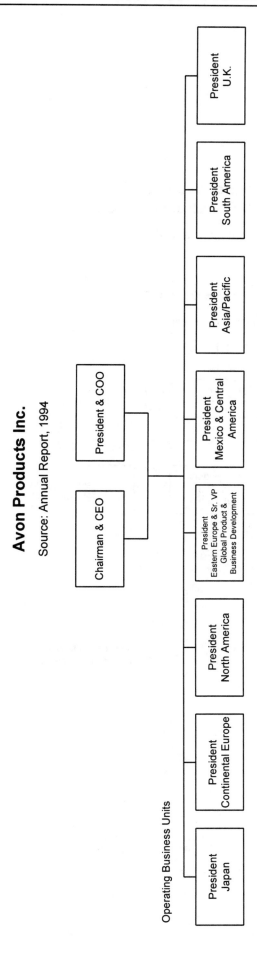

Avon Products Inc.

Source: Annual Report, 1994

Chairman & CEO

President & COO

Operating Business Units

President Japan

President Continental Europe

President North America

President Eastern Europe & Sr. VP Global Product & Business Development

President Mexico & Central America

President Asia/Pacific

President South America

President U.K.

Babcock and Wilcox Co.*
Engineering & Construction Group

Source: McDermott International, Inc., 1996

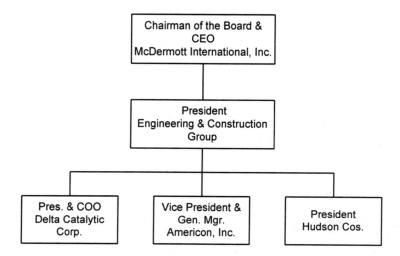

*A wholly-owned subsidiary of
McDermott International, Inc.

Babcock and Wilcox Co.
Government Group

Source: McDermott International, Inc., 1996

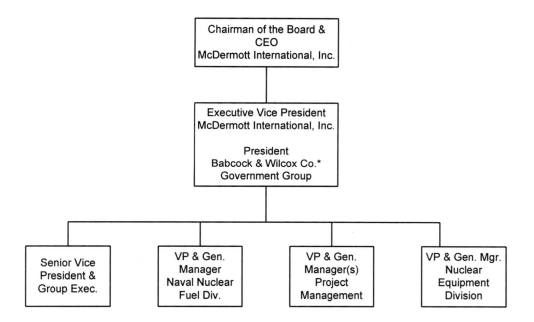

*A wholly-owned subsidiary of
McDermott International, Inc.

Babcock & Wilcox Co.
Power Generation Group

Source: McDermott International, Inc., 1996

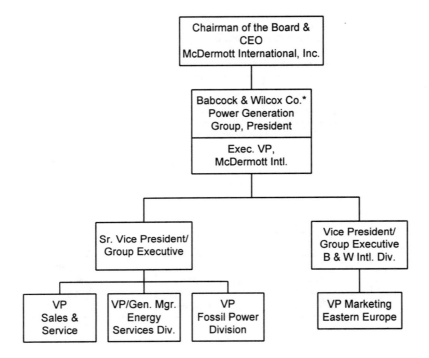

*A wholly-owned Subsidiary of
McDermott International, Inc.

Babcock and Wilcox Co.*
Technical & Shipbuilding Operations

Source: McDermott International, Inc., 1996

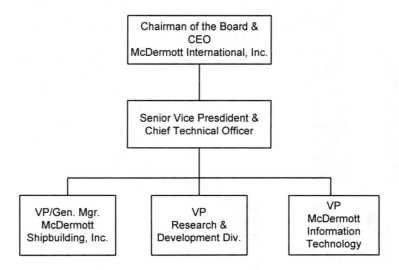

*A wholly-owned subsidiary of
McDermott International, Inc.

Bangkok Bank Public Company Limited (Thailand)

Source: Annual report, 1994

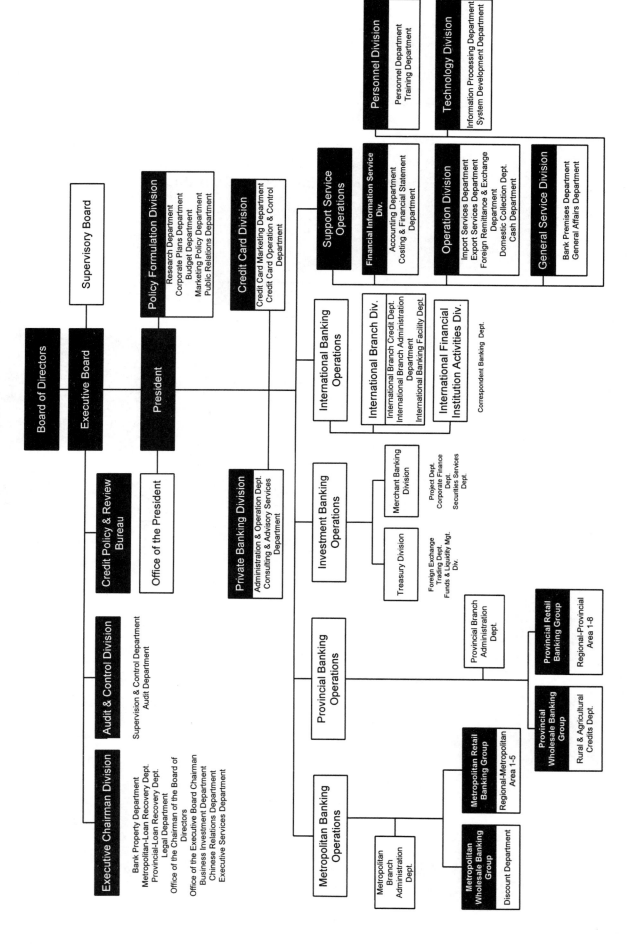

Bass PLC (England)

Source: Annual report, 1996

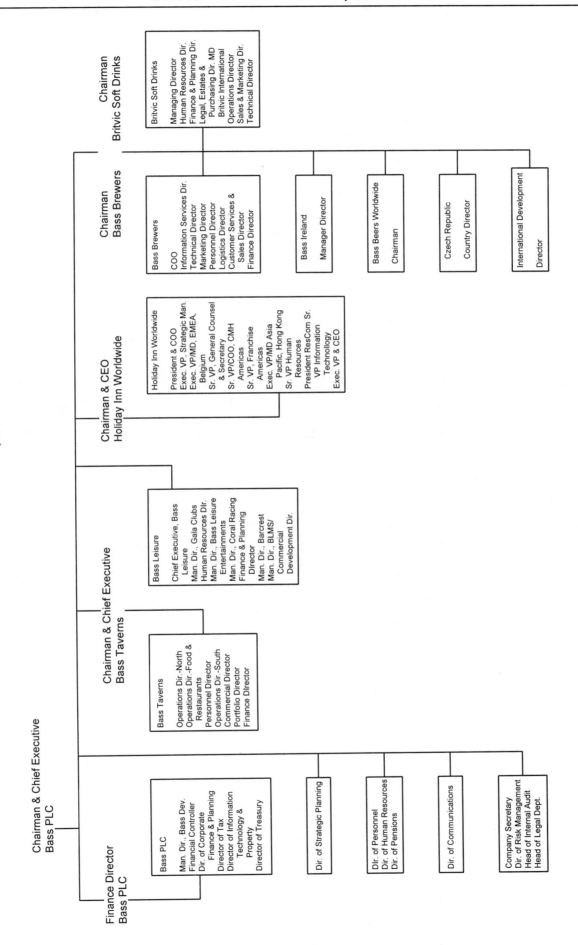

Battelle Memorial Institute Corp.

Source: Battelle Memorial Institute Corp., 1996

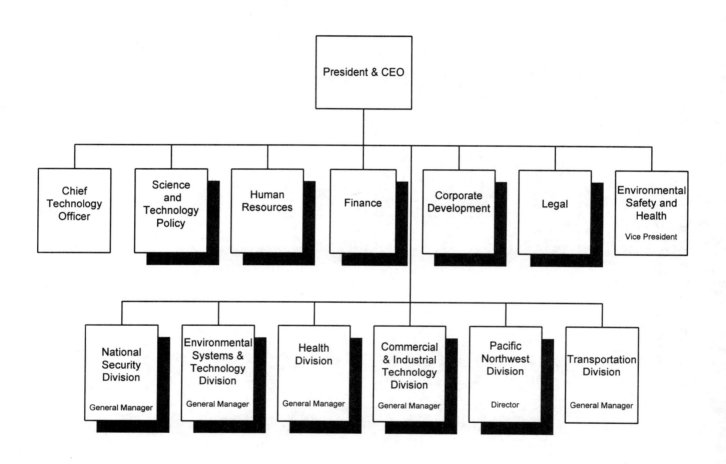

Senior Vice
President, BMI

Bay View Federal Bank F.S.B.

Source: Bay View Federal Bank F.S.B., 1996

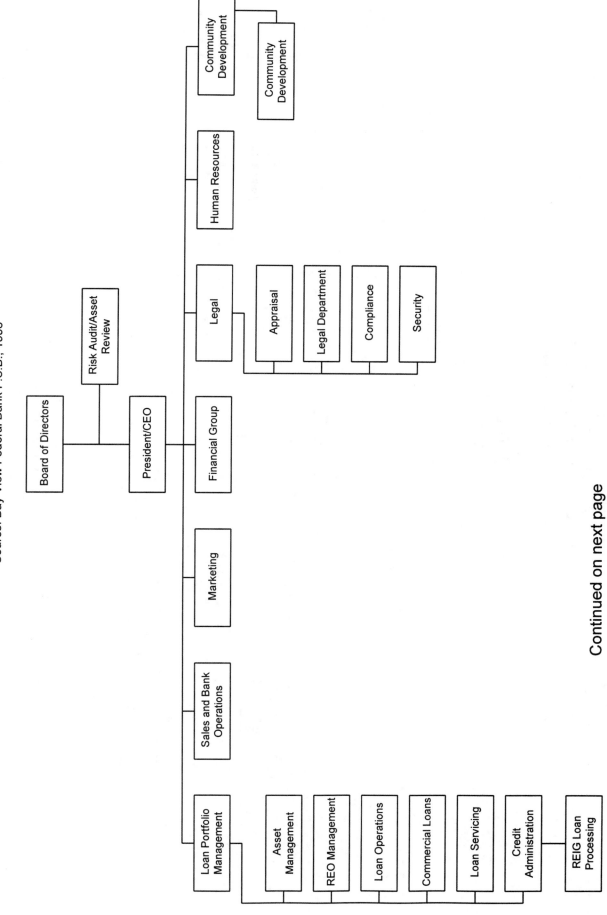

Continued on next page

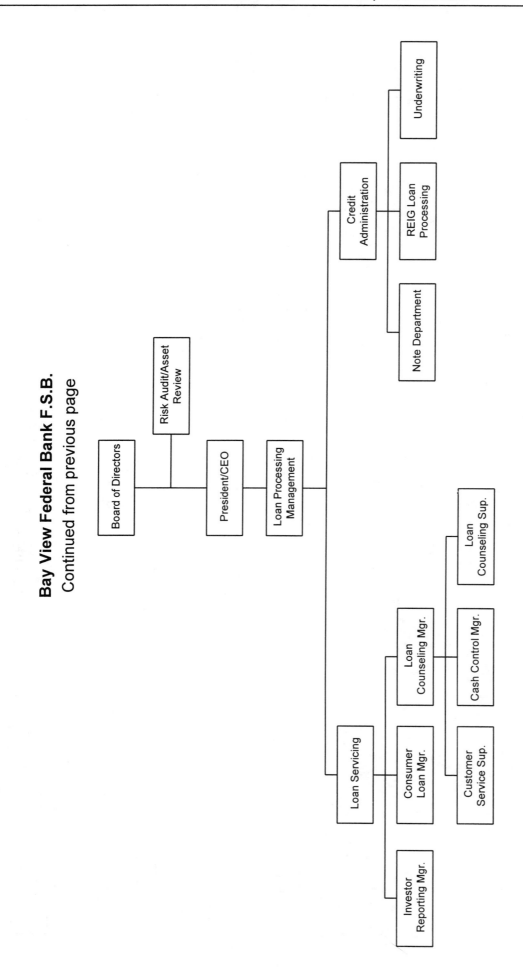

Bay View Federal Bank F.S.B.
Continued from previous page

Continued on next page

Bay View Federal Bank F.S.B.
Continued from previous page

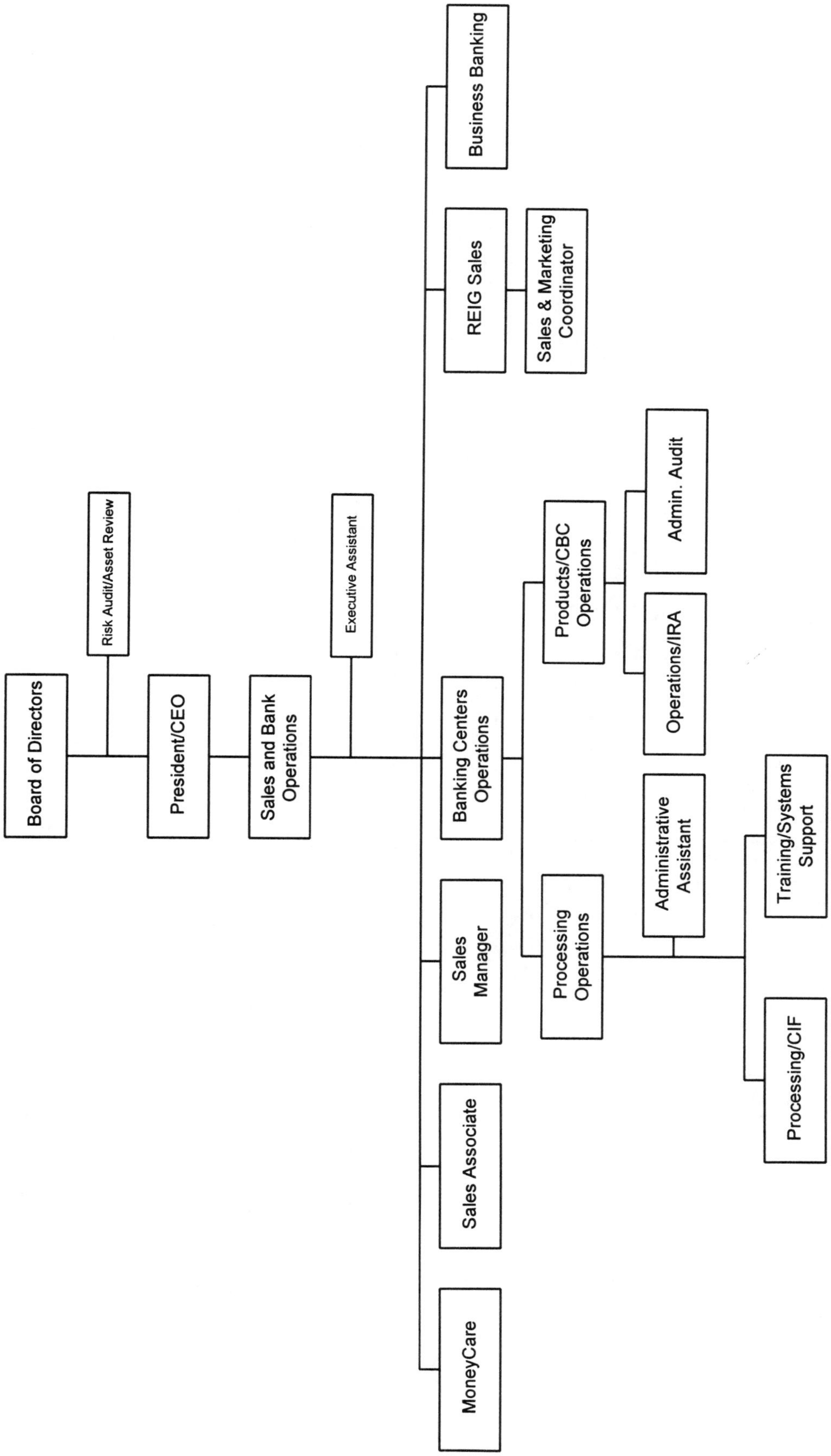

Board of Directors

Risk Audit/Asset Review

President/CEO

Sales and Bank Operations

Executive Assistant

Banking Centers Operations

MoneyCare

Sales Associate

Sales Manager

Processing Operations

Administrative Assistant

Processing/CIF

Training/Systems Support

Products/CBC Operations

Operations/IRA

Admin. Audit

REIG Sales

Sales & Marketing Coordinator

Business Banking

Continued on next page

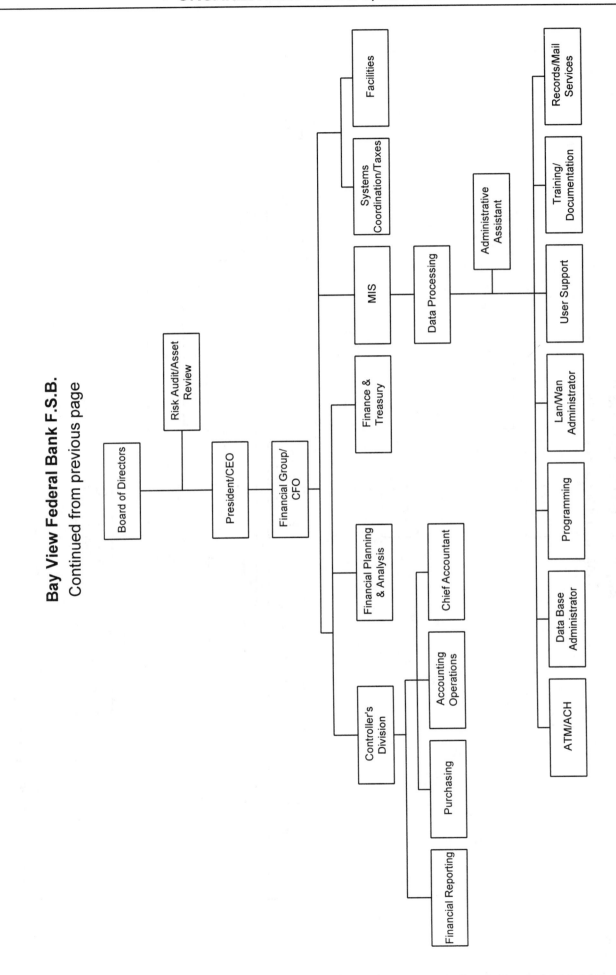

Bay View Federal Bank F.S.B.
Continued from previous page

BellSouth Corporation

Source: BellSouth Corporation, 1996

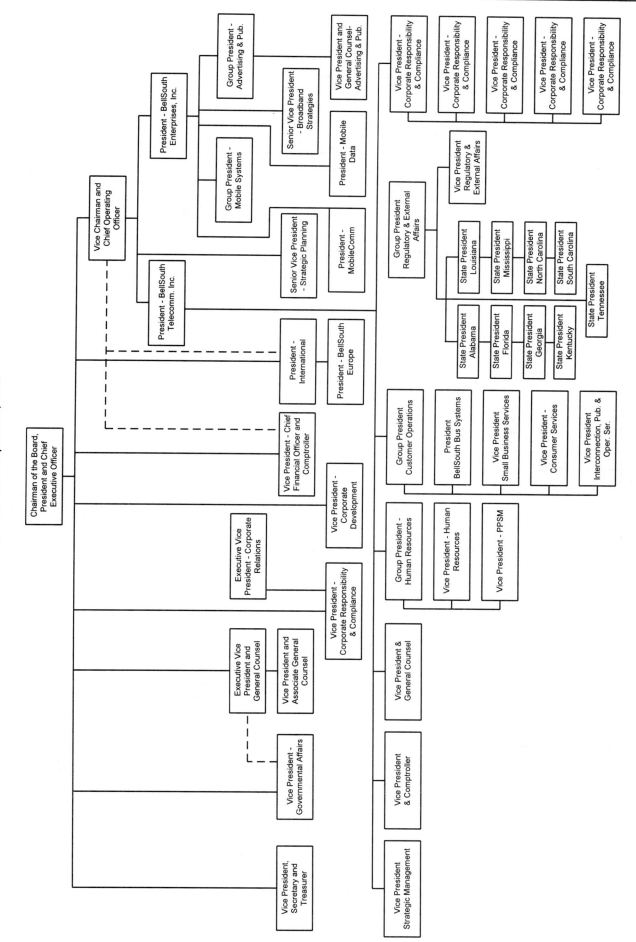

Beth Israel Hospital (Boston)

Source: Beth Israel Hospital, 1996

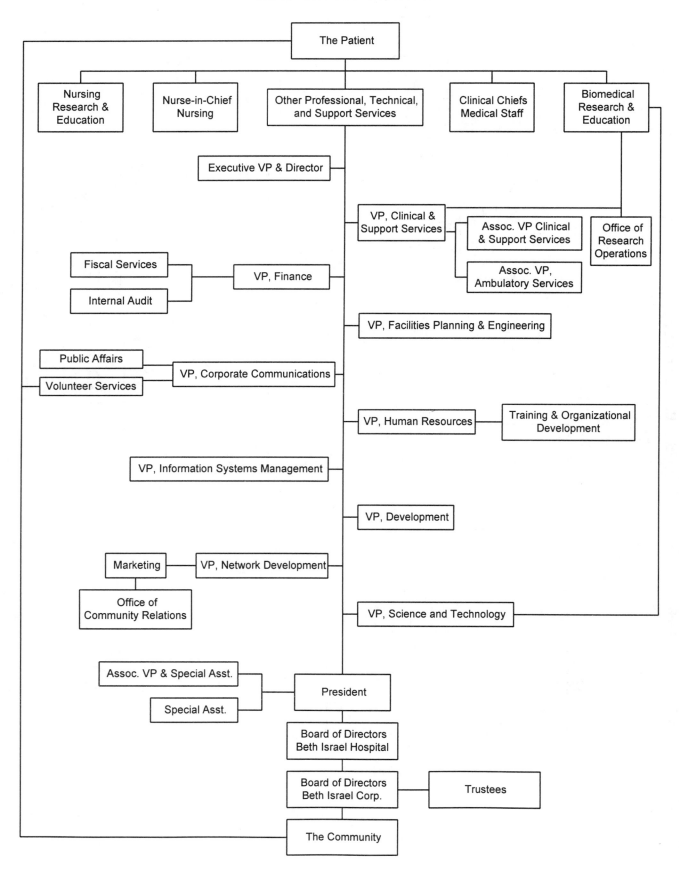

Bethlehem Steel Corporation

Source: Bethlehem Steel Corporation, 1996

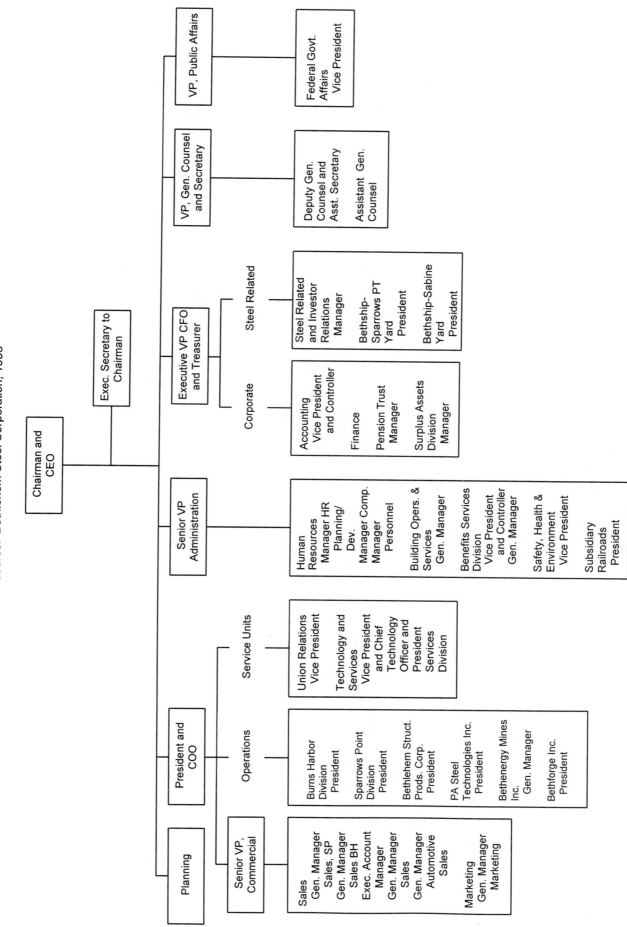

Blount International, Inc.

Source: Blount International, Inc., 1996

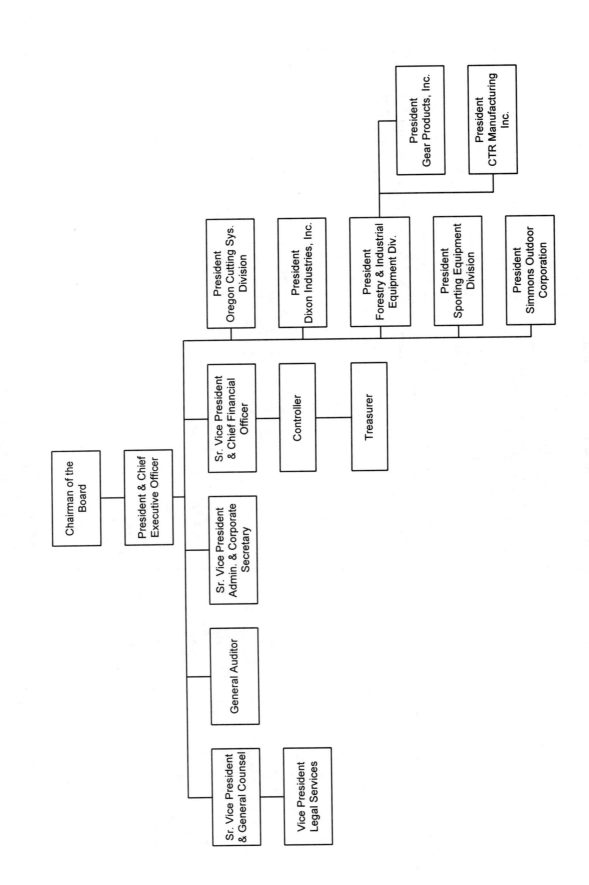

Bob Evans Farms, Inc.

Source: Bob Evans Farms, Inc., 1996

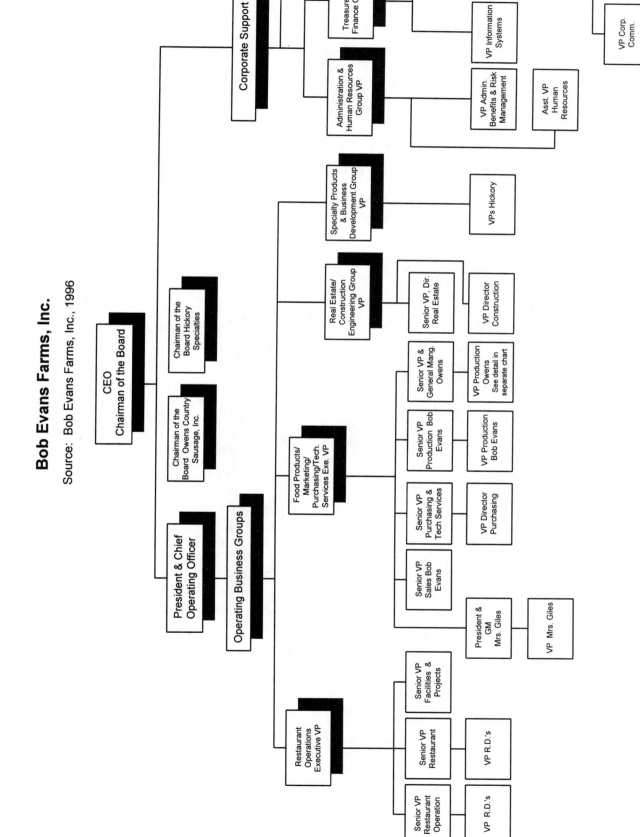

Bob Evans Farms, Inc.
Plant Production Structure

Source: Bob Evans Farms, Inc., 1996

Bob Evans Farms, Inc.
Xenia Plant

Source: Bob Evans Farms, Inc.,1996

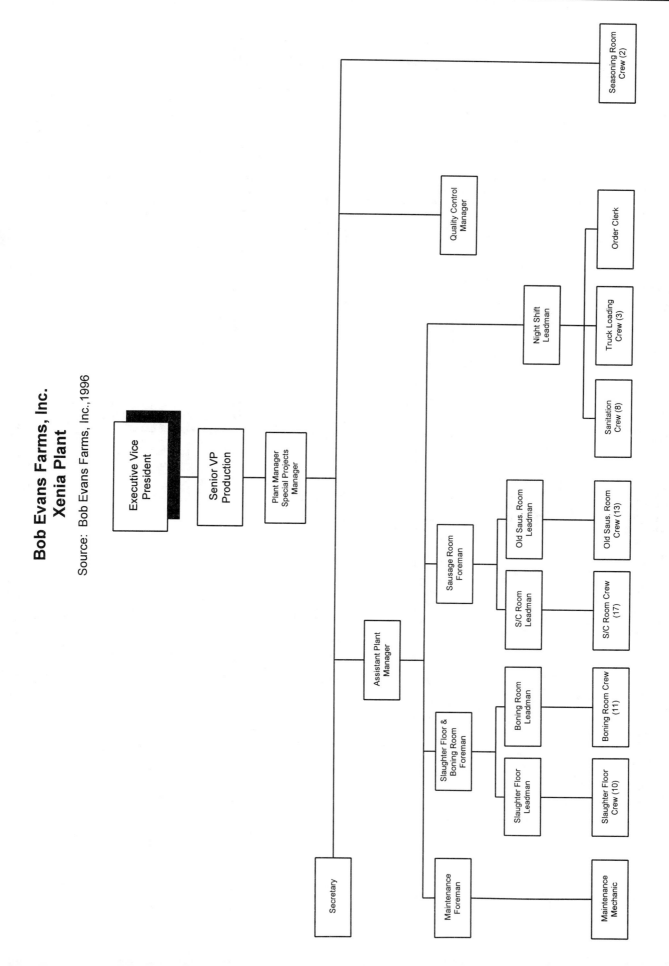

Boise Cascade Corp.

Source: Boise Cascade Corp., 1996

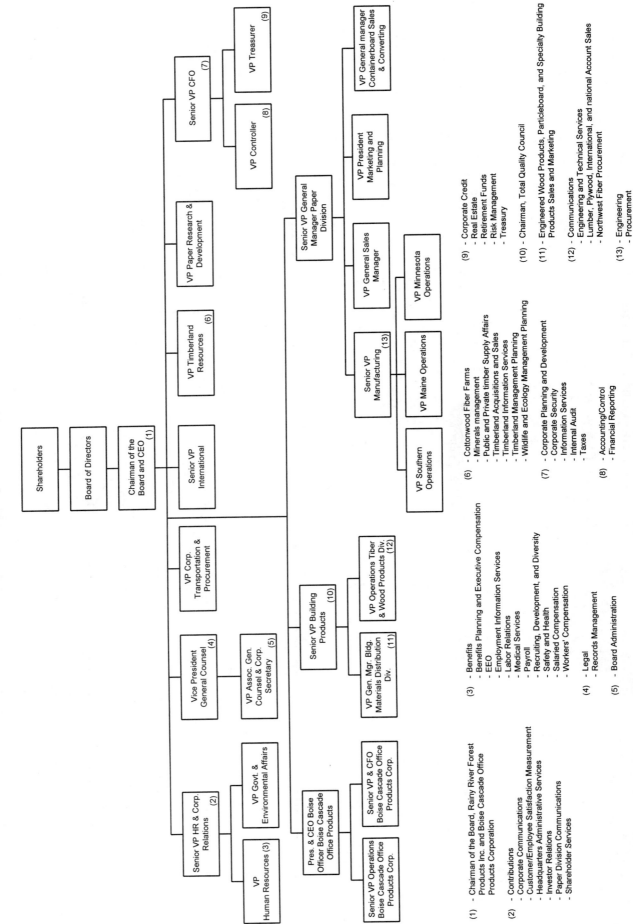

(1) - Chairman of the Board, Rainy River Forest
      Products Inc. and Boise Cascade Office
      Products Corporation
(2) - Contributions
    - Corporate Communications
    - Customer/Employee Satisfaction Measurement
    - Headquarters Administrative Services
    - Investor Relations
    - Paper Division Communications
    - Shareholder Services

(3) - Benefits
    - Benefits Planning and Executive Compensation
    - EEO
    - Employment Information Services
    - Labor Relations
    - Medical Services
    - Payroll
    - Recruiting, Development, and Diversity
    - Safety and Health
    - Salaried Compensation
    - Workers' Compensation

(4) - Legal
    - Records Management

(5) - Board Administration

(6) - Cottonwood Fiber Farms
    - Minerals management
    - Public and Private timber Supply Affairs
    - Timberland Acquisitions and Sales
    - Timberland Information Services
    - Timberland Management Planning
    - Wildlife and Ecology Management Planning

(7) - Corporate Planning and Development
    - Corporate Security
    - Information Services
    - Internal Audit
    - Taxes

(8) - Accounting/Control
    - Financial Reporting

(9) - Corporate Credit
    - Real Estate
    - Retirement Funds
    - Risk Management
    - Treasury

(10) - Chairman, Total Quality Council

(11) - Engineered Wood Products, Particleboard, and Specialty Building
       Products Sales and Marketing

(12) - Communications
     - Engineering and Technical Services
     - Lumber, Plywood, International, and national Account Sales
     - Northwest Fiber Procurement

(13) - Engineering
     - Procurement

Brasfield & Gorrie General Contractor, Inc.

Source: Brasfield & Gorrie General Contractor, Inc., 1996

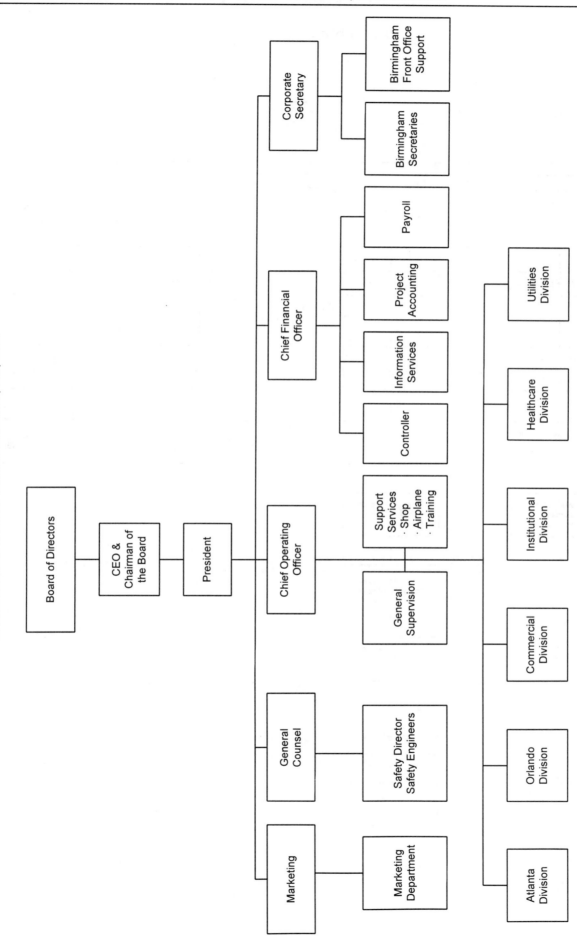

British Steel PLC (England)

Source: Company update, 1996

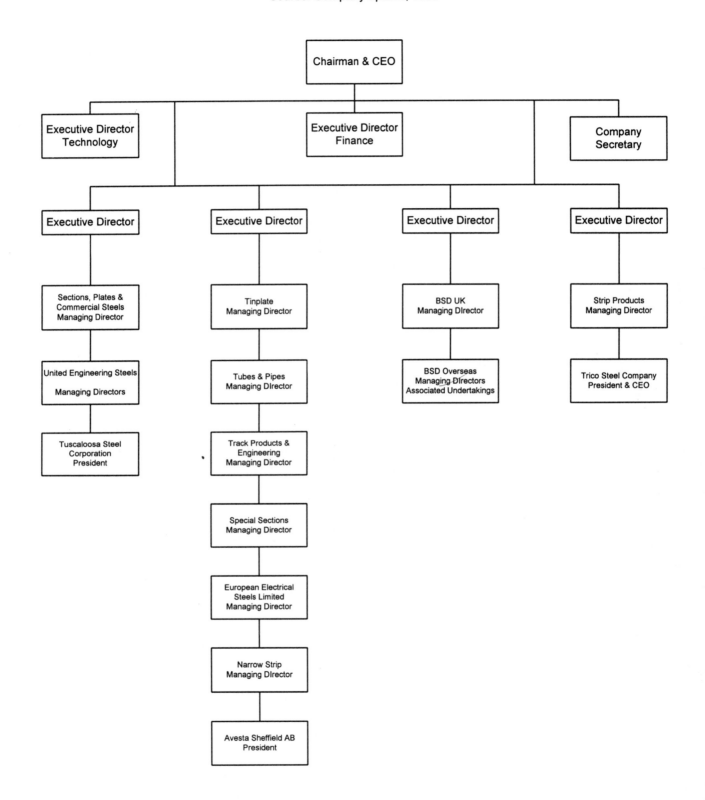

Bronner's Christmas Wonderland

Source: Bronner's Christmas Wonderland, 1996

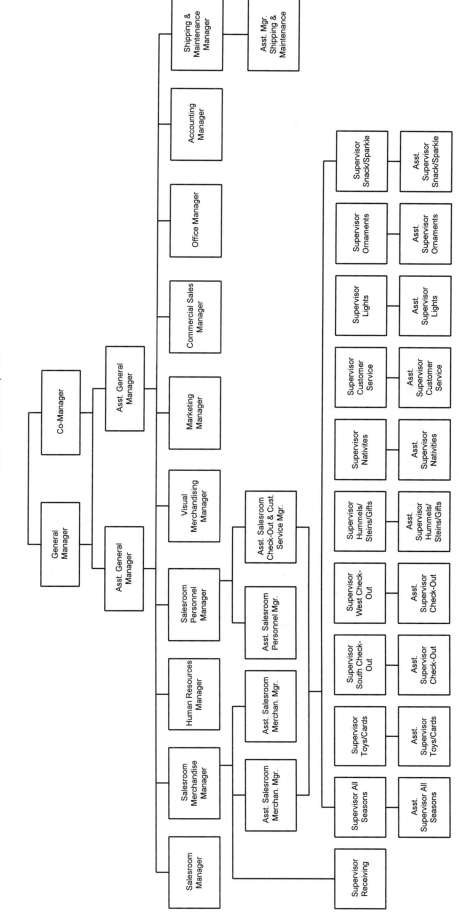

Campbell Soup Co.

Source: Campbell Soup Co., 1996

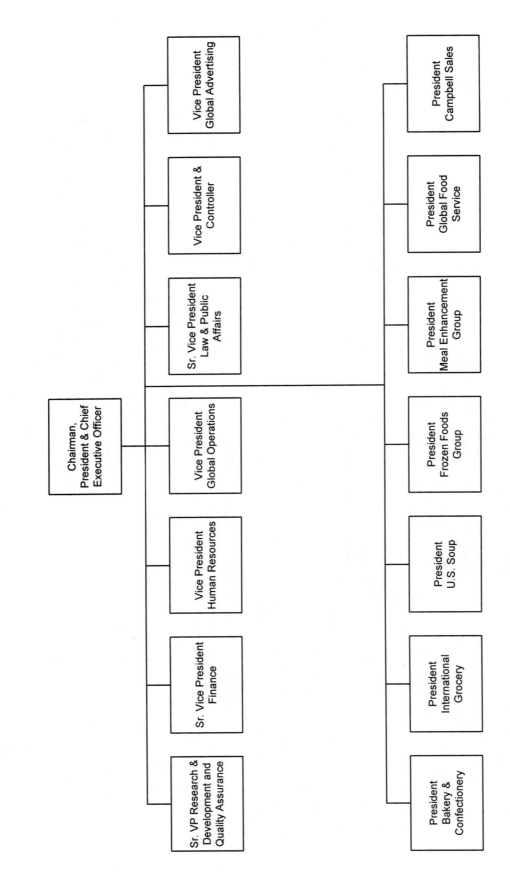

Caterpillar Inc.

Source: Caterpillar Inc., 1996

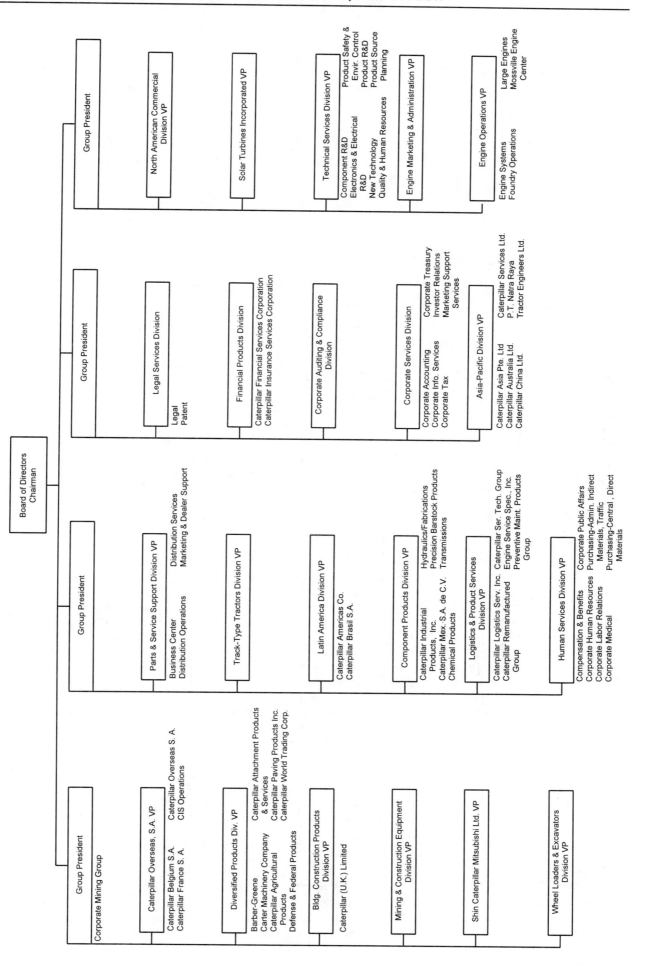

Centerior Energy Corporation

Source: Centerior Energy Corporation, 1996

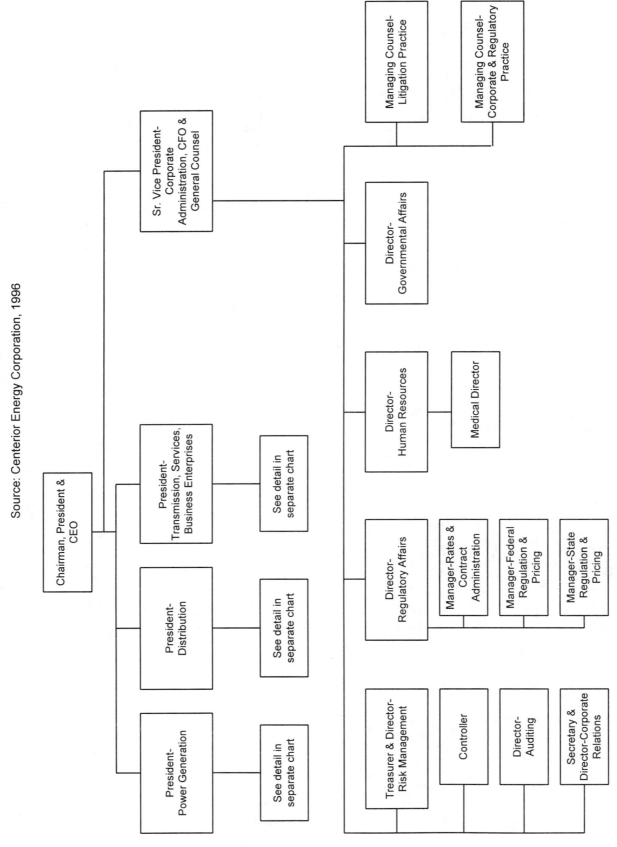

Centerior Energy Corporation Distribution

Source: Centerior Energy Corporation, 1996

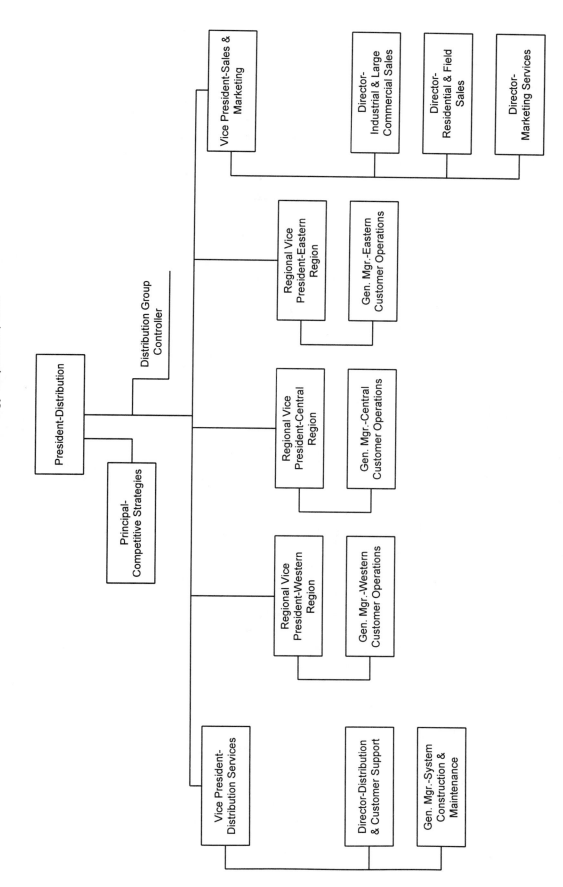

Centerior Energy Corporation Power Generation

Source: Centerior Energy Corporation, 1996

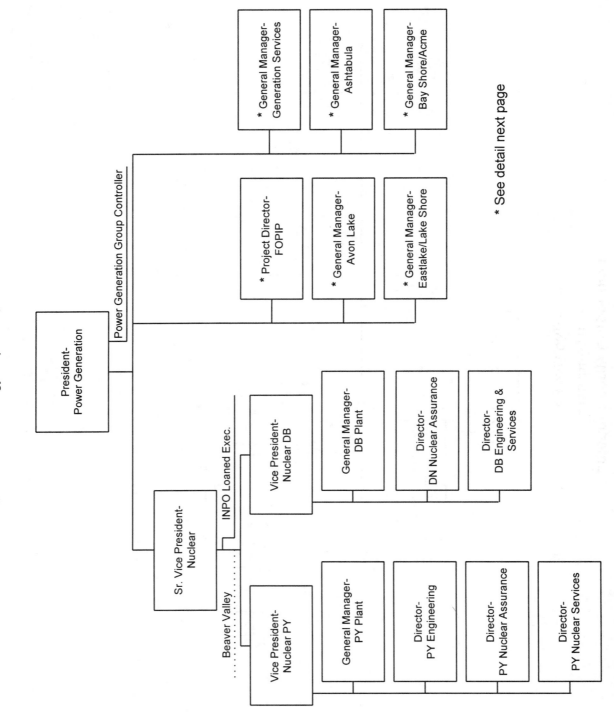

Centerior Energy Corporation Power Generation

Continued from previous page

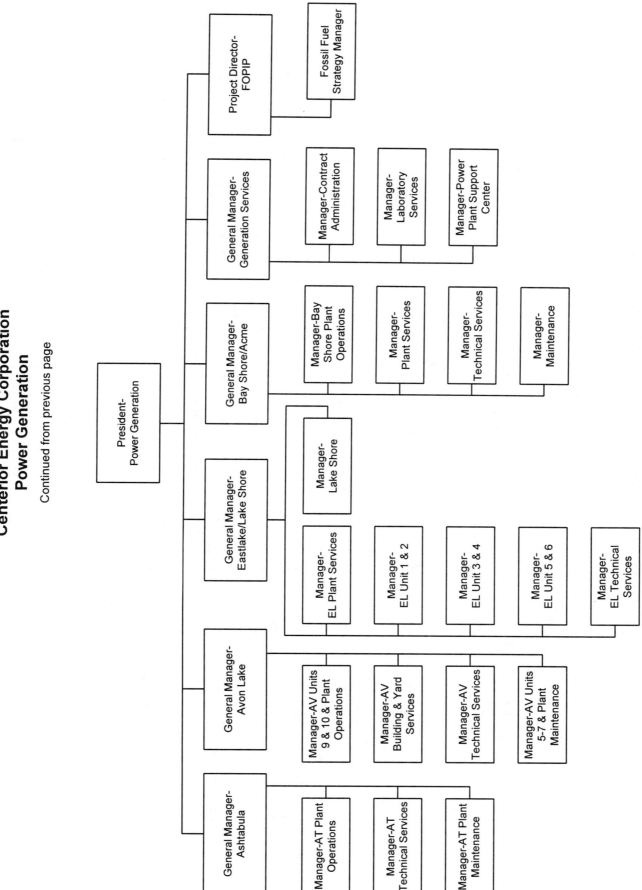

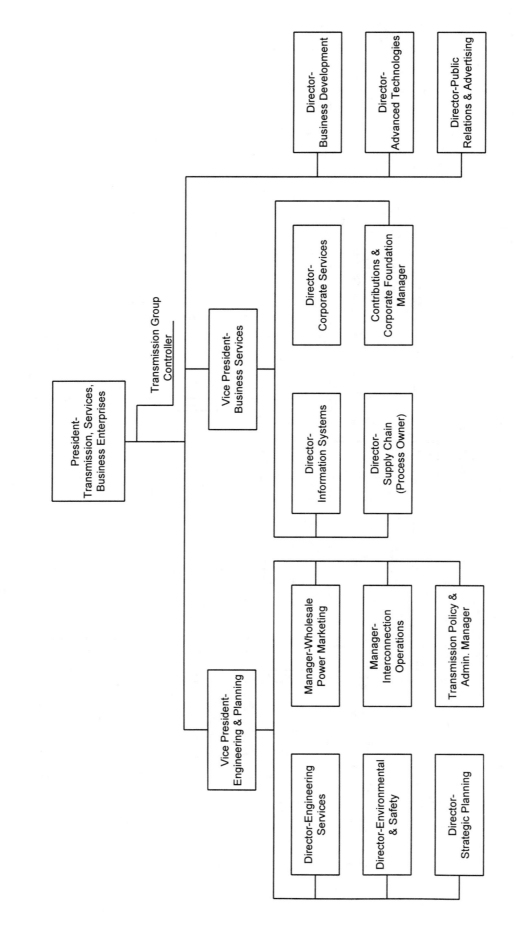

Centerior Energy Corporation
Transmission, Services, Business Enterprises

Source: Centerior Energy Corporation, 1996

Chinese Petroleum Corp. (Taiwan)

Source: Chinese Petroleum Corp., 1996

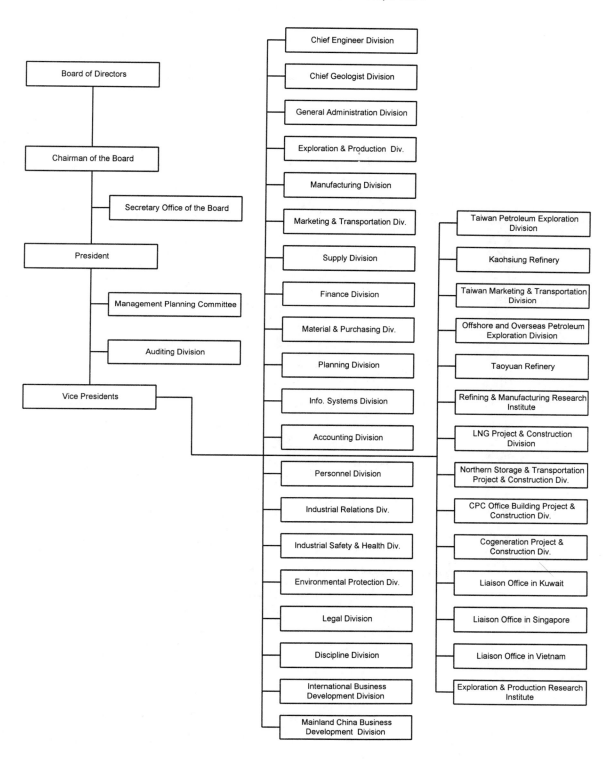

Chrysler Corporation

Source: Chrysler Corporation, 1996

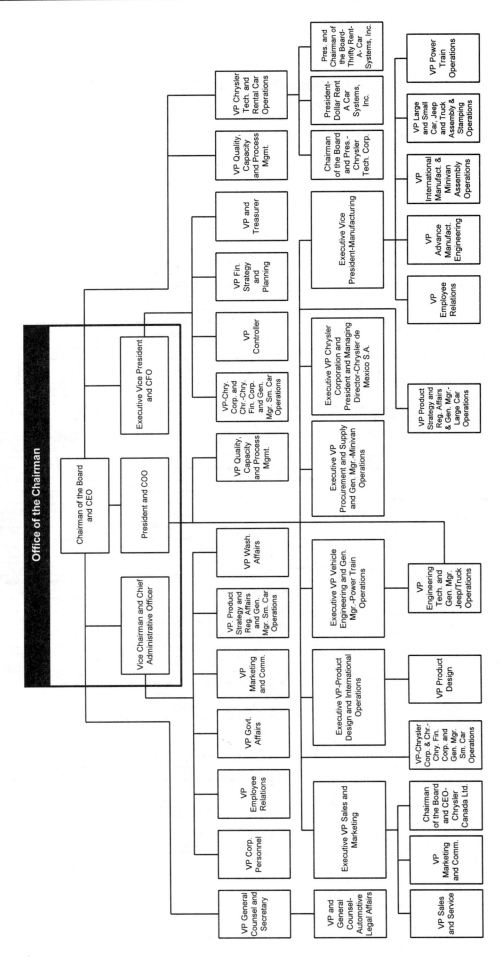

Chubu Electric Power Co., Inc. (Japan)

Source: Chubu Electric Power Co., Inc., 1996

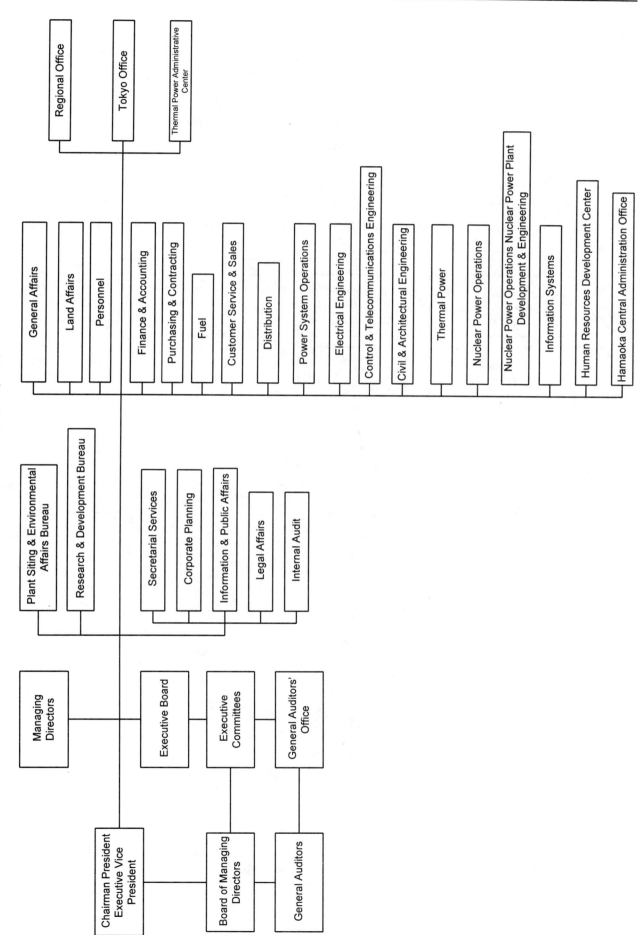

The Chugoku Electric Power Co., Inc. (Japan)

Source: Chugoku Electric Power Co., Inc., 1996

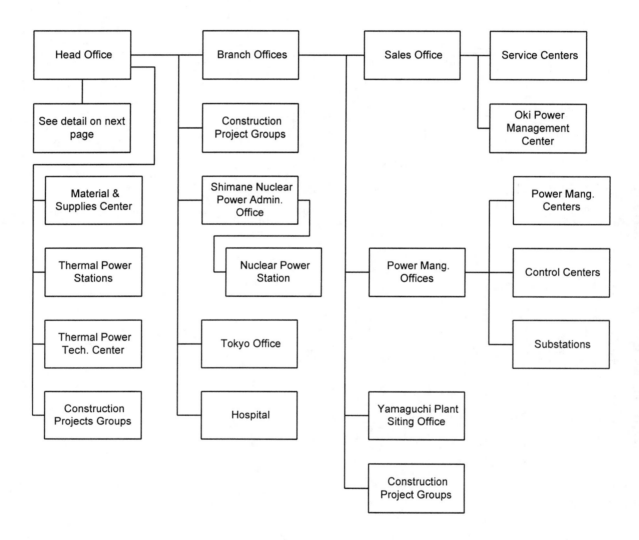

Chugoku Electric Power Co., Inc. (Japan)
Head Office

Source: Chugoku Electric Power Co., Inc., 1996

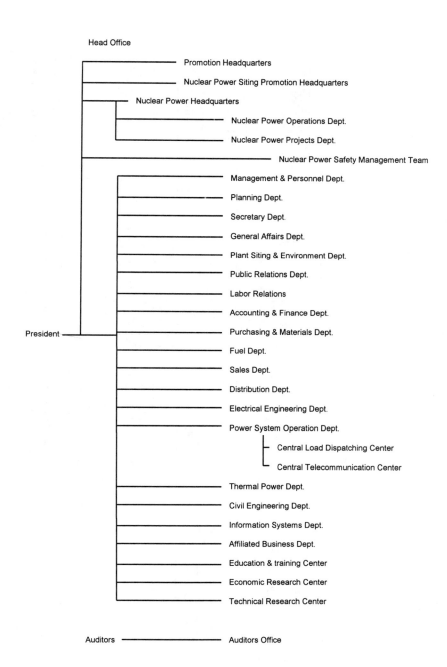

Head Office

Promotion Headquarters

Nuclear Power Siting Promotion Headquarters

Nuclear Power Headquarters

Nuclear Power Operations Dept.

Nuclear Power Projects Dept.

Nuclear Power Safety Management Team

Management & Personnel Dept.

Planning Dept.

Secretary Dept.

General Affairs Dept.

Plant Siting & Environment Dept.

Public Relations Dept.

Labor Relations

Accounting & Finance Dept.

President —— Purchasing & Materials Dept.

Fuel Dept.

Sales Dept.

Distribution Dept.

Electrical Engineering Dept.

Power System Operation Dept.

Central Load Dispatching Center

Central Telecommunication Center

Thermal Power Dept.

Civil Engineering Dept.

Information Systems Dept.

Affiliated Business Dept.

Education & training Center

Economic Research Center

Technical Research Center

Auditors ———————— Auditors Office

Consumers Power Co.

Source: Consumers Power Co., 1996

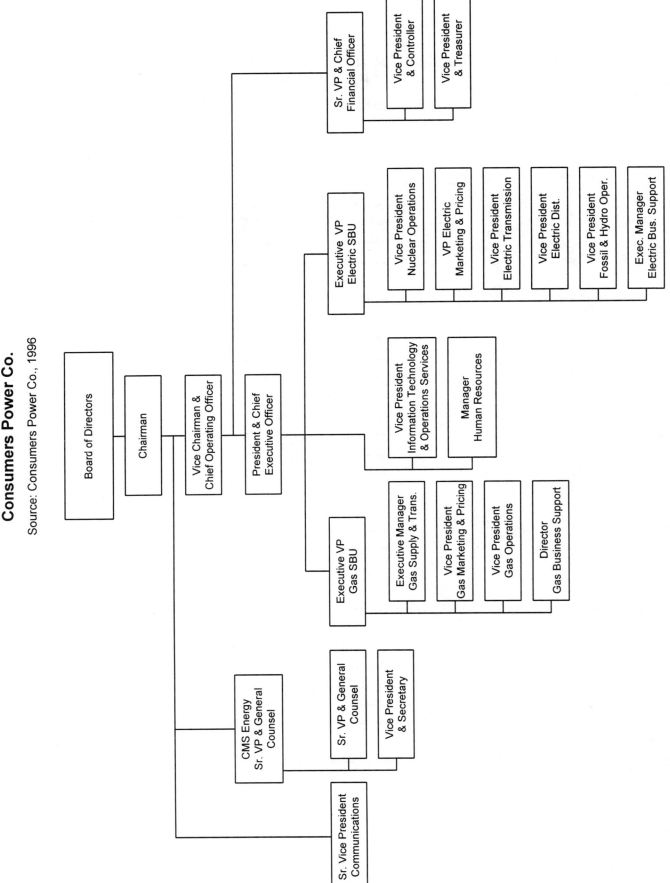

Credit Suisse (Switzerland)
Source: Credit Suisse, 1996

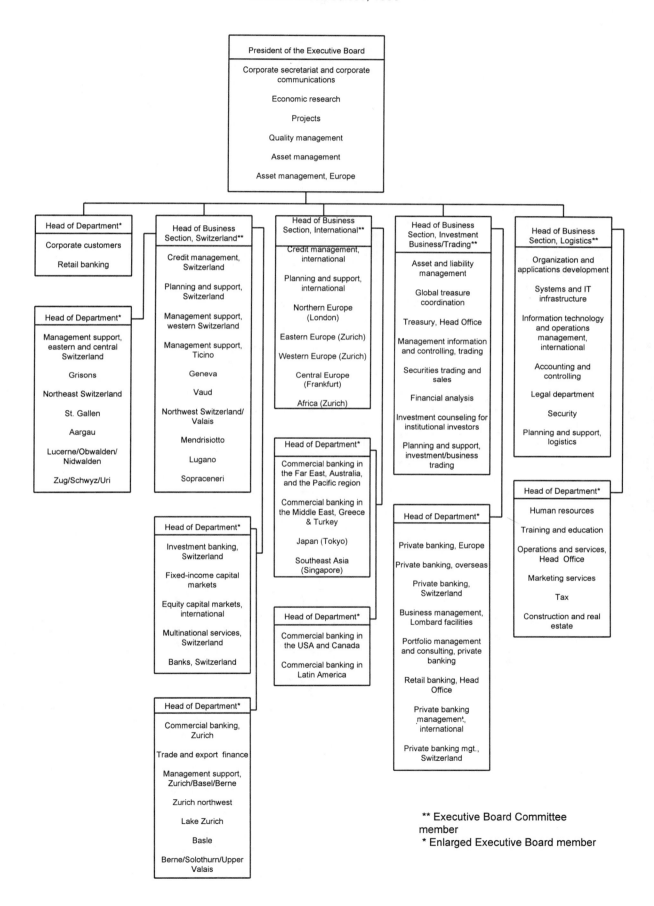

President of the Executive Board

Corporate secretariat and corporate communications

Economic research

Projects

Quality management

Asset management

Asset management, Europe

Head of Department*

Corporate customers

Retail banking

Head of Department*

Management support, eastern and central Switzerland

Grisons

Northeast Switzerland

St. Gallen

Aargau

Lucerne/Obwalden/Nidwalden

Zug/Schwyz/Uri

Head of Business Section, Switzerland**

Credit management, Switzerland

Planning and support, Switzerland

Management support, western Switzerland

Management support, Ticino

Geneva

Vaud

Northwest Switzerland/Valais

Mendrisiotto

Lugano

Sopraceneri

Head of Department*

Investment banking, Switzerland

Fixed-income capital markets

Equity capital markets, international

Multinational services, Switzerland

Banks, Switzerland

Head of Department*

Commercial banking, Zurich

Trade and export finance

Management support, Zurich/Basel/Berne

Zurich northwest

Lake Zurich

Basle

Berne/Solothurn/Upper Valais

Head of Business Section, International**

Credit management, international

Planning and support, international

Northern Europe (London)

Eastern Europe (Zurich)

Western Europe (Zurich)

Central Europe (Frankfurt)

Africa (Zurich)

Head of Department*

Commercial banking in the Far East, Australia, and the Pacific region

Commercial banking in the Middle East, Greece & Turkey

Japan (Tokyo)

Southeast Asia (Singapore)

Head of Department*

Commercial banking in the USA and Canada

Commercial banking in Latin America

Head of Business Section, Investment Business/Trading**

Asset and liability management

Global treasure coordination

Treasury, Head Office

Management information and controlling, trading

Securities trading and sales

Financial analysis

Investment counseling for institutional investors

Planning and support, investment/business trading

Head of Department*

Private banking, Europe

Private banking, overseas

Private banking, Switzerland

Business management, Lombard facilities

Portfolio management and consulting, private banking

Retail banking, Head Office

Private banking management, international

Private banking mgt., Switzerland

Head of Business Section, Logistics**

Organization and applications development

Systems and IT infrastructure

Information technology and operations management, international

Accounting and controlling

Legal department

Security

Planning and support, logistics

Head of Department*

Human resources

Training and education

Operations and services, Head Office

Marketing services

Tax

Construction and real estate

** Executive Board Committee member

* Enlarged Executive Board member

Dai-ichi Mutual Life Insurance Co.

Source: Dai-ichi Mutual Life Insurance Co., 1996

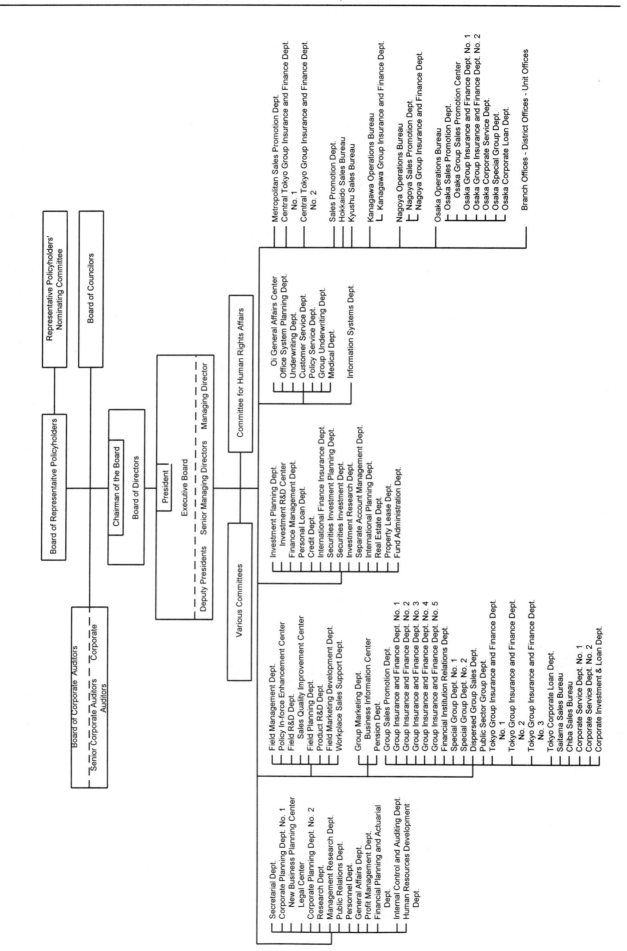

The Daiei, Inc.

Source: The Daiei, Inc., 1996

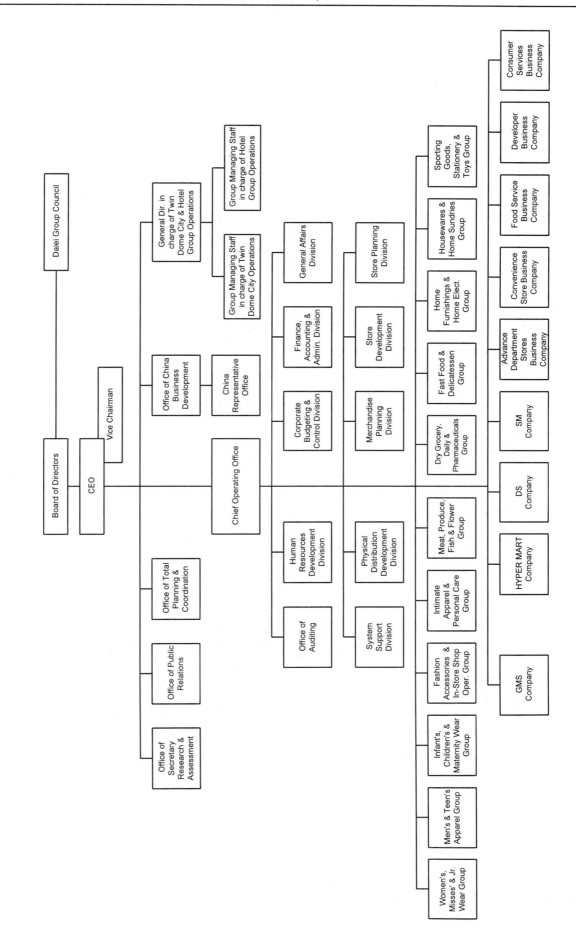

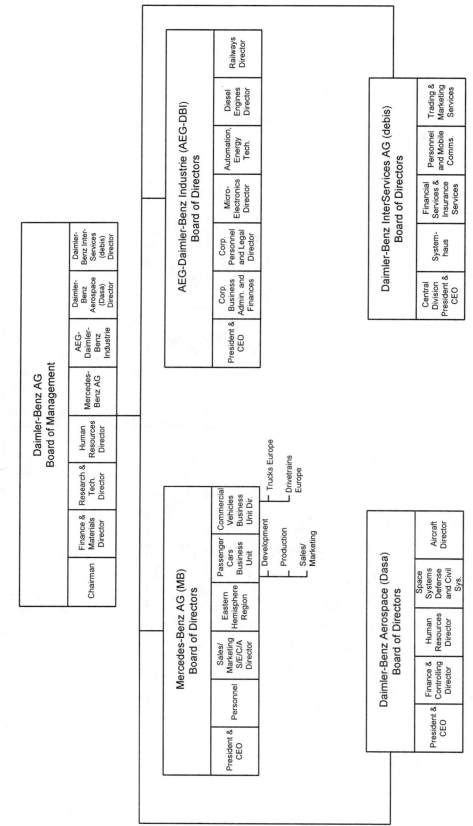

Daimler-Benz AG (Germany)

Source: Daimler-Benz AG, 1996

Dana Corp. and North American Operations

Source: Dana Corp., 1996

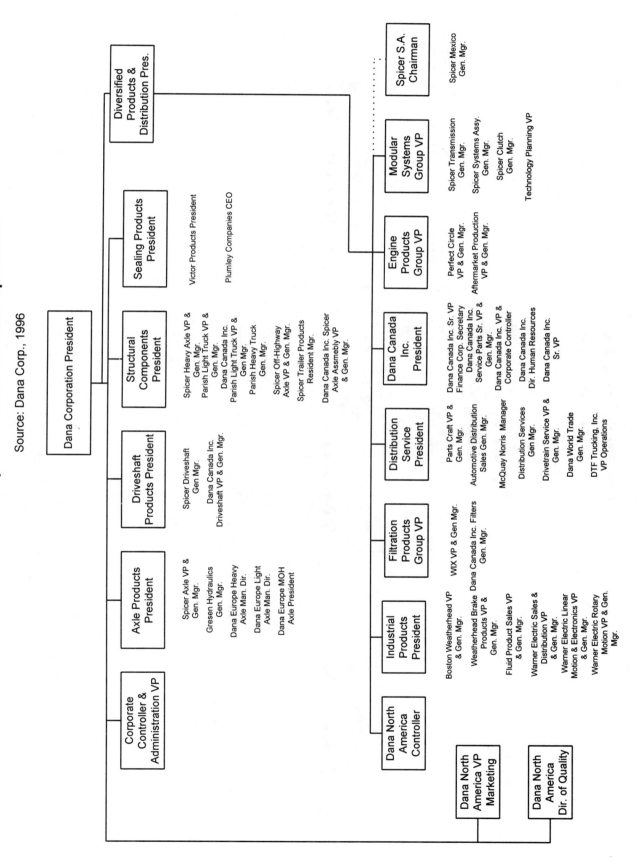

Dana World Trade Corp.

Source: Dana Corp., 1996

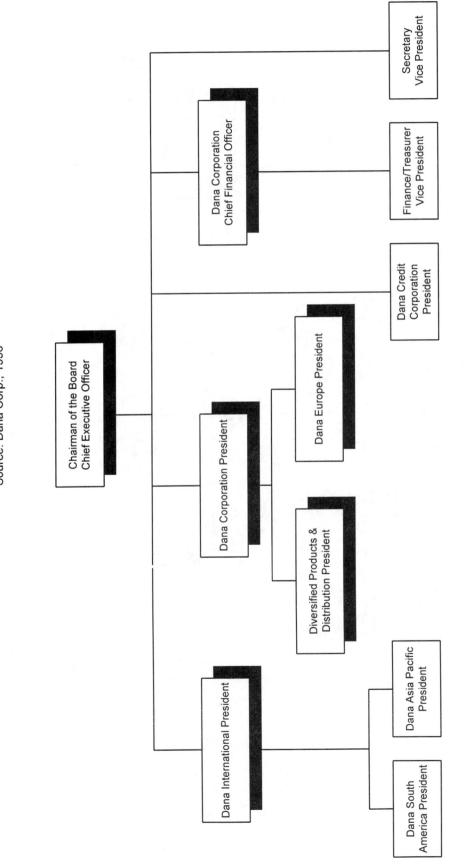

Degussa AG (Germany)

Source: Degussa AG, 1996

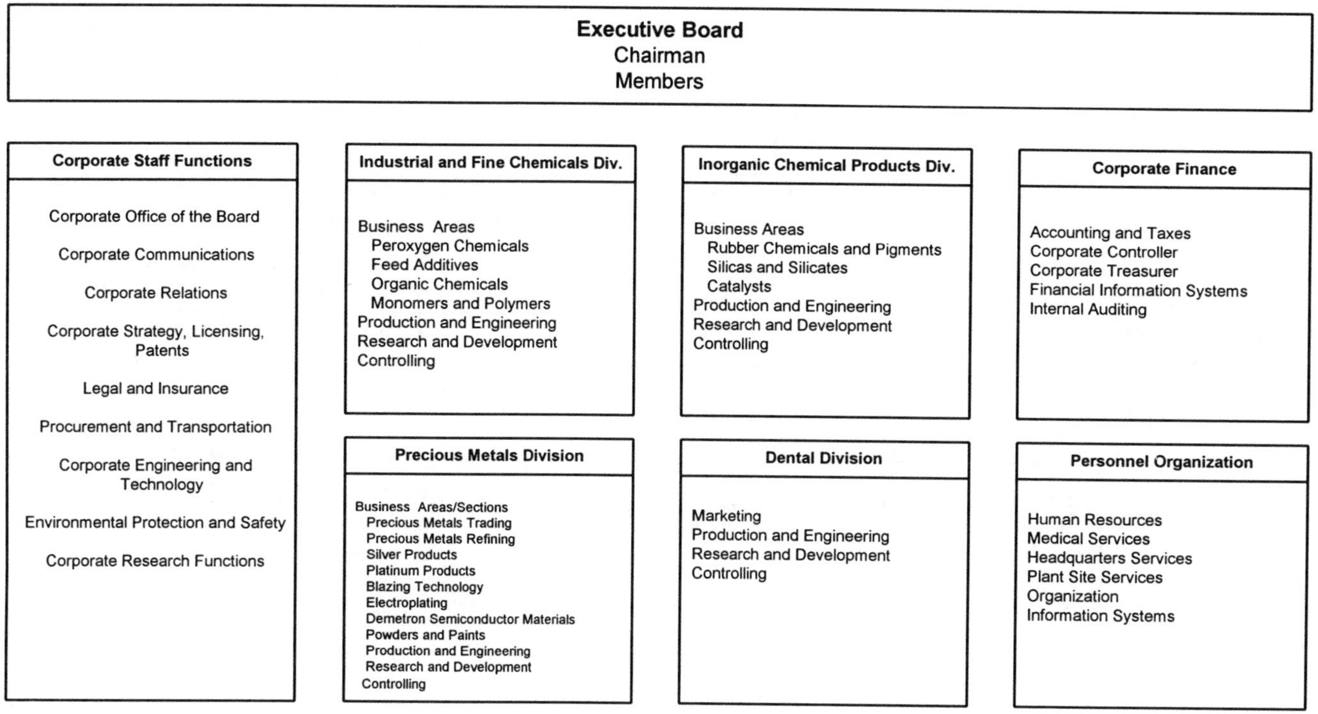

Executive Board
Chairman
Members

Corporate Staff Functions

Corporate Office of the Board

Corporate Communications

Corporate Relations

Corporate Strategy, Licensing, Patents

Legal and Insurance

Procurement and Transportation

Corporate Engineering and Technology

Environmental Protection and Safety

Corporate Research Functions

Industrial and Fine Chemicals Div.

Business Areas
Peroxygen Chemicals
Feed Additives
Organic Chemicals
Monomers and Polymers
Production and Engineering
Research and Development
Controlling

Inorganic Chemical Products Div.

Business Areas
Rubber Chemicals and Pigments
Silicas and Silicates
Catalysts
Production and Engineering
Research and Development
Controlling

Corporate Finance

Accounting and Taxes
Corporate Controller
Corporate Treasurer
Financial Information Systems
Internal Auditing

Precious Metals Division

Business Areas/Sections
Precious Metals Trading
Precious Metals Refining
Silver Products
Platinum Products
Blazing Technology
Electroplating
Demetron Semiconductor Materials
Powders and Paints
Production and Engineering
Research and Development
Controlling

Dental Division

Marketing
Production and Engineering
Research and Development
Controlling

Personnel Organization

Human Resources
Medical Services
Headquarters Services
Plant Site Services
Organization
Information Systems

Responsibility within the Board: Some members of the Executive Board are responsible for Corporate Staff Functions and some of the Divisions.

Detroit Edison Company
Source: Detroit Edison Company, 1996

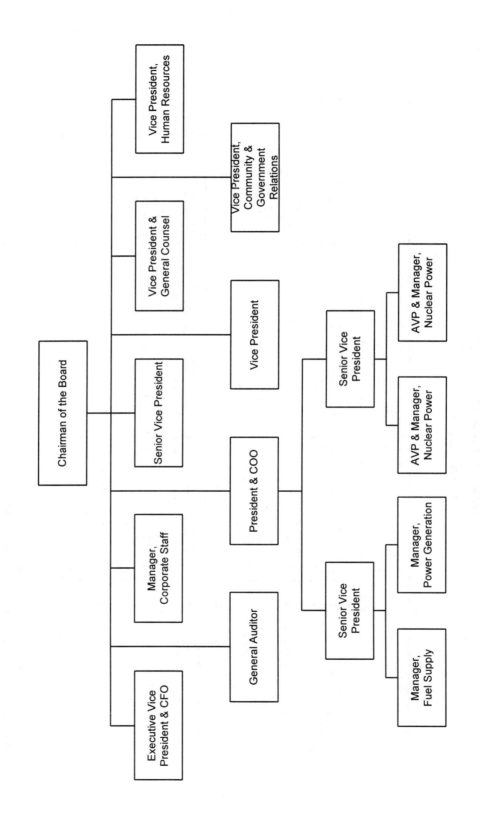

Deutsche Bundespost Postdienst (Germany)
New Business Sectors, Purchasing, Legal Affairs

Source: Deutsche Post AG, 1996

Continued on next page

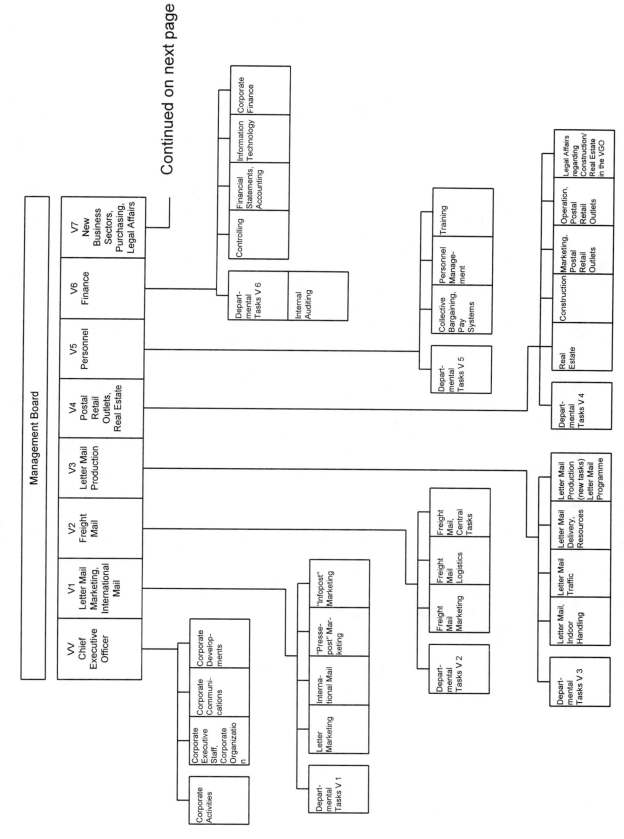

Deutsche Bundespost Postdienst (Germany)
New Business Sectors, Purchasing, Legal Affairs

Continued from previous page

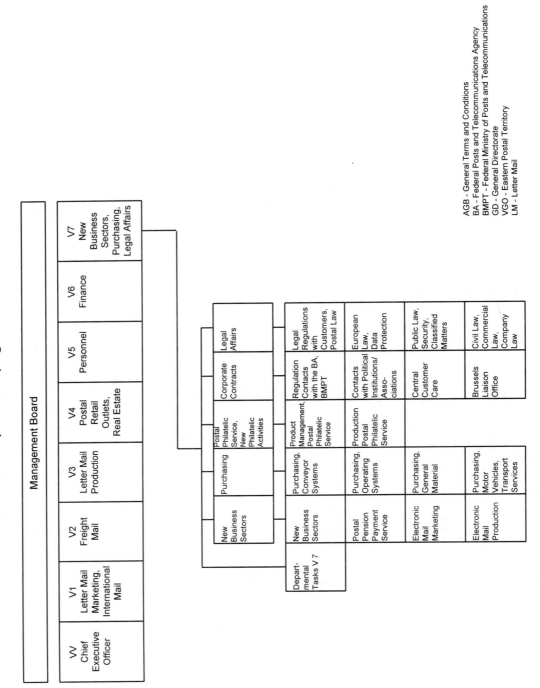

Management Board

| VV Chief Executive Officer | V1 Letter Mail Marketing, International Mail | V2 Freight Mail | V3 Letter Mail Production | V4 Postal Retail Outlets, Real Estate | V5 Personnel | V6 Finance | V7 New Business Sectors, Purchasing, Legal Affairs |

| New Business Sectors | Purchasing | Postal Philatelic Service, New Philatelic Activities | Corporate Contracts | Legal Affairs |

Depart-mental Tasks V 7	New Business Sectors	Purchasing, Conveyor Systems	Product Management, Postal Philatelic Service	Regulation Contacts with the BA, BMPT	Legal Regulations with Customers, Postal Law
	Postal Pension Payment Service	Purchasing, Operating Systems	Production Postal Philatelic Service	Contacts with Political Institutions/ Asso-ciations	European Law, Data Protection
	Electronic Mail Marketing	Purchasing, General Material		Central Customer Care	Public Law, Security, Classified Matters
	Electronic Mail Production	Purchasing, Motor Vehicles, Transport Services		Brussels Liaison Office	Civil Law, Commercial Law, Company Law

AGB - General Terms and Conditions
BA - Federal Posts and Telecommunications Agency
BMPT - Federal Ministry of Posts and Telecommunications
GD - General Directorate
VGO - Eastern Postal Territory
LM - Letter Mail

Douglas Aircraft Company

Source: McDonnell Douglas Corporation, 1996

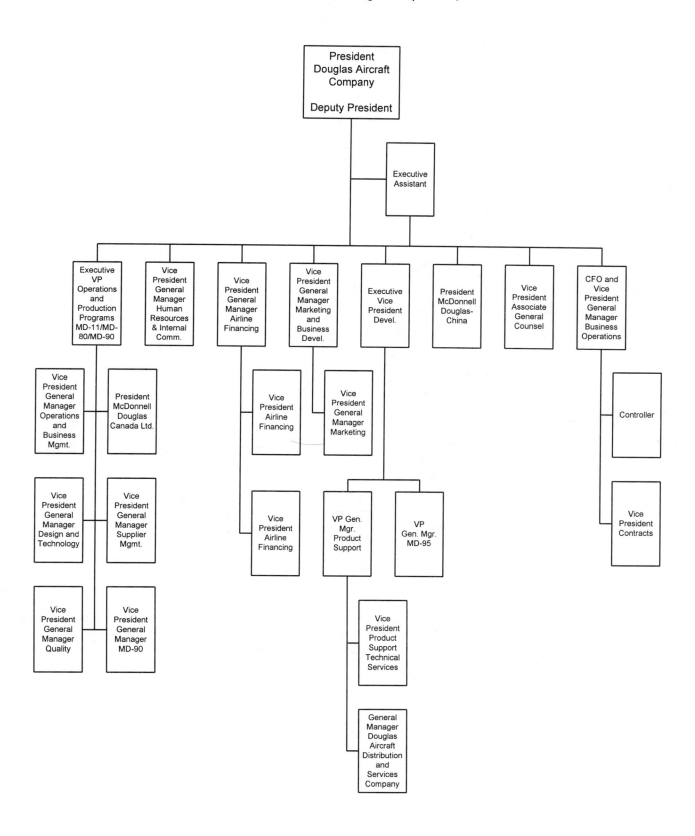

Edeka Zentrale AG (Germany)

Source: Edeka Zentrale AG, 1996

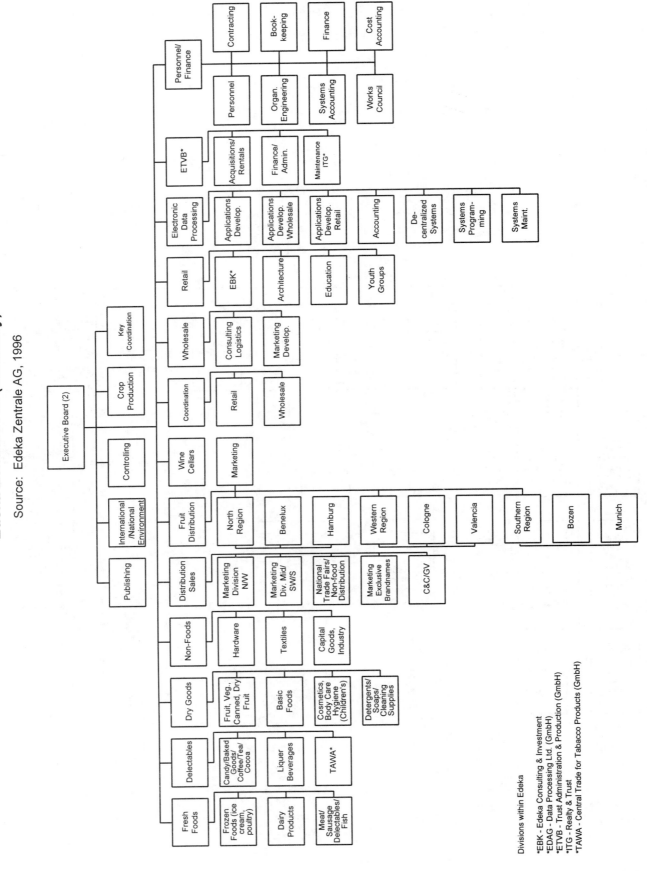

Divisions within Edeka

*EBK - Edeka Consulting & Investment
*EDAG - Data Processing Ltd. (GmbH)
*ETVB - Trust Administration & Production (GmbH)
*ITG - Realty & Trust
*TAWA - Central Trade for Tabacco Products (GmbH)

Elf Aquitaine (France)

Source: Annual report, 1994*

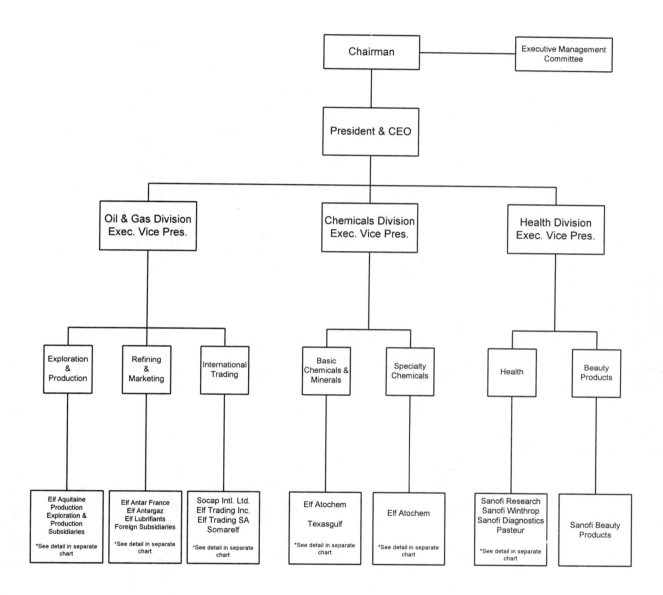

* Dec. 31, 1994

Elf Aquitaine (France)
Financial Structure
Continued from previous page

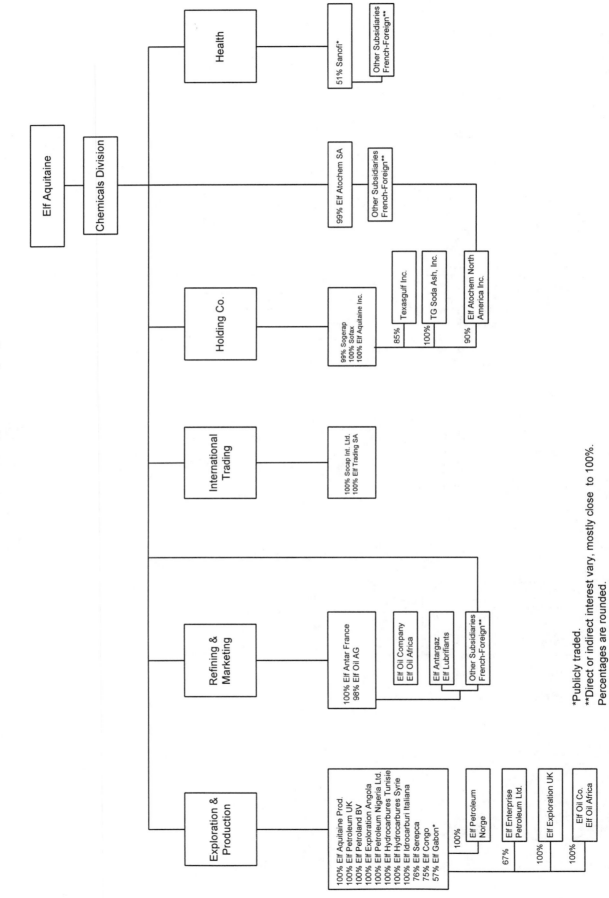

*Publicly traded.
**Direct or indirect interest vary, mostly close to 100%.
Percentages are rounded.

Eskom (Republic of South Africa)

Source: Eskom, 1996

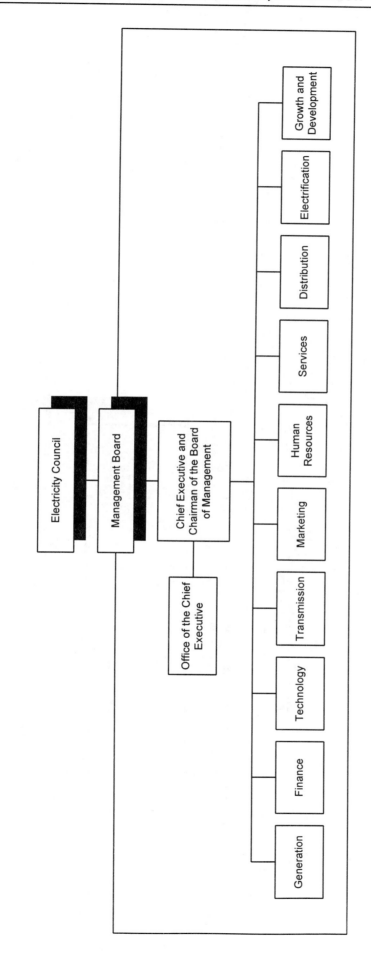

Ethyl Corporation

Source: Ethyl Corporation, 1996

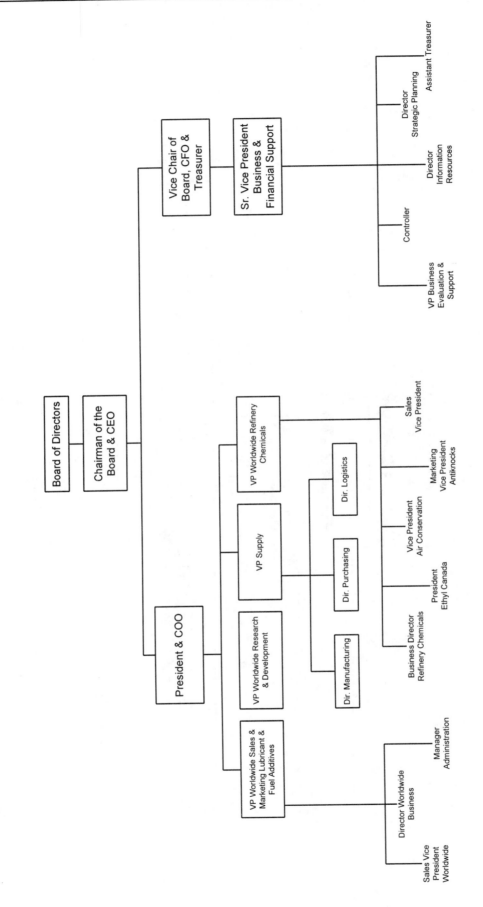

European Union (Belgium)

Source: Acceuil Jeunes ASBL, 1996

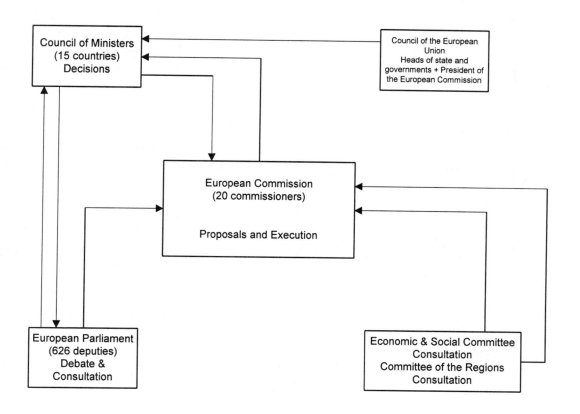

Exxon Corp.

Source: Exxon Corp., 1996

Board of Directors

- Executive Committee
- Audit Committee
- Board Advisory Committee on Contributions
- Board Compensation Committee
- Finance Committee
- Nominating Committee
- Public Issues Committee

Chief Executive Officer / Chairman of the Board
Senior Vice Presidents

- Management Committee
- Compensation & Executive Development Committee

- Controller's Vice President & Controller
- Corporate Planning General Mgr.
- Environment & Safety Vice President
- Human Resources Vice President
- Investor Relations & Office of the Secretary VP & Secretary
- Law Vice President & General Counsel
- Medicine & Occupational Health Vice President
- Public Affairs Vice President
- Tax Vice President & General Tax Counsel
- Treasurer's Vice President & Treasurer

- Exxon Chemical President
- Exxon Coal and Minerals President
- Exxon Company, International President
- Exxon Company, U.S.A. President
- Exxon Exploration President
- Exxon Production Research President
- Exxon Research & Engineering President
- Imperial Chairman

Fina Oil and Chemical Company, Inc.

Source: Fina Oil and Chemical Company, Inc., 1996

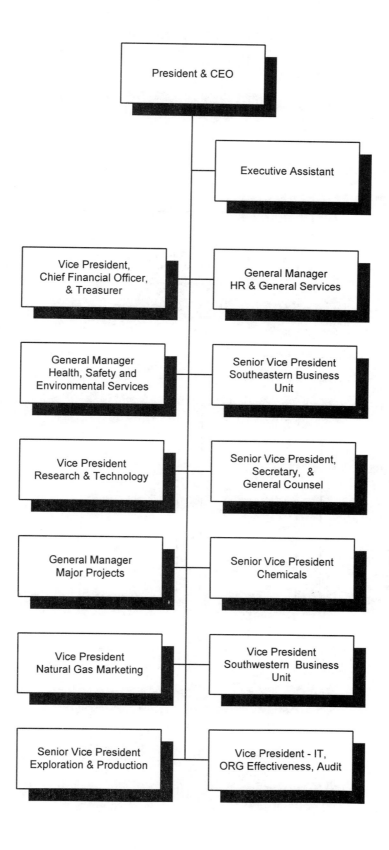

Fortis (The Netherlands)

Source: Fortis, 1996

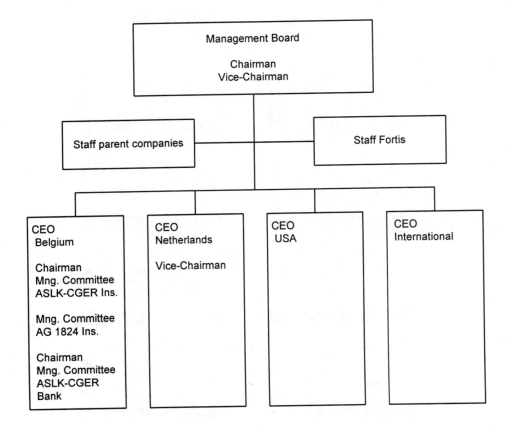

Fuji Electric Co., Ltd. (Japan)

Source: Fuji Electric Co., Ltd., 1996

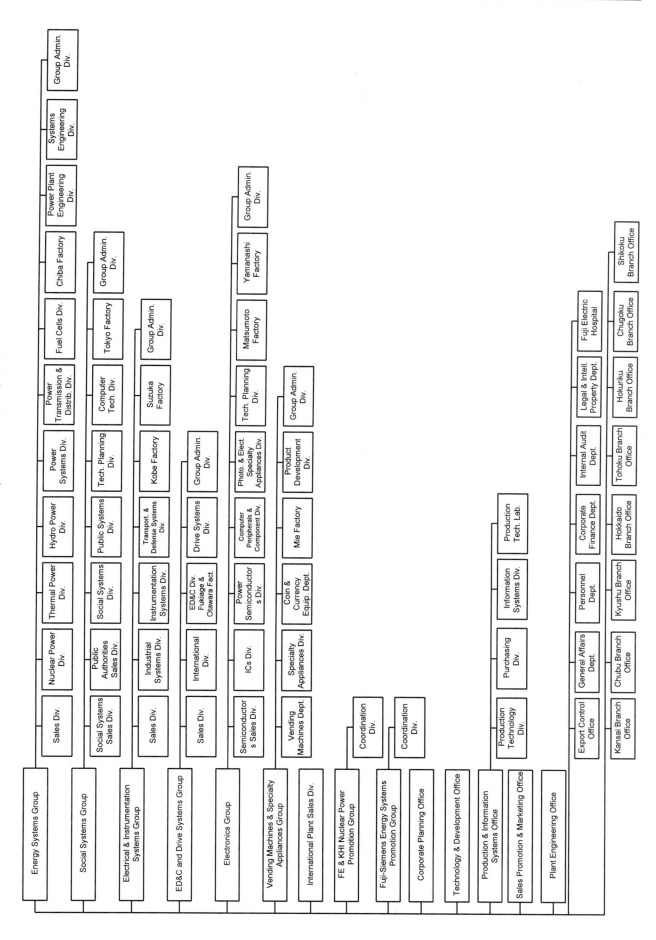

Fuji Heavy Industries Ltd. (Japan)

Source: Fuji Heavy Industries Ltd., 1996

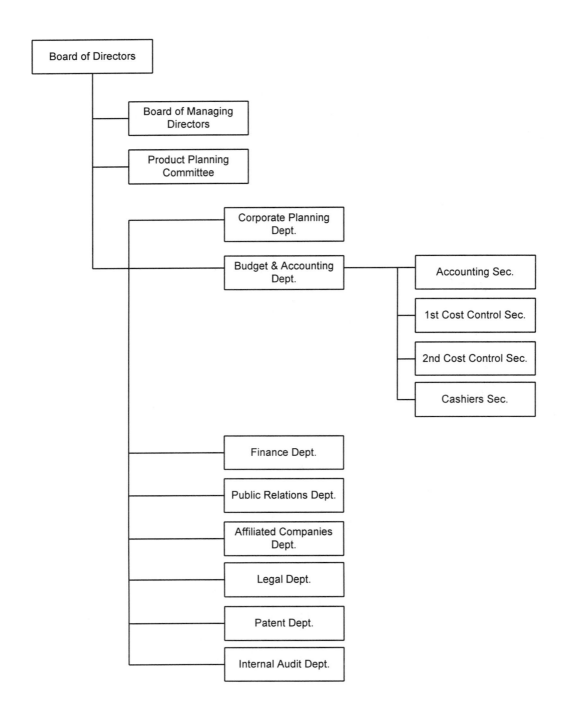

Continued on next page

Fuji Heavy Industries Ltd. (Japan)

Continued from previous page

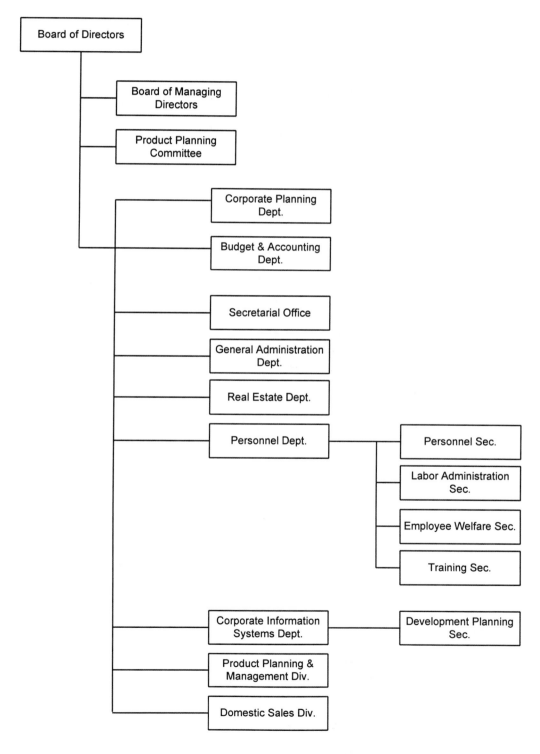

Continued on next page

Fuji Heavy Industries Ltd. (Japan)

Continued from previous page

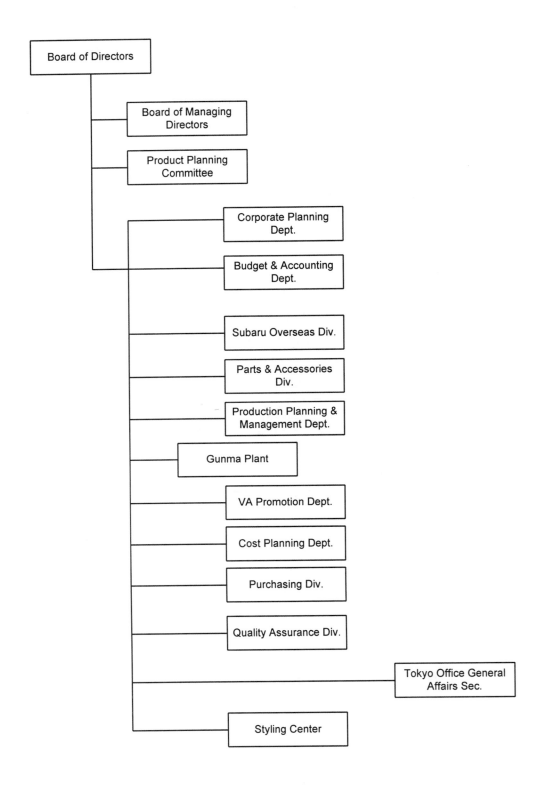

Continued on next page

Fuji Heavy Industries Ltd. (Japan)

Continued from previous page

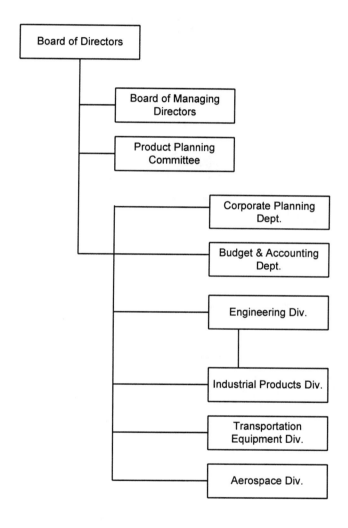

Gebroeders De Rycke n.v. (Belgium)

Source: Gebroeders De Rycke n.v., 1996

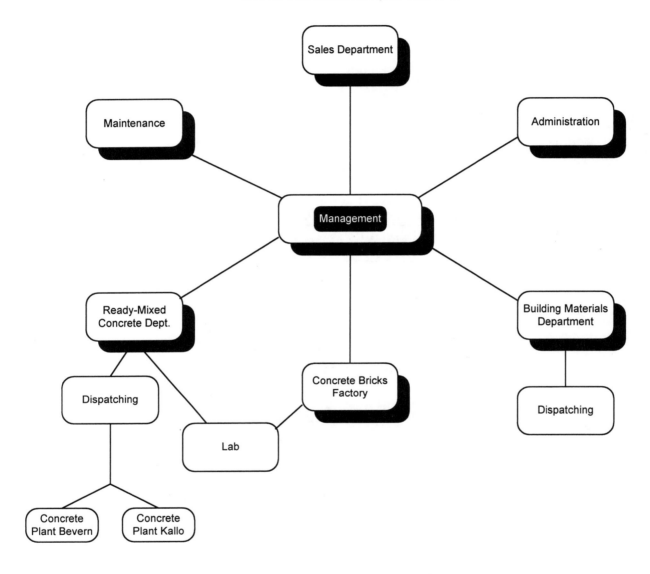

General Electric Co.

Source: General Electric Co., 1996

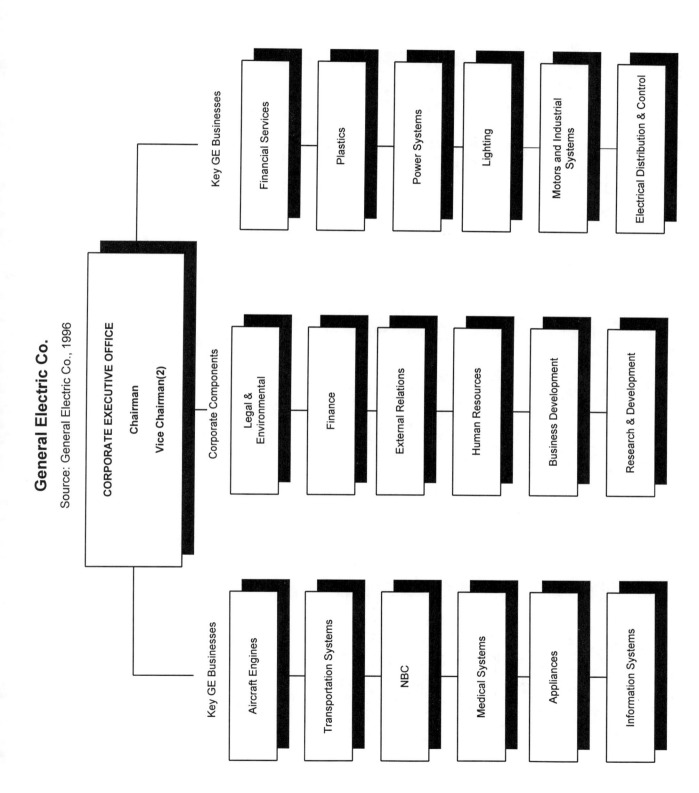

CORPORATE EXECUTIVE OFFICE

Chairman

Vice Chairman(2)

Key GE Businesses

- Financial Services
- Plastics
- Power Systems
- Lighting
- Motors and Industrial Systems
- Electrical Distribution & Control

Corporate Components

- Legal & Environmental
- Finance
- External Relations
- Human Resources
- Business Development
- Research & Development

Key GE Businesses

- Aircraft Engines
- Transportation Systems
- NBC
- Medical Systems
- Appliances
- Information Systems

General Motors Corp.

Source: General Motors Corp., 1996

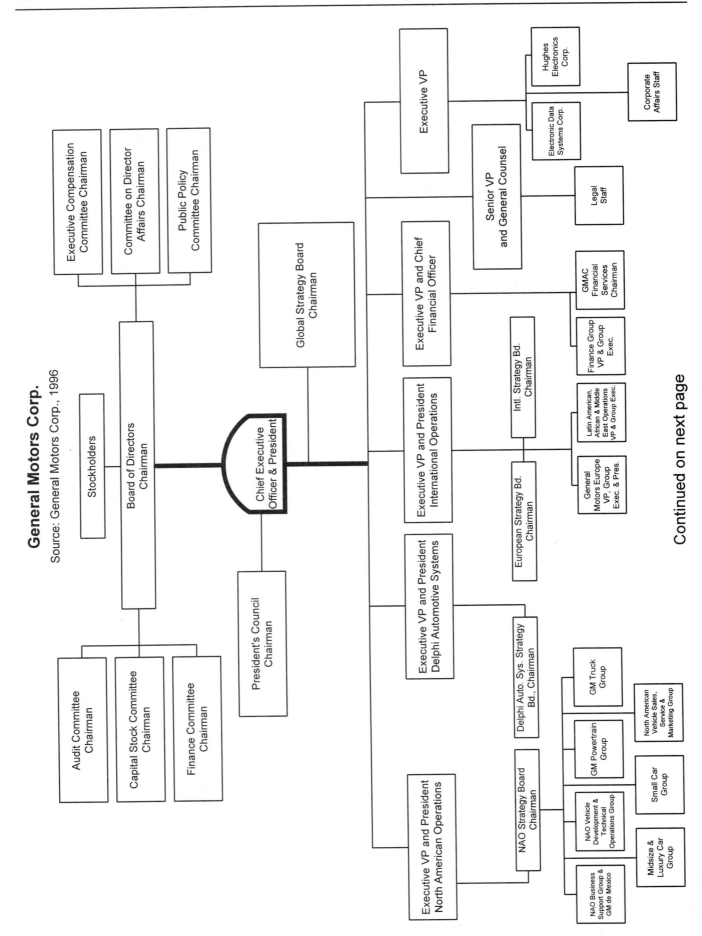

Continued on next page

General Motors Corp.

Continued from previous page

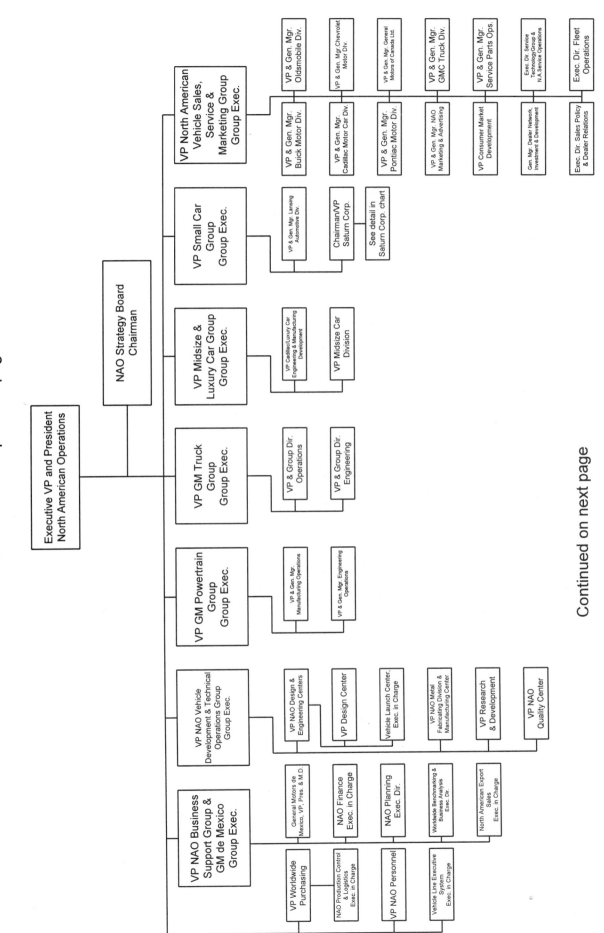

Continued on next page

General Motors Corp.
Continued from previous page

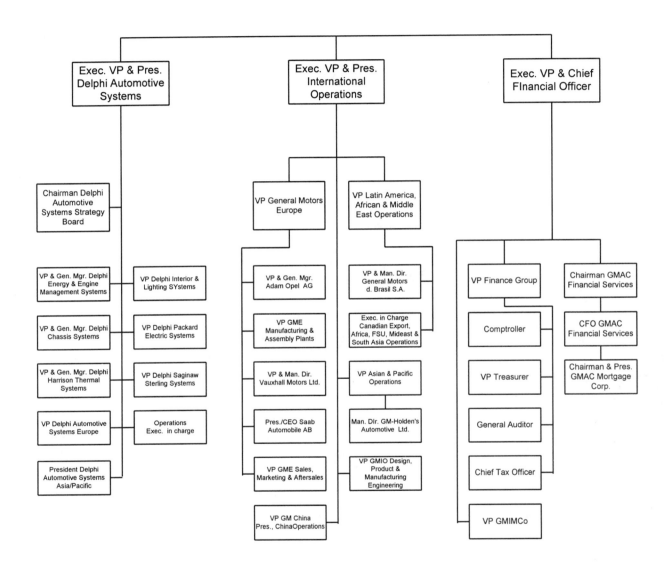

Continued on next page

General Motors Corp.
Continued from previous page

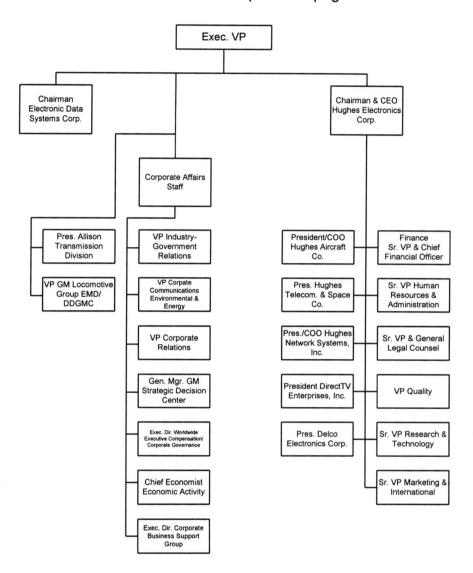

Exec. VP

Chairman Electronic Data Systems Corp.

Chairman & CEO Hughes Electronics Corp.

Corporate Affairs Staff

Pres. Allison Transmission Division

VP GM Locomotive Group EMD/ DDGMC

VP Industry-Government Relations

VP Corpate Communications Environmental & Energy

VP Corporate Relations

Gen. Mgr. GM Strategic Decision Center

Exec. Dir. Worldwide Executive Compensation/ Corporate Governance

Chief Economist Economic Activity

Exec. Dir. Corporate Business Support Group

President/COO Hughes Aircraft Co.

Pres. Hughes Telecom. & Space Co.

Pres./COO Hughes Network Systems, Inc.

President DirectTV Enterprises, Inc.

Pres. Delco Electronics Corp.

Finance Sr. VP & Chief Financial Officer

Sr. VP Human Resources & Administration

Sr. VP & General Legal Counsel

VP Quality

Sr. VP Research & Technology

Sr. VP Marketing & International

Green Bay Packers, Inc.

Source: Green Bay Packers, Inc., 1996

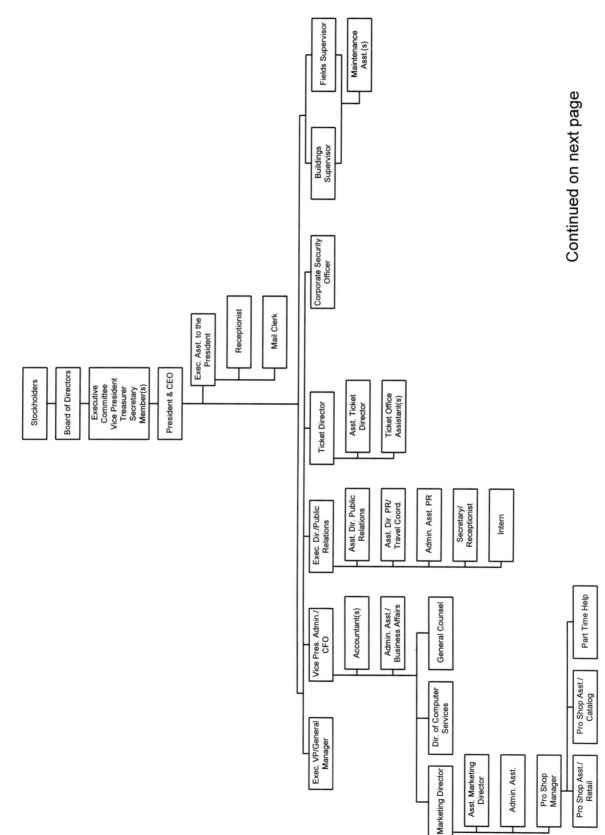

Continued on next page

Green Bay Packers, Inc.
Continued from previous page

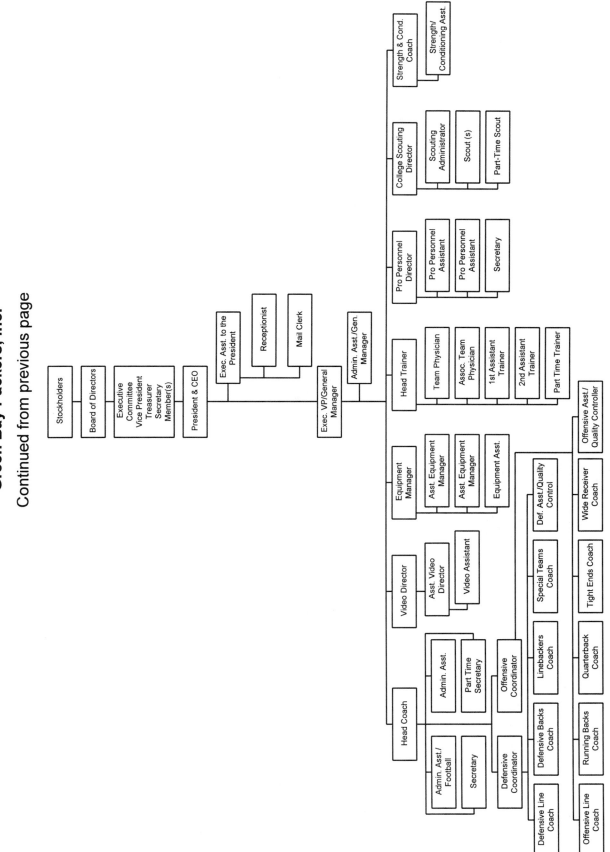

Harrah's Entertainment, Inc.
Source: Harrah's Entertainment, Inc., 1996

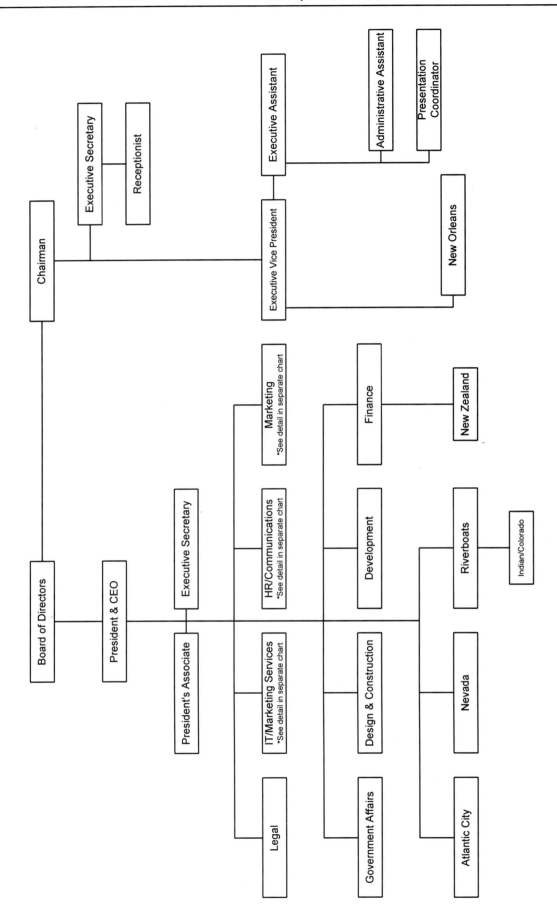

Harrah's Entertainment, Inc.
Human Resources & Communications

Source: Harrah's Entertainment, Inc., 1996

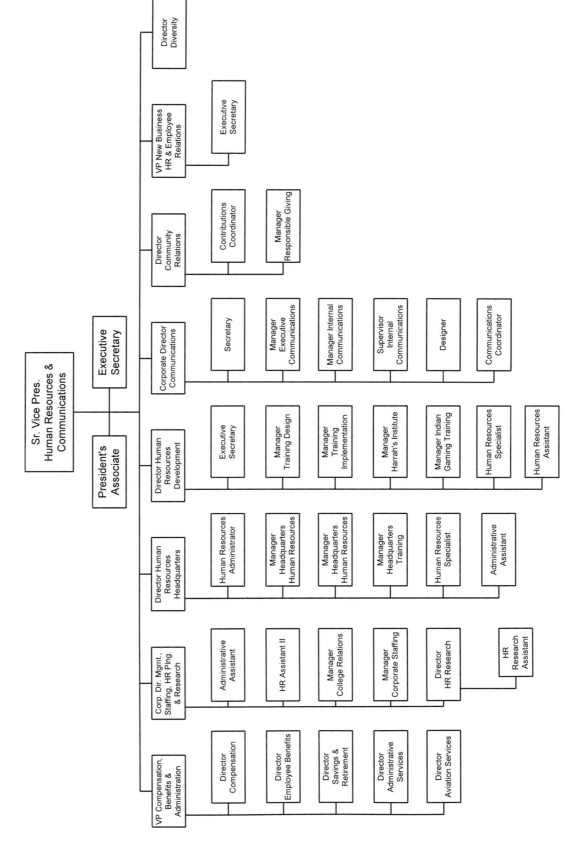

Harrah's Entertainment, Inc.
Information Technology & Marketing Services

Source: Harrah's Entertainment, Inc., 1996

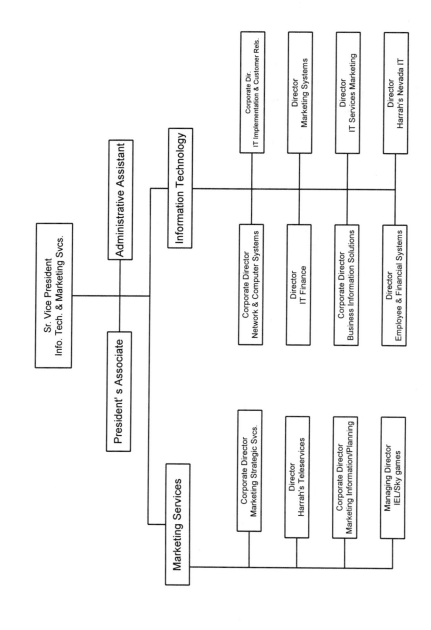

Harrah's Entertainment, Inc.
Marketing

Source: Harrah's Entertainment, Inc., 1996

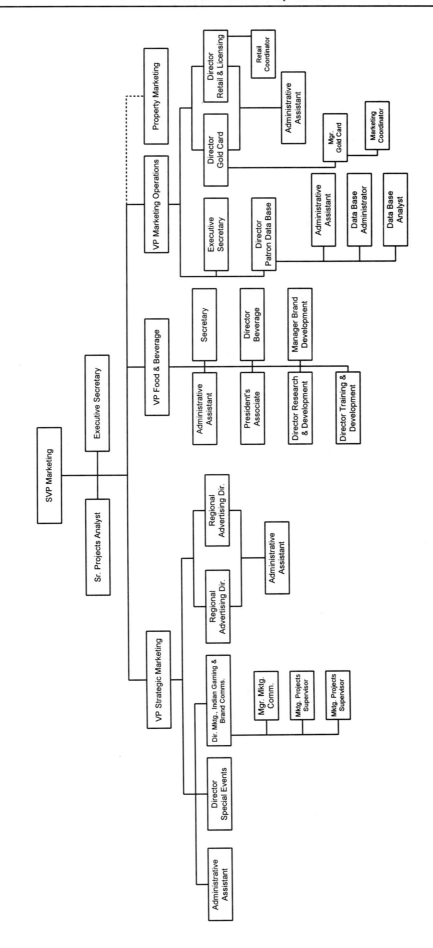

Henry Ford Health System

Source: Henry Ford Health System, 1996

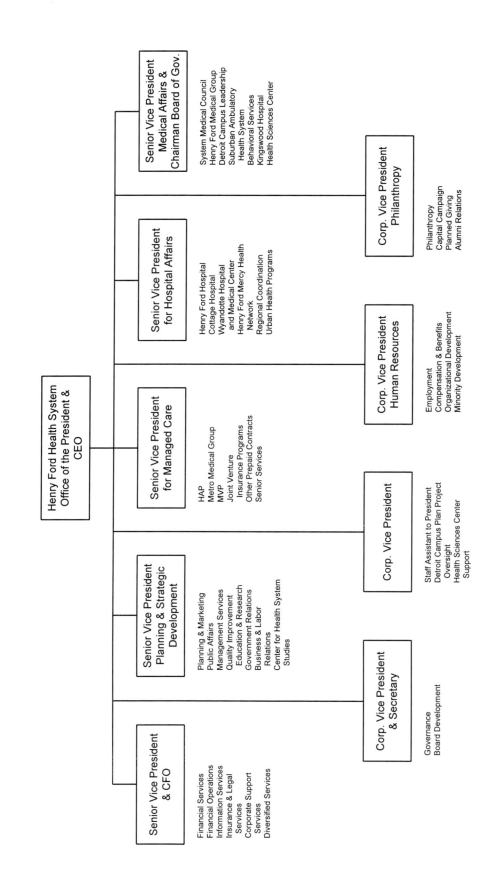

Henry Ford Health System
Office of the President & CEO

Senior Vice President & CFO
Financial Services
Financial Operations
Information Services
Insurance & Legal Services
Corporate Support Services
Diversified Services

Corp. Vice President & Secretary
Governance
Board Development

Senior Vice President Planning & Strategic Development
Planning & Marketing
Public Affairs
Management Services
Quality Improvement
Education & Research
Government Relations
Business & Labor Relations
Center for Health System Studies

Corp. Vice President
Staff Assistant to President
Detroit Campus Plan Project Oversight
Health Sciences Center Support

Senior Vice President for Managed Care
HAP
Metro Medical Group
MVP
Joint Venture
Insurance Programs
Other Prepaid Contracts
Senior Services

Corp. Vice President Human Resources
Employment
Compensation & Benefits
Organizational Development
Minority Development

Senior Vice President for Hospital Affairs
Henry Ford Hospital
Cottage Hospital
Wyandotte Hospital and Medical Center
Henry Ford Mercy Health Network
Regional Coordination
Urban Health Programs

Corp. Vice President Philanthropy
Philanthropy
Capital Campaign
Planned Giving
Alumni Relations

Senior Vice President Medical Affairs & Chairman Board of Gov.
System Medical Council
Henry Ford Medical Group
Detroit Campus Leadership
Suburban Ambulatory Health System
Behavioral Services
Kingswood Hospital
Health Sciences Center

Henry Ford Museum & Greenfield Village

Source: Henry Ford Museum & Greenfield Village, 1996

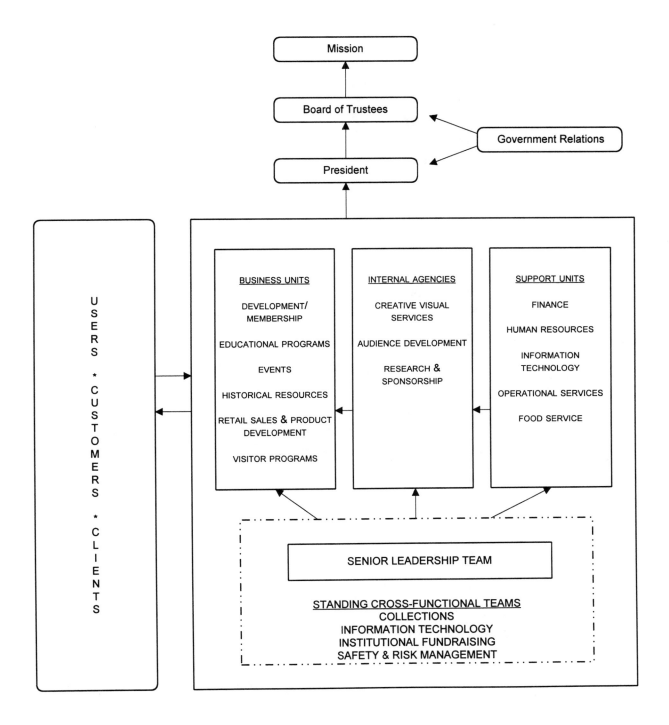

Hewlett-Packard Co.

Source: Hewlett-Packard Co., 1996

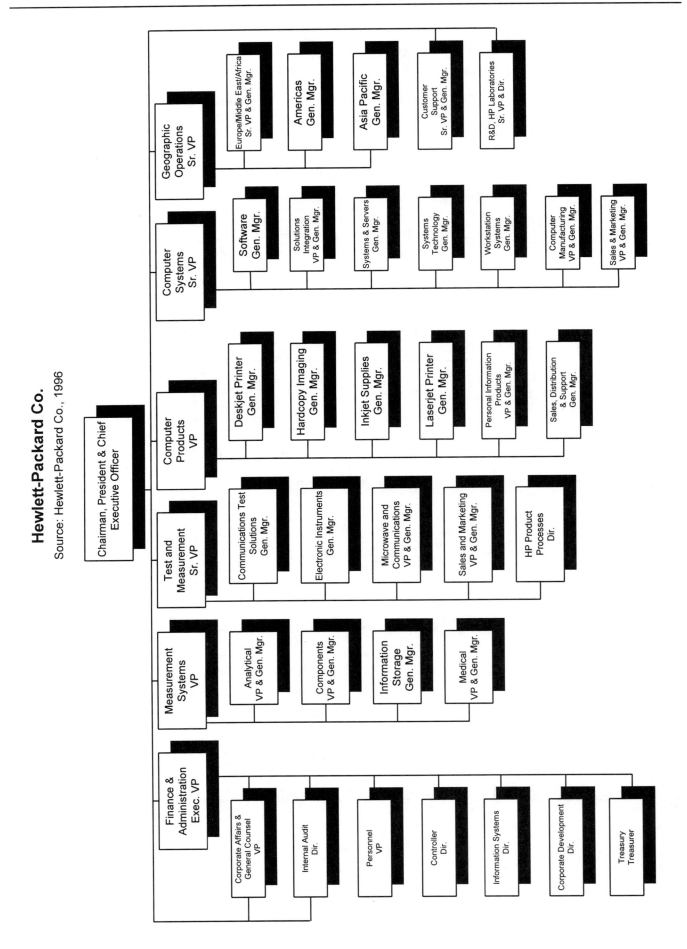

Chairman, President & Chief Executive Officer

Geographic Operations Sr. VP
- Europe/Middle East/Africa Sr. VP & Gen. Mgr.
- Americas Gen. Mgr.
- Asia Pacific Gen. Mgr.
- Customer Support Sr. VP & Gen. Mgr.
- R&D, HP Laboratories Sr. VP & Dir.

Computer Systems Sr. VP
- Software Gen. Mgr.
- Solutions Integration VP & Gen. Mgr.
- Systems & Servers Gen. Mgr.
- Systems Technology Gen. Mgr.
- Workstation Systems Gen. Mgr.
- Computer Manufacturing VP & Gen. Mgr.
- Sales & Marketing VP & Gen. Mgr.

Computer Products VP
- Deskjet Printer Gen. Mgr.
- Hardcopy Imaging Gen. Mgr.
- Inkjet Supplies Gen. Mgr.
- Laserjet Printer Gen. Mgr.
- Personal Information Products VP & Gen. Mgr.
- Sales, Distribution & Support Gen. Mgr.

Test and Measurement Sr. VP
- Communications Test Solutions Gen. Mgr.
- Electronic Instruments Gen. Mgr.
- Microwave and Communications VP & Gen. Mgr.
- Sales and Marketing VP & Gen. Mgr.
- HP Product Processes Dir.

Measurement Systems VP
- Analytical VP & Gen. Mgr.
- Components VP & Gen. Mgr.
- Information Storage Gen. Mgr.
- Medical VP & Gen. Mgr.

Finance & Administration Exec. VP
- Corporate Affairs & General Counsel VP
- Internal Audit Dir.
- Personnel VP
- Controller Dir.
- Information Systems Dir.
- Corporate Development Dir.
- Treasury Treasurer

Hitachi, Ltd. (Japan)

Source: Hitachi, Ltd., 1996

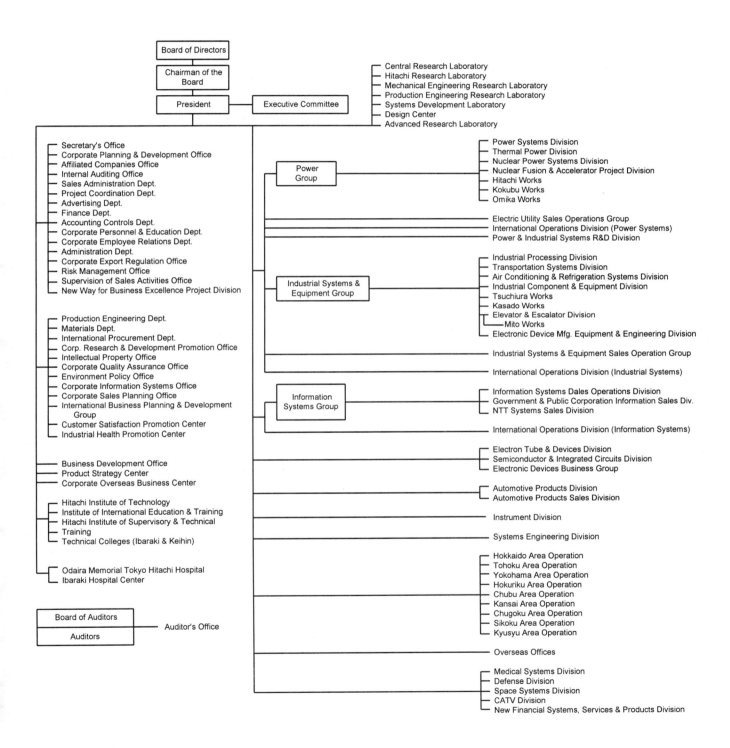

- Board of Directors
- Chairman of the Board
- President
- Executive Committee

- Central Research Laboratory
- Hitachi Research Laboratory
- Mechanical Engineering Research Laboratory
- Production Engineering Research Laboratory
- Systems Development Laboratory
- Design Center
- Advanced Research Laboratory

- Secretary's Office
- Corporate Planning & Development Office
- Affiliated Companies Office
- Internal Auditing Office
- Sales Administration Dept.
- Project Coordination Dept.
- Advertising Dept.
- Finance Dept.
- Accounting Controls Dept.
- Corporate Personnel & Education Dept.
- Corporate Employee Relations Dept.
- Administration Dept.
- Corporate Export Regulation Office
- Risk Management Office
- Supervision of Sales Activities Office
- New Way for Business Excellence Project Division

- Production Engineering Dept.
- Materials Dept.
- International Procurement Dept.
- Corp. Research & Development Promotion Office
- Intellectual Property Office
- Corporate Quality Assurance Office
- Environment Policy Office
- Corporate Information Systems Office
- Corporate Sales Planning Office
- International Business Planning & Development Group
- Customer Satisfaction Promotion Center
- Industrial Health Promotion Center

- Business Development Office
- Product Strategy Center
- Corporate Overseas Business Center

- Hitachi Institute of Technology
- Institute of International Education & Training
- Hitachi Institute of Supervisory & Technical Training
- Technical Colleges (Ibaraki & Keihin)

- Odaira Memorial Tokyo Hitachi Hospital
- Ibaraki Hospital Center

- Board of Auditors
- Auditors
  - Auditor's Office

Power Group
- Power Systems Division
- Thermal Power Division
- Nuclear Power Systems Division
- Nuclear Fusion & Accelerator Project Division
- Hitachi Works
- Kokubu Works
- Omika Works

- Electric Utility Sales Operations Group
- International Operations Division (Power Systems)
- Power & Industrial Systems R&D Division

Industrial Systems & Equipment Group
- Industrial Processing Division
- Transportation Systems Division
- Air Conditioning & Refrigeration Systems Division
- Industrial Component & Equipment Division
- Tsuchiura Works
- Kasado Works
- Elevator & Escalator Division
  - Mito Works
- Electronic Device Mfg. Equipment & Engineering Division

- Industrial Systems & Equipment Sales Operation Group

- International Operations Division (Industrial Systems)

Information Systems Group
- Information Systems Dales Operations Division
- Government & Public Corporation Information Sales Div.
- NTT Systems Sales Division

- International Operations Division (Information Systems)

- Electron Tube & Devices Division
- Semiconductor & Integrated Circuits Division
- Electronic Devices Business Group

- Automotive Products Division
- Automotive Products Sales Division

- Instrument Division

- Systems Engineering Division

- Hokkaido Area Operation
- Tohoku Area Operation
- Yokohama Area Operation
- Hokuriku Area Operation
- Chubu Area Operation
- Kansai Area Operation
- Chugoku Area Operation
- Sikoku Area Operation
- Kyusyu Area Operation

- Overseas Offices

- Medical Systems Division
- Defense Division
- Space Systems Division
- CATV Division
- New Financial Systems, Services & Products Division

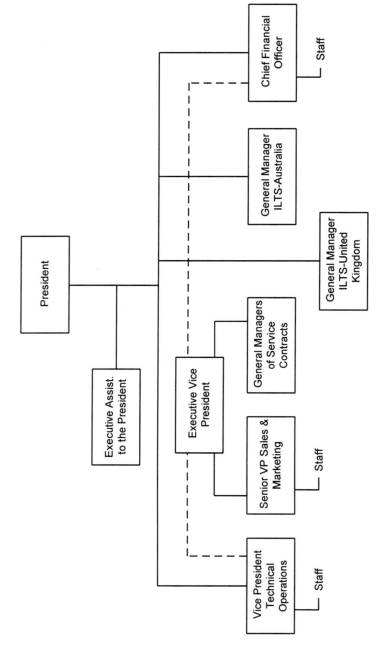

International Lottery & Totalizator Systems, Inc. (ILTS)

Source: International Lottery & Totalizator Systems, Inc. (ILTS), 1996

Invetech Co.

Source: Invetech Co., 1996

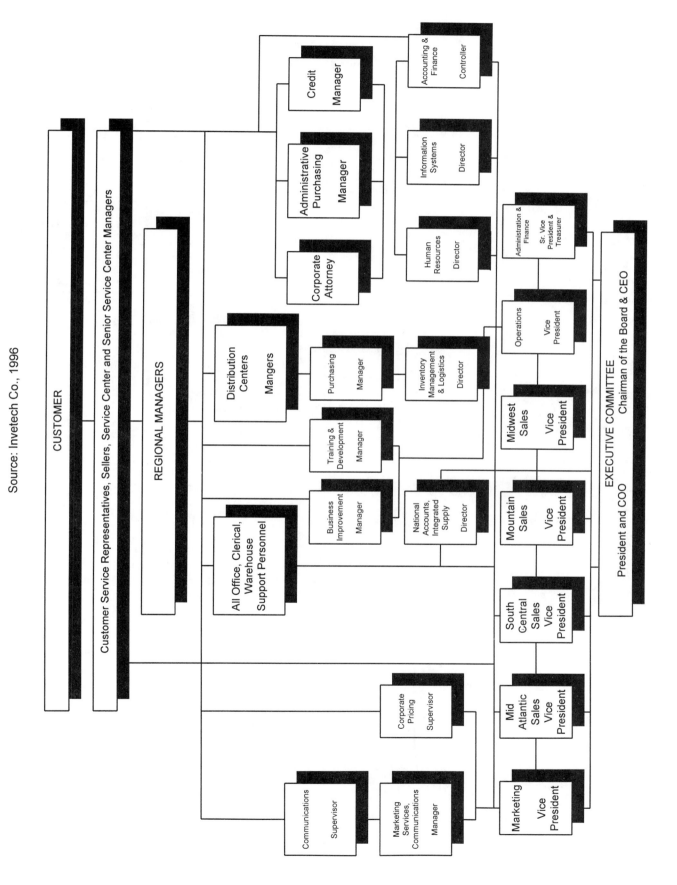

Ishikawajima-Harima Heavy Industries Co., Ltd. (Japan)

Source: Ishikawajima-Harima Heavy Industries Co., Ltd., 1996

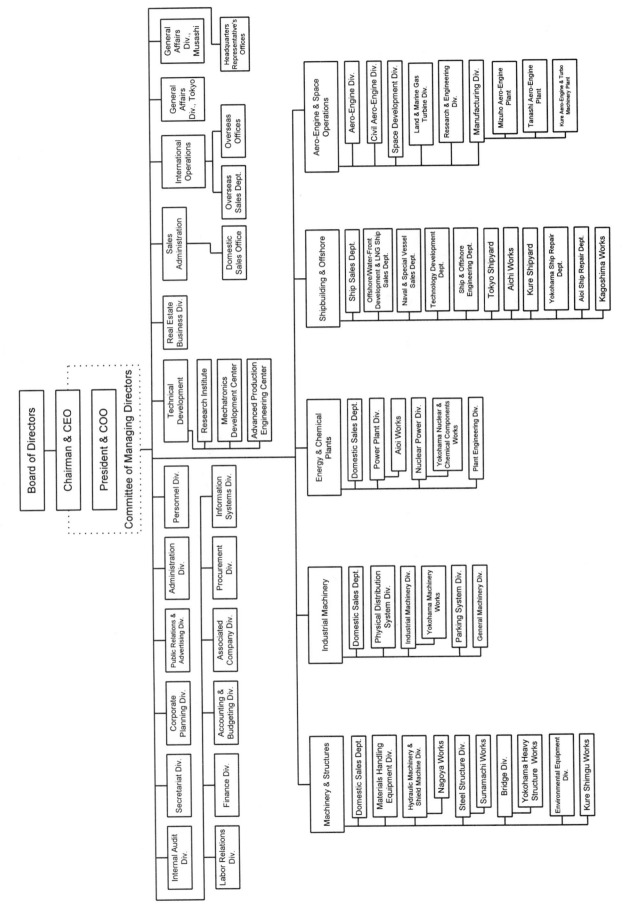

Ito-Yokado Co., Ltd. (Japan)

Source: Ito-Yokado Co., Ltd., 1996

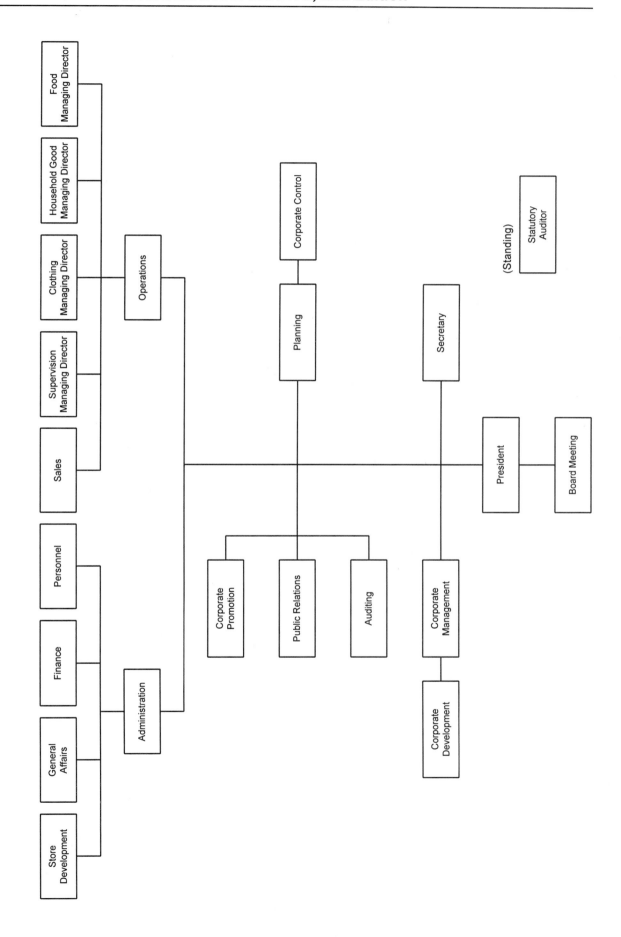

The Kansai Electric Power Co., Inc. (Japan)

Source: The Kansai Electric Power Co., Inc., 1995

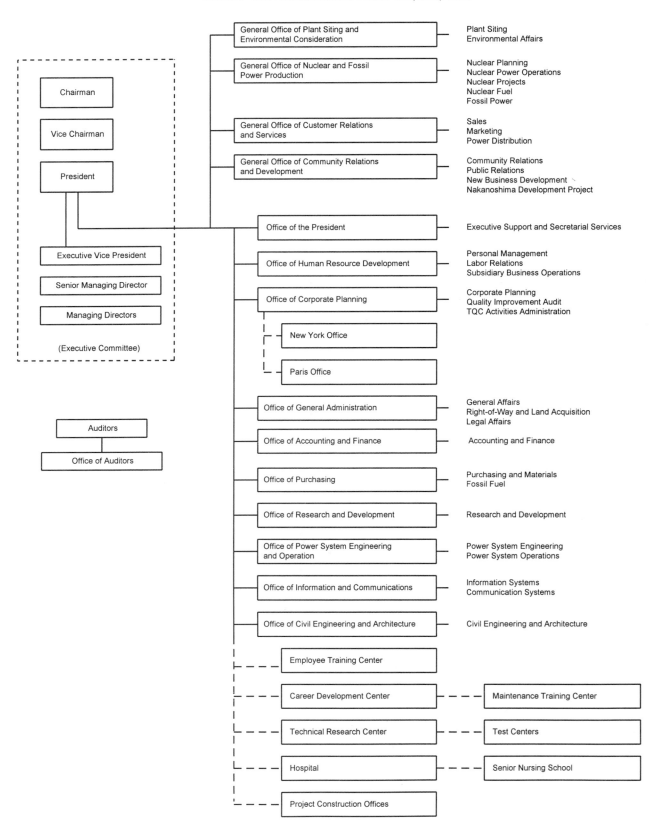

General Office of Plant Siting and Environmental Consideration	Plant Siting Environmental Affairs
General Office of Nuclear and Fossil Power Production	Nuclear Planning Nuclear Power Operations Nuclear Projects Nuclear Fuel Fossil Power
General Office of Customer Relations and Services	Sales Marketing Power Distribution
General Office of Community Relations and Development	Community Relations Public Relations New Business Development Nakanoshima Development Project
Office of the President	Executive Support and Secretarial Services
Office of Human Resource Development	Personal Management Labor Relations Subsidiary Business Operations
Office of Corporate Planning	Corporate Planning Quality Improvement Audit TQC Activities Administration
New York Office	
Paris Office	
Office of General Administration	General Affairs Right-of-Way and Land Acquisition Legal Affairs
Office of Accounting and Finance	Accounting and Finance
Office of Purchasing	Purchasing and Materials Fossil Fuel
Office of Research and Development	Research and Development
Office of Power System Engineering and Operation	Power System Engineering Power System Operations
Office of Information and Communications	Information Systems Communication Systems
Office of Civil Engineering and Architecture	Civil Engineering and Architecture
Employee Training Center	
Career Development Center	Maintenance Training Center
Technical Research Center	Test Centers
Hospital	Senior Nursing School
Project Construction Offices	

Chairman

Vice Chairman

President

Executive Vice President

Senior Managing Director

Managing Directors

(Executive Committee)

Auditors

Office of Auditors

Kawasaki Steel Corp. (Japan)

Source: Annual report, 1994

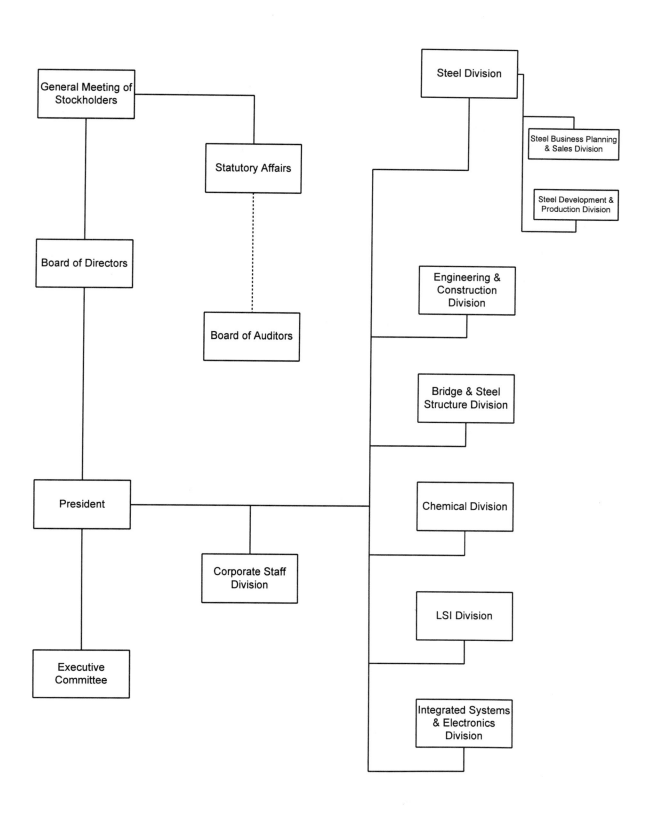

Kirin Brewery Company, Ltd. (Japan)

Source: Kirin Brewery Company, Ltd., 1996

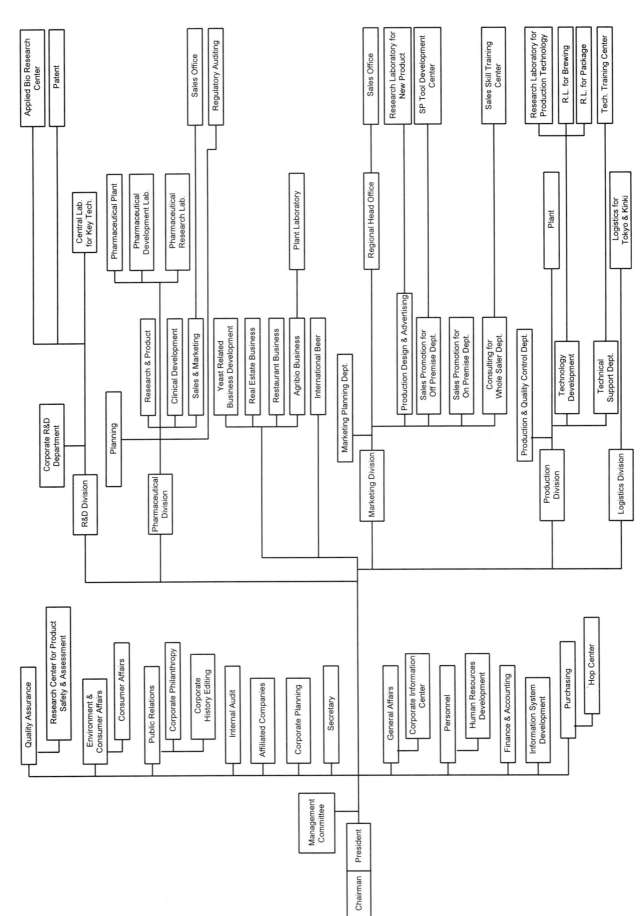

Komatsu Ltd. (Japan)

Source: Komatsu Ltd., 1996

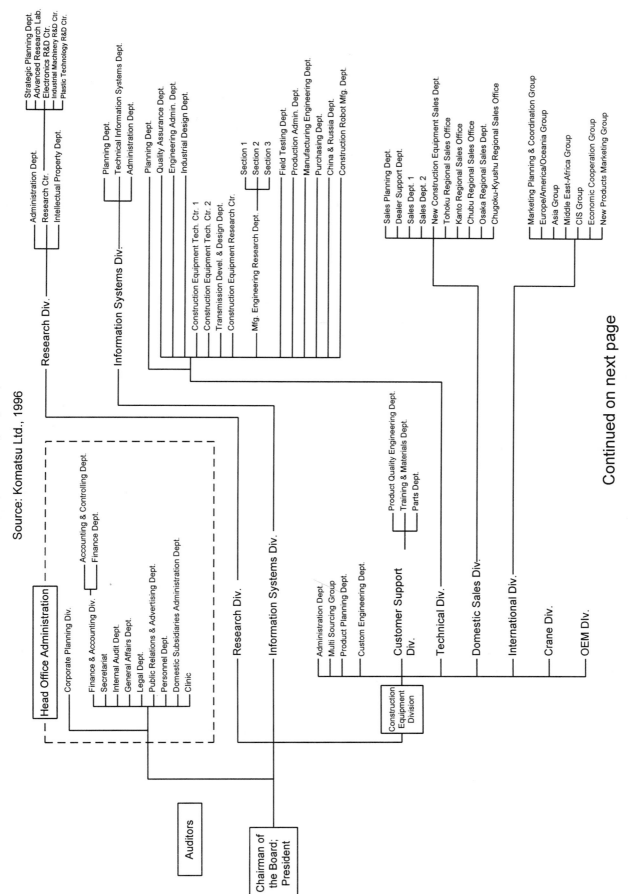

Continued on next page

Komatsu Ltd. (Japan)
Continued from previous page

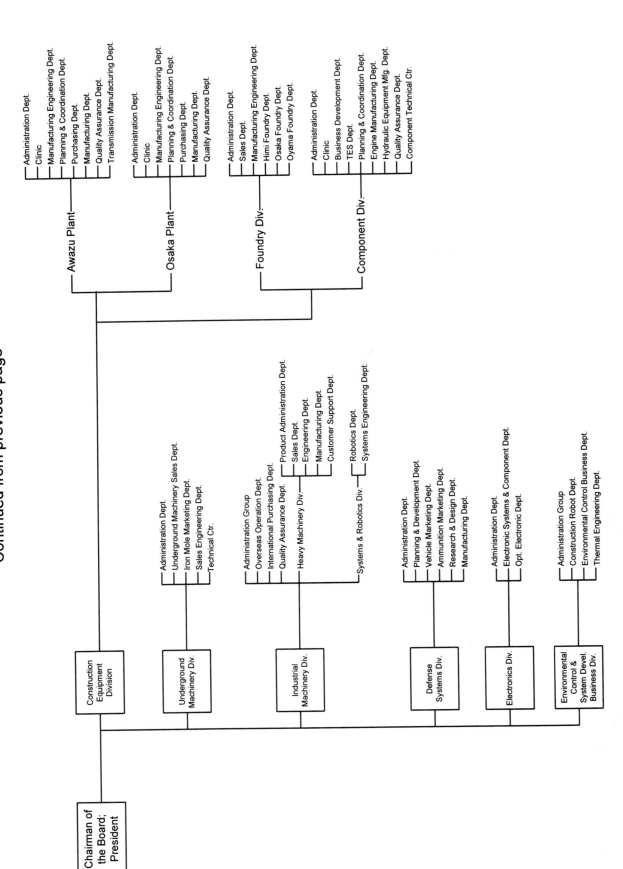

K.P.R. Sports International, Inc.

Source: KPR Sports International, 1996

Kubota Corporation (Japan)

Source: Kubota Corporation, 1996

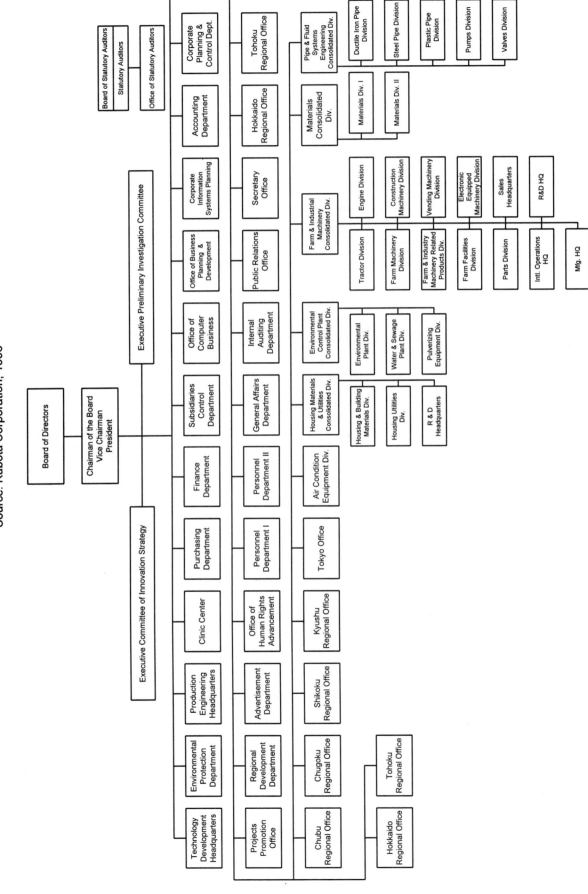

The Kyoei Life Insurance Co., Ltd. (Japan)

Source: The Kyoei Life Insurance Co., Ltd., 1996

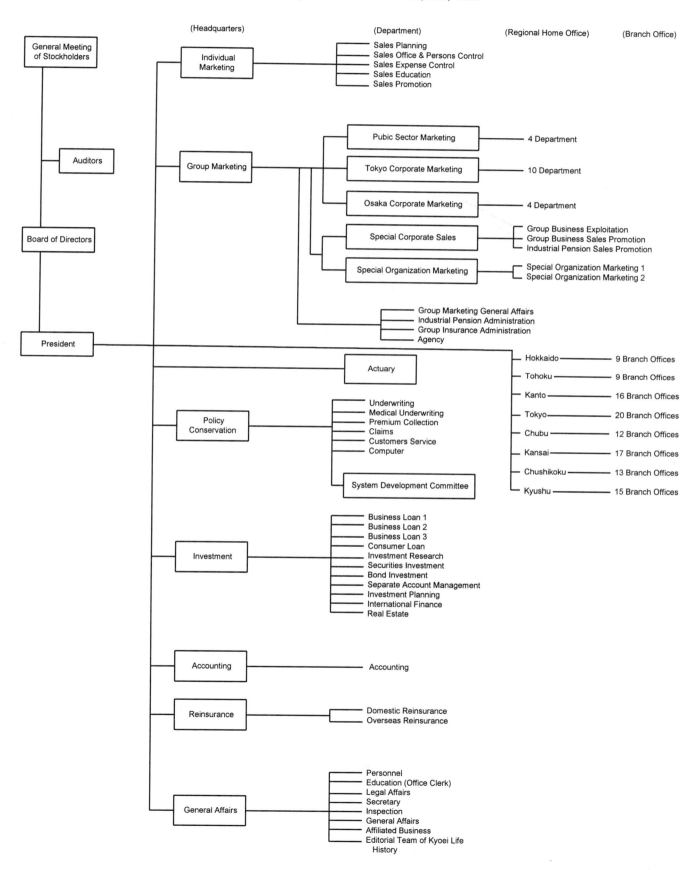

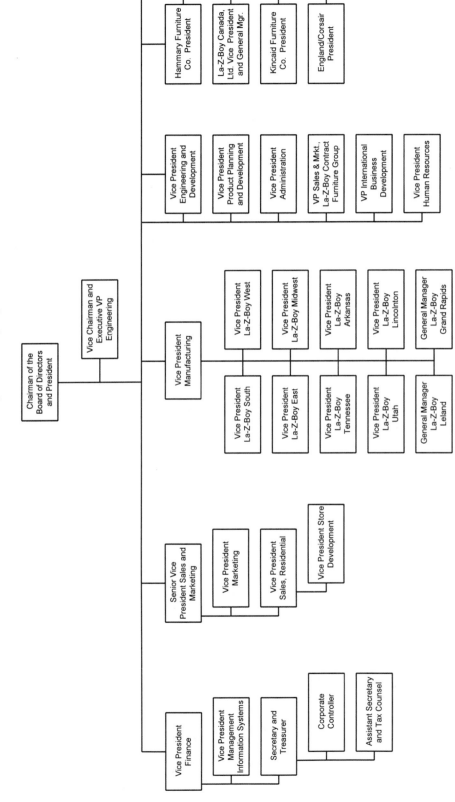

La-Z-Boy Chair Company

Source: La-Z-Boy Chair Company, 1996

Landis & Gyr AG (Switzerland)

Source: Landis & Gyr AG, 1996

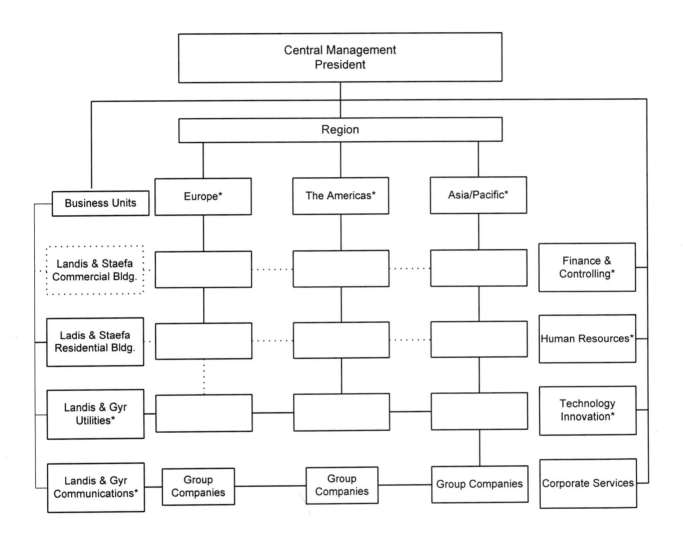

*Central Management members.

Company provided chart with blank shapes (above).

Livonia Historical Society

Source: Livonia Historical Society, 1996

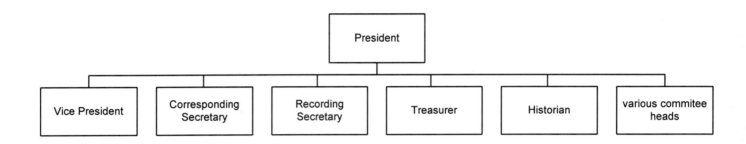

The Livonia Historical Society conducts
activities and confers with the following groups
on an informal basis: the Friends of
Greenmead, the Livonia Historical
Commission, and local Questers groups.

Long John Silver's, Inc.

Source: Long John Silver's, Inc., 1996

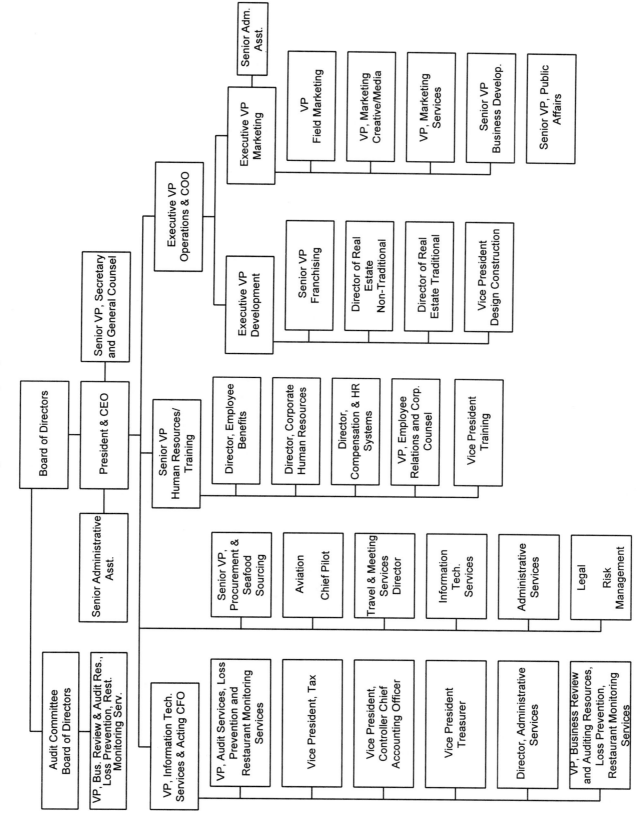

Long-Term Credit Bank of Japan, Ltd. (Japan)

Source: Annual Report, 1996

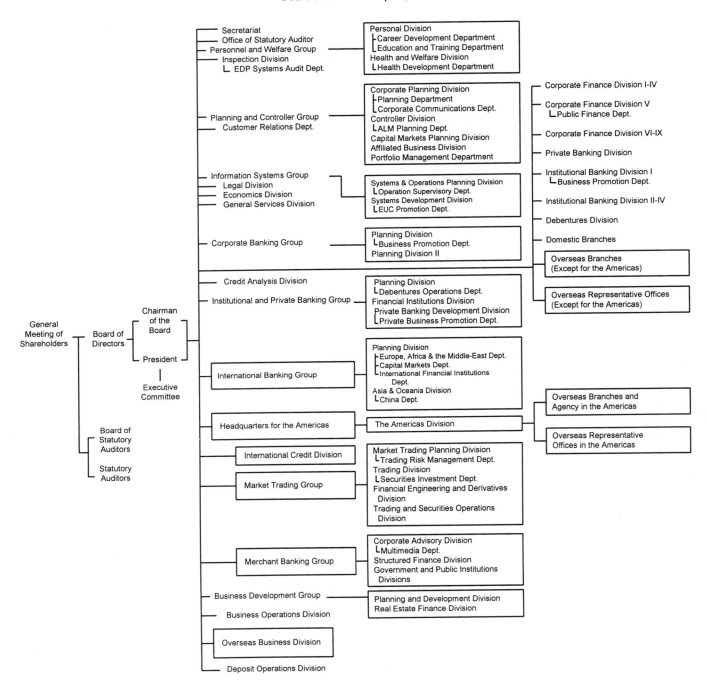

MagneTek Inc.

Source: Annual report, 1995

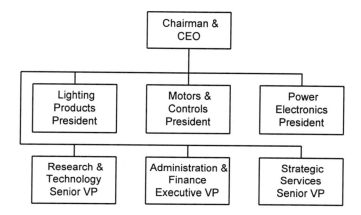

Maruha Corporation (Japan)

Source: Maruha Corporation, 1996

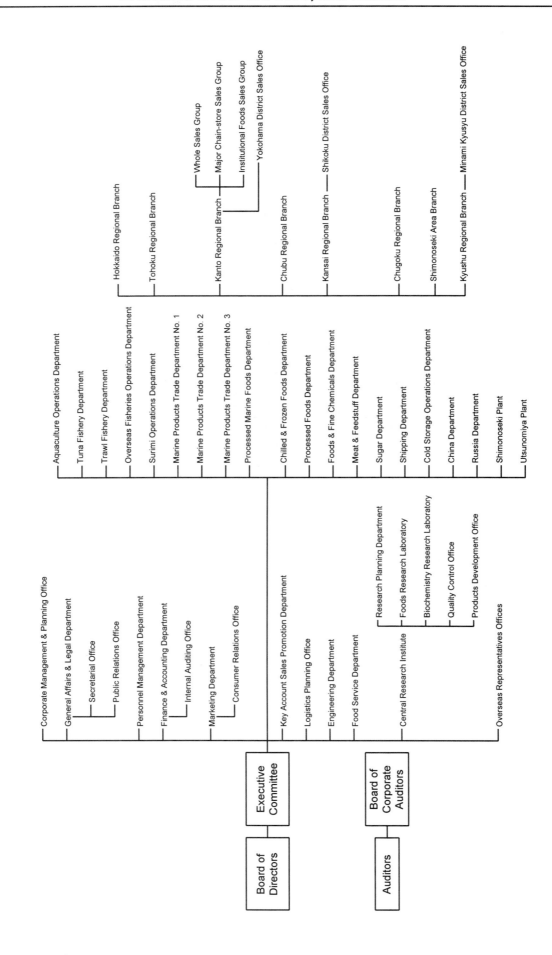

Matsushita Electric Works, Ltd. (Japan)

Source: Matsushita Electric Works, Ltd., 1996

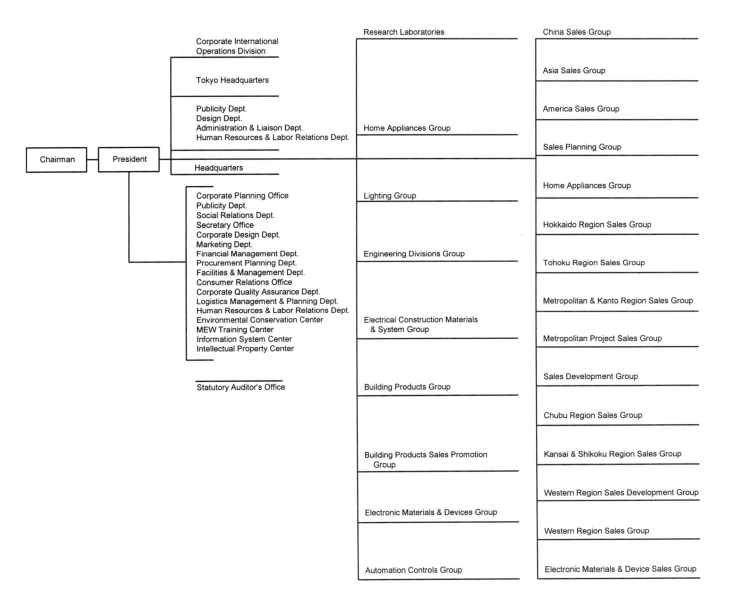

Mazda Motor Corp. (Japan)

Source: Mazda Motor Corp., 1996

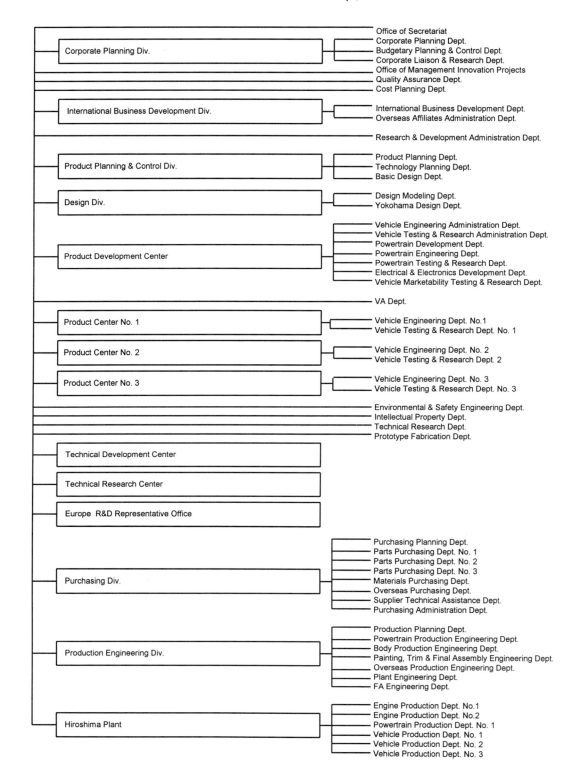

Continued on next page

Mazda Motor Corp.
Continued from previous page

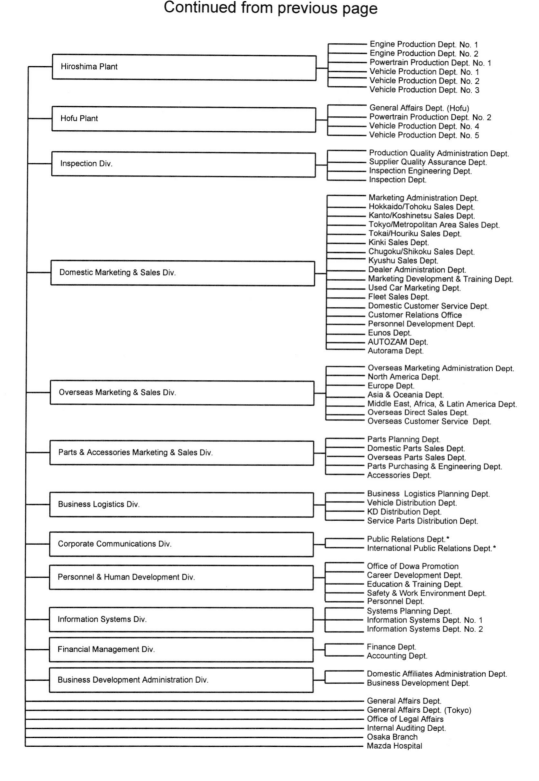

Hiroshima Plant
- Engine Production Dept. No. 1
- Engine Production Dept. No. 2
- Powertrain Production Dept. No. 1
- Vehicle Production Dept. No. 1
- Vehicle Production Dept. No. 2
- Vehicle Production Dept. No. 3

Hofu Plant
- General Affairs Dept. (Hofu)
- Powertrain Production Dept. No. 2
- Vehicle Production Dept. No. 4
- Vehicle Production Dept. No. 5

Inspection Div.
- Production Quality Administration Dept.
- Supplier Quality Assurance Dept.
- Inspection Engineering Dept.
- Inspection Dept.

Domestic Marketing & Sales Div.
- Marketing Administration Dept.
- Hokkaido/Tohoku Sales Dept.
- Kanto/Koshinetsu Sales Dept.
- Tokyo/Metropolitan Area Sales Dept.
- Tokai/Houriku Sales Dept.
- Kinki Sales Dept.
- Chugoku/Shikoku Sales Dept.
- Kyushu Sales Dept.
- Dealer Administration Dept.
- Marketing Development & Training Dept.
- Used Car Marketing Dept.
- Fleet Sales Dept.
- Domestic Customer Service Dept.
- Customer Relations Office
- Personnel Development Dept.
- Eunos Dept.
- AUTOZAM Dept.
- Autorama Dept.

Overseas Marketing & Sales Div.
- Overseas Marketing Administration Dept.
- North America Dept.
- Europe Dept.
- Asia & Oceania Dept.
- Middle East, Africa, & Latin America Dept.
- Overseas Direct Sales Dept.
- Overseas Customer Service Dept.

Parts & Accessories Marketing & Sales Div.
- Parts Planning Dept.
- Domestic Parts Sales Dept.
- Overseas Parts Sales Dept.
- Parts Purchasing & Engineering Dept.
- Accessories Dept.

Business Logistics Div.
- Business Logistics Planning Dept.
- Vehicle Distribution Dept.
- KD Distribution Dept.
- Service Parts Distribution Dept.

Corporate Communications Div.
- Public Relations Dept.*
- International Public Relations Dept.*

Personnel & Human Development Div.
- Office of Dowa Promotion
- Career Development Dept.
- Education & Training Dept.
- Safety & Work Environment Dept.
- Personnel Dept.

Information Systems Div.
- Systems Planning Dept.
- Information Systems Dept. No. 1
- Information Systems Dept. No. 2

Financial Management Div.
- Finance Dept.
- Accounting Dept.

Business Development Administration Div.
- Domestic Affiliates Administration Dept.
- Business Development Dept.

- General Affairs Dept.
- General Affairs Dept. (Tokyo)
- Office of Legal Affairs
- Internal Auditing Dept.
- Osaka Branch
- Mazda Hospital

*Dept. names changed as
of March 20, 1995

McDermott International, Inc.

Source: McDermott International Inc., 1996

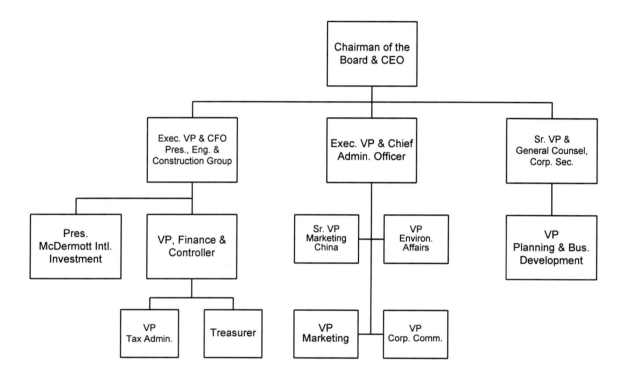

J. Ray McDermott, S.A.

Source: McDermott International Inc., 1996

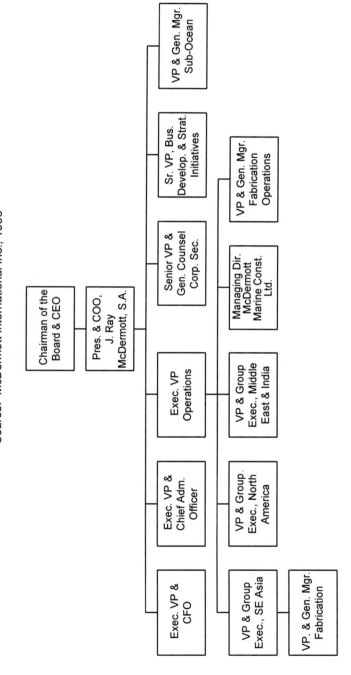

McDonnell Douglas Aerospace

Source: McDonnell Douglas Corporation, 1996

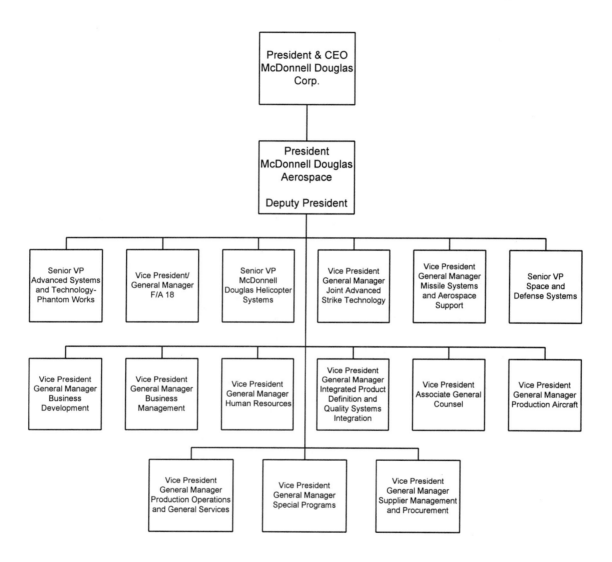

McDonnell Douglas Corporation

Source: McDonnell Douglas Corporation, 1996

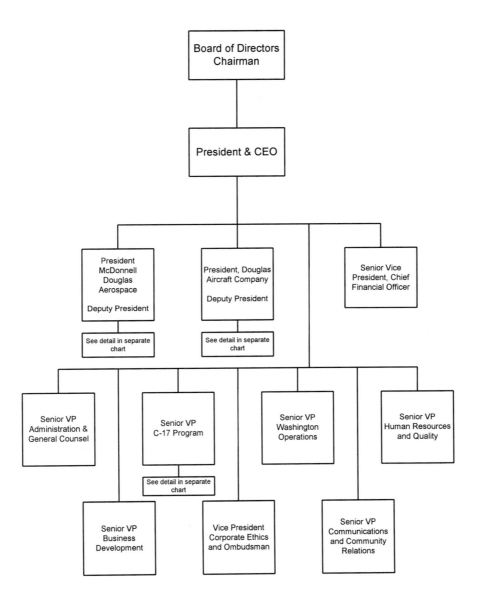

McDonnell Douglas Corporation
C-17 Program

Source: McDonnell Douglas Corporation, 1996

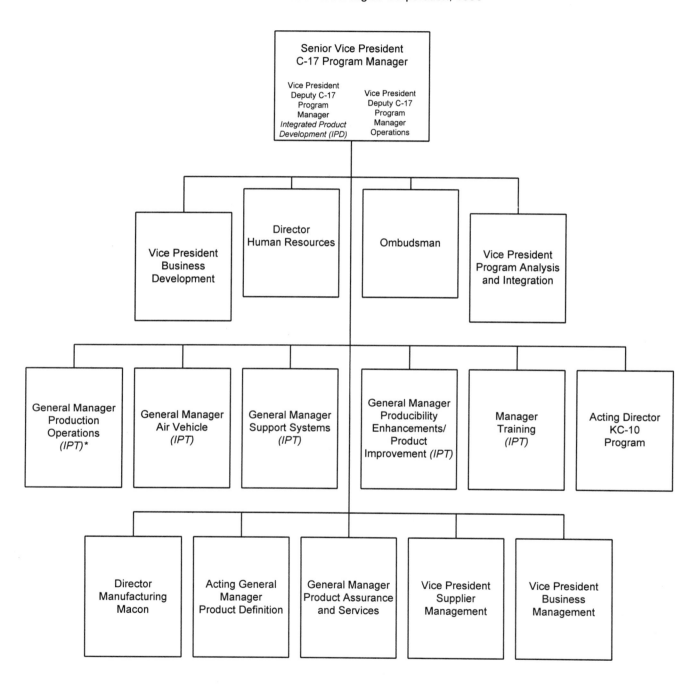

*Integrated Product Team

Memorial Health System

Source: Memorial Health System, 1996

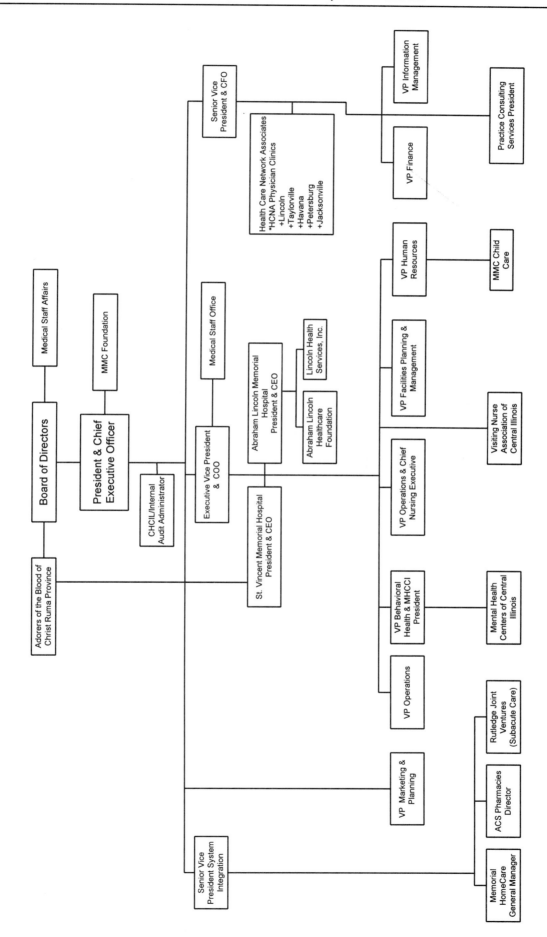

Methodist Health Systems, Inc.

Source: Methodist Health Systems, Inc., 1996

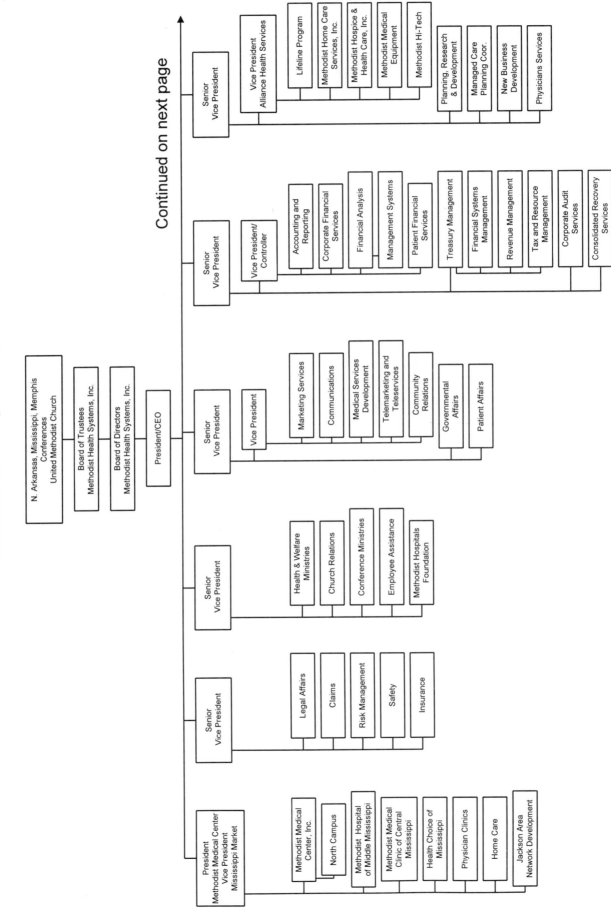

Continued on next page

Methodist Health Systems, Inc.
Continued from previous page

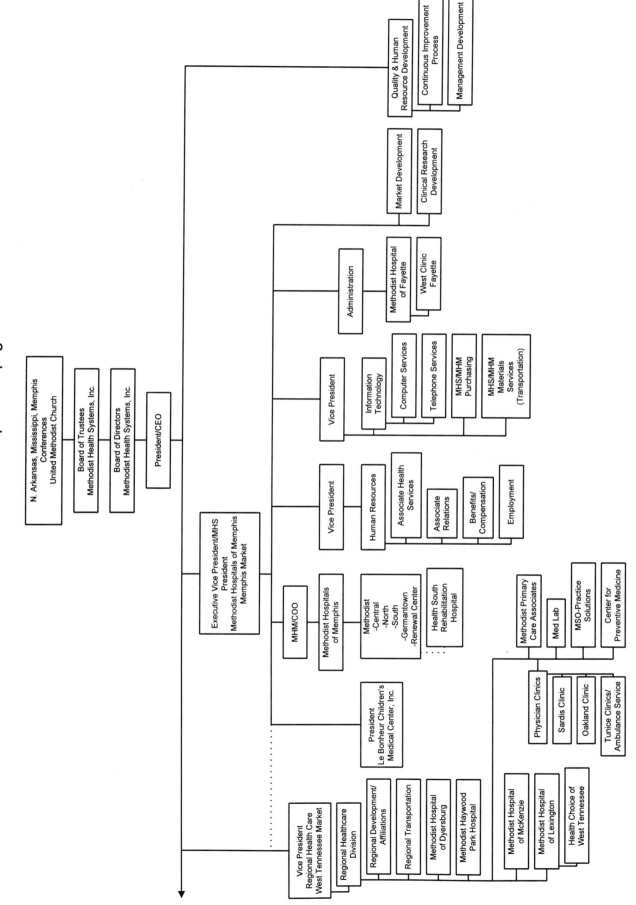

Methodist Hospitals of Memphis

Source: Methodist Health Systems, 1996

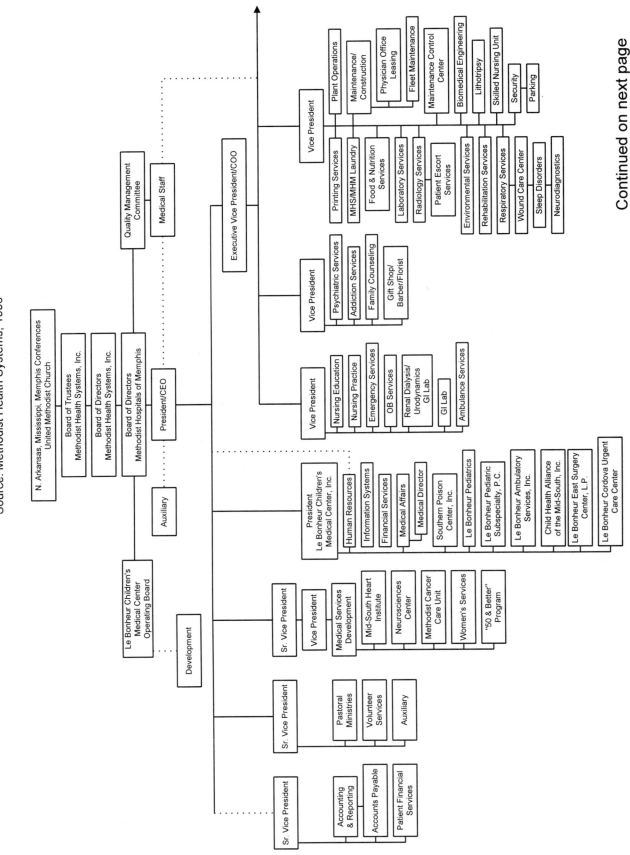

Continued on next page

Methodist Hospitals of Memphis
Continued from previous page

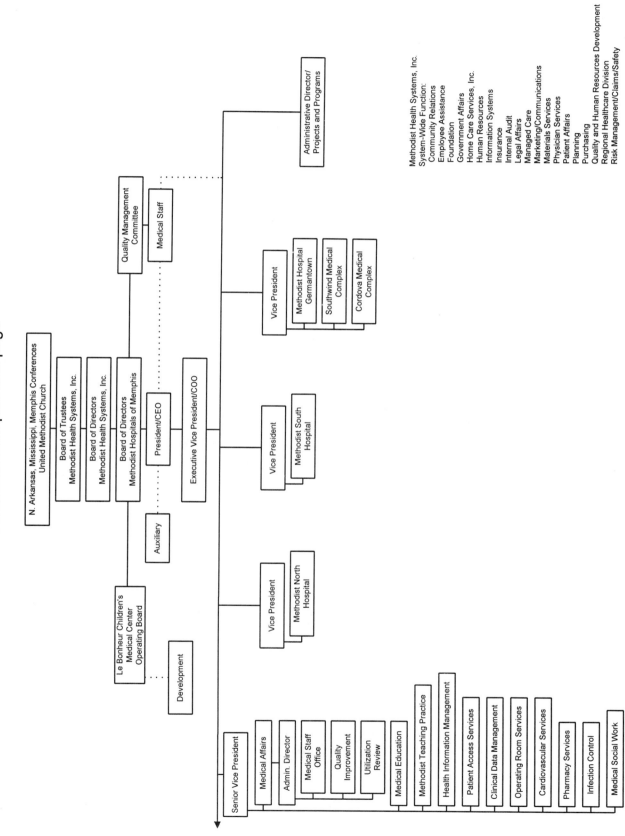

Methodist Health Systems, Inc.
System-Wide Function:
Community Relations
Employee Assistance
Foundation
Government Affairs
Home Care Services, Inc.
Human Resources
Information Systems
Insurance
Internal Audit
Legal Affairs
Managed Care
Marketing/Communications
Materials Services
Physician Services
Patient Affairs
Planning
Purchasing
Quality and Human Resources Development
Regional Healthcare Division
Risk Management/Claims/Safety

N. Arkansas, Mississippi, Memphis Conferences
United Methodist Church

Board of Trustees
Methodist Health Systems, Inc.

Board of Directors
Methodist Health Systems, Inc.

Board of Directors
Methodist Hospitals of Memphis

President/CEO

Executive Vice President/COO

Quality Management Committee

Medical Staff

Administrative Director/
Projects and Programs

Auxiliary

Le Bonheur Children's
Medical Center
Operating Board

Development

Vice President
Methodist North Hospital

Vice President
Methodist South Hospital

Vice President
Methodist Hospital Germantown
Southwind Medical Complex
Cordova Medical Complex

Senior Vice President
Medical Affairs
Admin. Director
Medical Staff Office
Quality Improvement
Utilization Review
Medical Education
Methodist Teaching Practice
Health Information Management
Patient Access Services
Clinical Data Management
Operating Room Services
Cardiovascular Services
Pharmacy Services
Infection Control
Medical Social Work

MicroHelp, Inc.

Source: MicroHelp, Inc., 1996

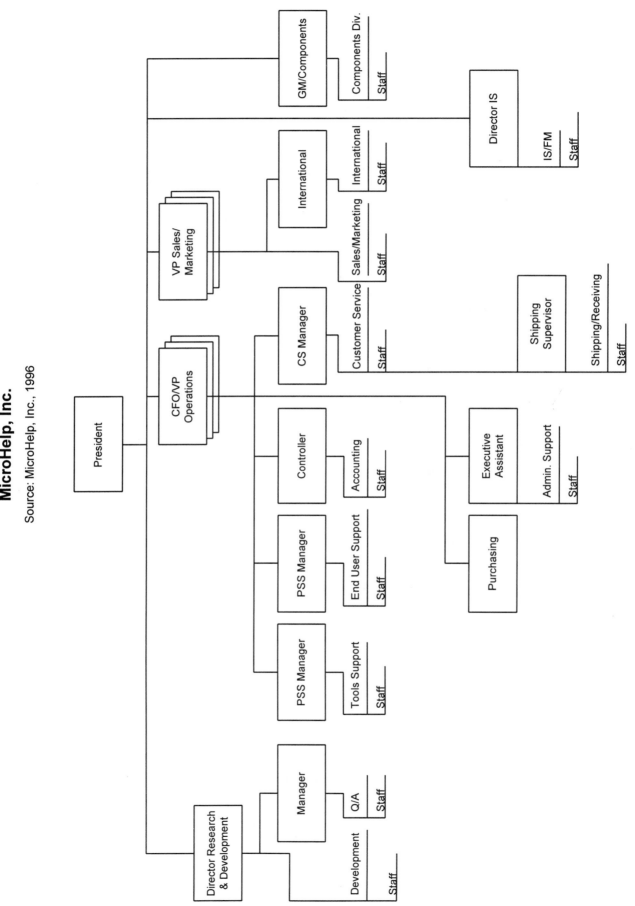

Micron Technology, Inc.

Source: Micron Technology, Inc., 1996

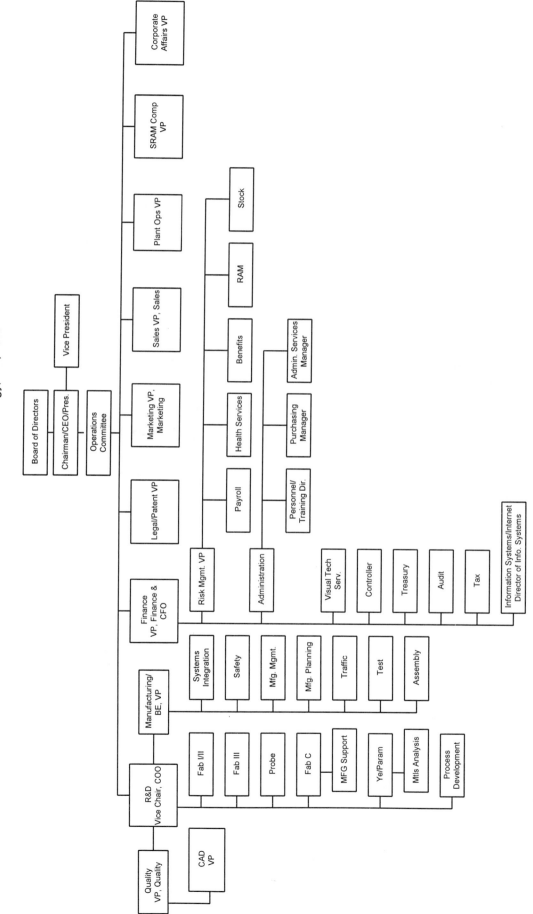

Mid-America Dairymen, Inc.

Source: Company update, 1995

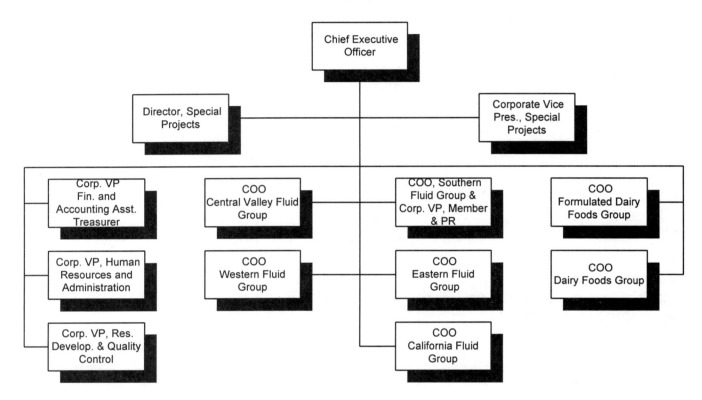

Migros Cooperative (Switzerland)

Source: Migros Cooperative, 1996

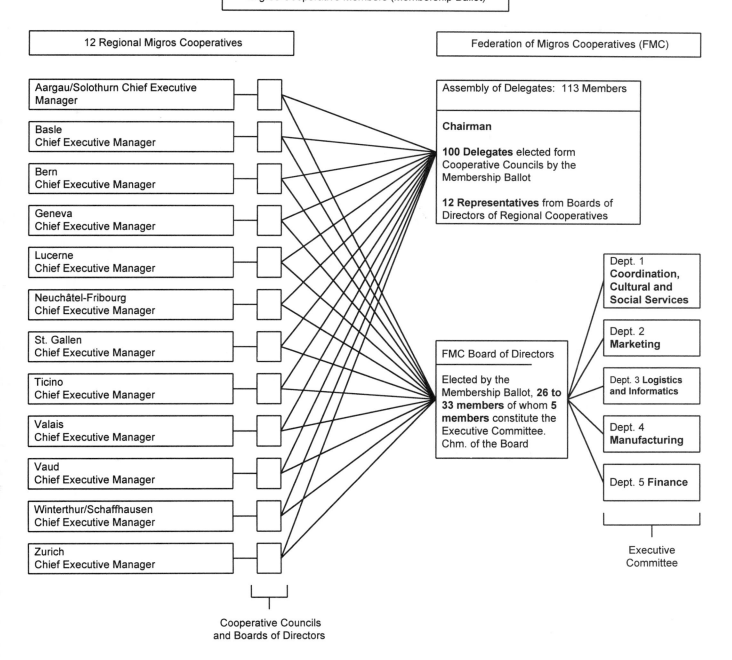

Migros Cooperative Members (Membership Ballot)

12 Regional Migros Cooperatives

Federation of Migros Cooperatives (FMC)

Aargau/Solothurn Chief Executive Manager

Basle Chief Executive Manager

Bern Chief Executive Manager

Geneva Chief Executive Manager

Lucerne Chief Executive Manager

Neuchâtel-Fribourg Chief Executive Manager

St. Gallen Chief Executive Manager

Ticino Chief Executive Manager

Valais Chief Executive Manager

Vaud Chief Executive Manager

Winterthur/Schaffhausen Chief Executive Manager

Zurich Chief Executive Manager

Assembly of Delegates: 113 Members

Chairman

100 Delegates elected form Cooperative Councils by the Membership Ballot

12 Representatives from Boards of Directors of Regional Cooperatives

FMC Board of Directors

Elected by the Membership Ballot, **26 to 33 members** of whom **5 members** constitute the Executive Committee. Chm. of the Board

Dept. 1 **Coordination, Cultural and Social Services**

Dept. 2 **Marketing**

Dept. 3 **Logistics and Informatics**

Dept. 4 **Manufacturing**

Dept. 5 **Finance**

Executive Committee

Cooperative Councils and Boards of Directors

Ministry of Posts and Telecommunications (Japan)

Source: Ministry of Posts and Telecommunications, 1996

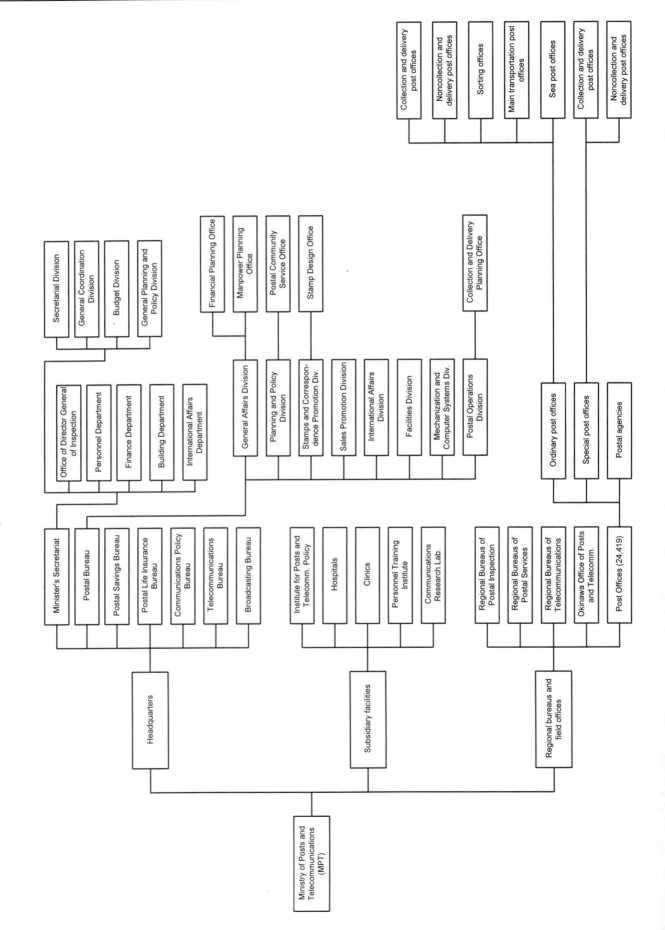

Minnesota Mining and Manufacturing Company

Source: Minnesota Mining and Manufacturing Company, 1996

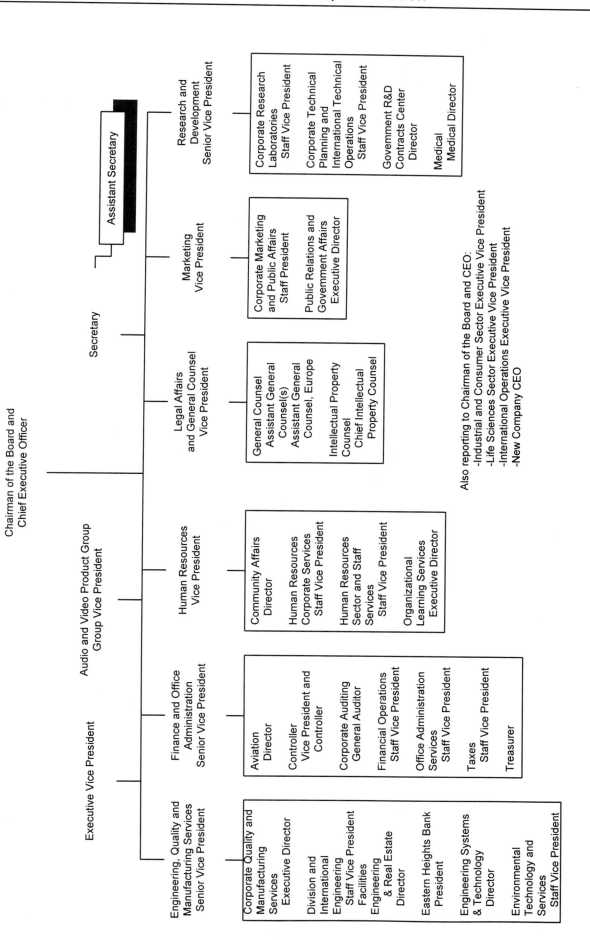

Chairman of the Board and
Chief Executive Officer

Secretary

Assistant Secretary

Executive Vice President

Audio and Video Product Group
Group Vice President

Engineering, Quality and
Manufacturing Services
Senior Vice President

Finance and Office
Administration
Senior Vice President

Human Resources
Vice President

Legal Affairs
and General Counsel
Vice President

Marketing
Vice President

Research and
Development
Senior Vice President

Corporate Quality and Manufacturing Services Executive Director

Division and International Engineering Staff Vice President

Engineering Facilities

Engineering & Real Estate Director

Eastern Heights Bank President

Engineering Systems & Technology Director

Environmental Technology and Services Staff Vice President

Aviation Director

Controller Vice President and Controller

Corporate Auditing General Auditor

Financial Operations Staff Vice President

Office Administration Services Staff Vice President

Taxes Staff Vice President

Treasurer

Community Affairs Director

Human Resources Corporate Services Staff Vice President

Human Resources Sector and Staff Services Staff Vice President

Organizational Learning Services Executive Director

General Counsel Assistant General Counsel(s)

Assistant General Counsel, Europe

Intellectual Property Counsel Chief Intellectual Property Counsel

Corporate Marketing and Public Affairs Staff President

Public Relations and Government Affairs Executive Director

Corporate Research Laboratories Staff Vice President

Corporate Technical Planning and International Technical Operations Staff Vice President

Government R&D Contracts Center Director

Medical Medical Director

Also reporting to Chairman of the Board and CEO:
-Industrial and Consumer Sector Executive Vice President
-Life Sciences Sector Executive Vice President
-International Operations Executive Vice President
-New Company CEO

Continued on next page

Minnesota Mining and Manufacturing Company

Continued from previous page

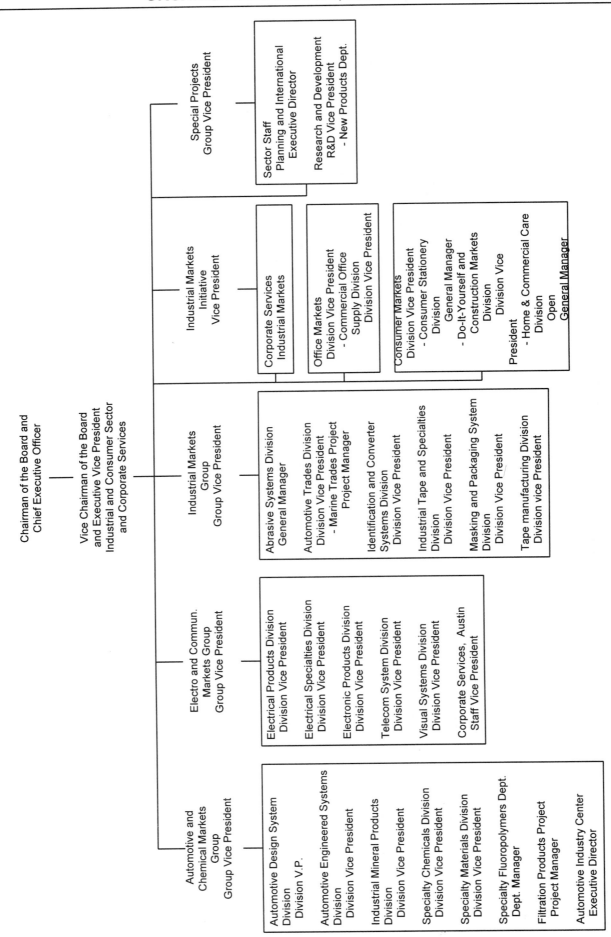

Continued on next page

Minnesota Mining and Manufacturing Company

Continued from previous page

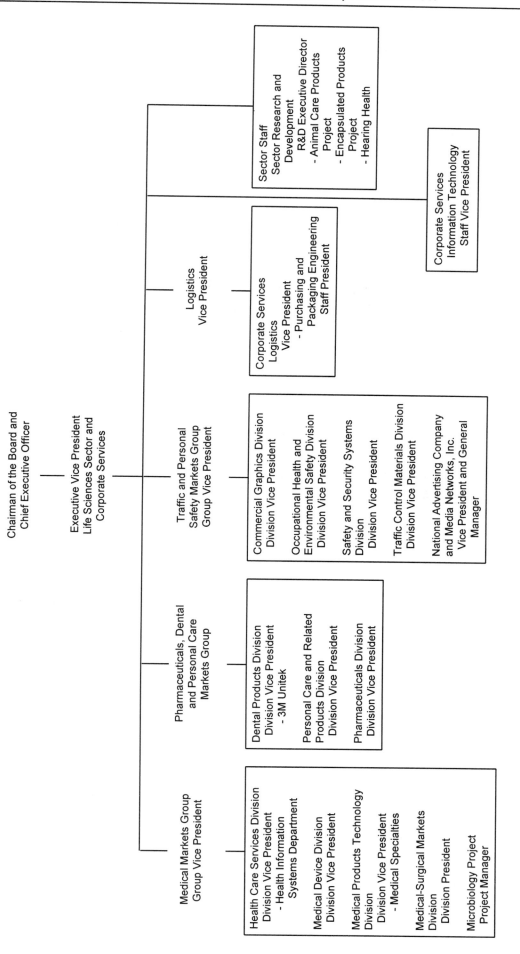

Chairman of the Board and Chief Executive Officer

Executive Vice President Life Sciences Sector and Corporate Services

Logistics Vice President

Sector Staff
Sector Research and Development
R&D Executive Director
- Animal Care Products Project
- Encapsulated Products Project
- Hearing Health

Corporate Services
Logistics Vice President
- Purchasing and Packaging Engineering Staff President

Corporate Services
Information Technology
Staff Vice President

Traffic and Personal Safety Markets Group Group Vice President

Commercial Graphics Division Division Vice President

Occupational Health and Environmental Safety Division Division Vice President

Safety and Security Systems Division Division Vice President

Traffic Control Materials Division Division Vice President

National Advertising Company and Media Networks, Inc. Vice President and General Manager

Pharmaceuticals, Dental and Personal Care Markets Group

Dental Products Division Division Vice President
- 3M Unitek

Personal Care and Related Products Division Division Vice President

Pharmaceuticals Division Division Vice President

Medical Markets Group Group Vice President

Health Care Services Division Division Vice President
- Health Information Systems Department

Medical Device Division Division Vice President

Medical Products Technology Division Division Vice President
- Medical Specialties

Medical-Surgical Markets Division Division President

Microbiology Project Project Manager

Continued on next page

Minnesota Mining and Manufacturing Company

Continued from previous page

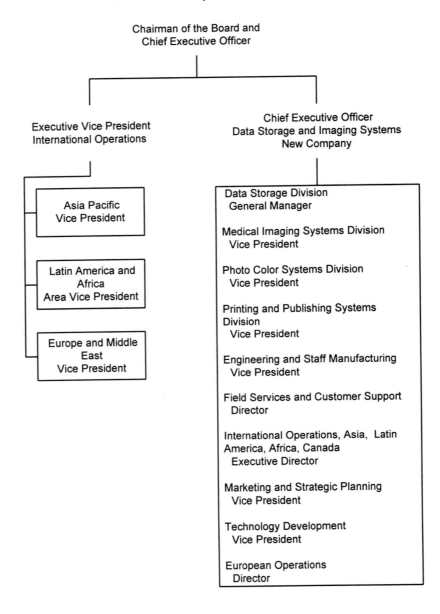

Mitsubishi Corporation (Japan)

Source: Annual report, 1996

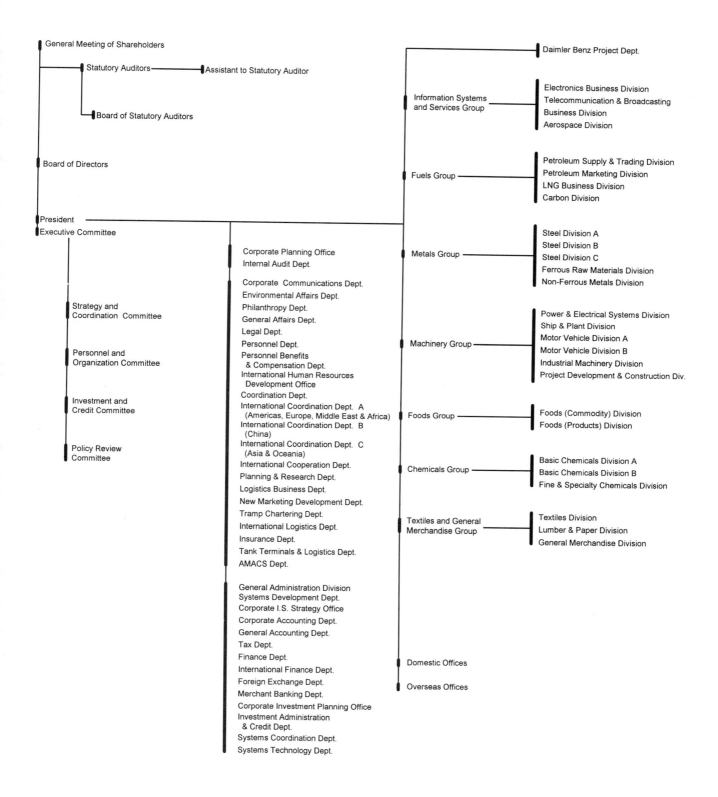

General Meeting of Shareholders

Statutory Auditors —— Assistant to Statutory Auditor

Board of Statutory Auditors

Board of Directors

President
Executive Committee

Strategy and
Coordination Committee

Personnel and
Organization Committee

Investment and
Credit Committee

Policy Review
Committee

Corporate Planning Office
Internal Audit Dept.

Corporate Communications Dept.
Environmental Affairs Dept.
Philanthropy Dept.
General Affairs Dept.
Legal Dept.
Personnel Dept.
Personnel Benefits
& Compensation Dept.
International Human Resources
Development Office
Coordination Dept.
International Coordination Dept. A
(Americas, Europe, Middle East & Africa)
International Coordination Dept. B
(China)
International Coordination Dept. C
(Asia & Oceania)
International Cooperation Dept.
Planning & Research Dept.
Logistics Business Dept.
New Marketing Development Dept.
Tramp Chartering Dept.
International Logistics Dept.
Insurance Dept.
Tank Terminals & Logistics Dept.
AMACS Dept.

General Administration Division
Systems Development Dept.
Corporate I.S. Strategy Office
Corporate Accounting Dept.
General Accounting Dept.
Tax Dept.
Finance Dept.
International Finance Dept.
Foreign Exchange Dept.
Merchant Banking Dept.
Corporate Investment Planning Office
Investment Administration
& Credit Dept.
Systems Coordination Dept.
Systems Technology Dept.

Information Systems
and Services Group

Daimler Benz Project Dept.

Electronics Business Division
Telecommunication & Broadcasting
Business Division
Aerospace Division

Fuels Group

Petroleum Supply & Trading Division
Petroleum Marketing Division
LNG Business Division
Carbon Division

Metals Group

Steel Division A
Steel Division B
Steel Division C
Ferrous Raw Materials Division
Non-Ferrous Metals Division

Machinery Group

Power & Electrical Systems Division
Ship & Plant Division
Motor Vehicle Division A
Motor Vehicle Division B
Industrial Machinery Division
Project Development & Construction Div.

Foods Group

Foods (Commodity) Division
Foods (Products) Division

Chemicals Group

Basic Chemicals Division A
Basic Chemicals Division B
Fine & Specialty Chemicals Division

Textiles and General
Merchandise Group

Textiles Division
Lumber & Paper Division
General Merchandise Division

Domestic Offices

Overseas Offices

Mitsubishi Heavy Industries, Ltd. (Japan)

Source: Annual report, 1994

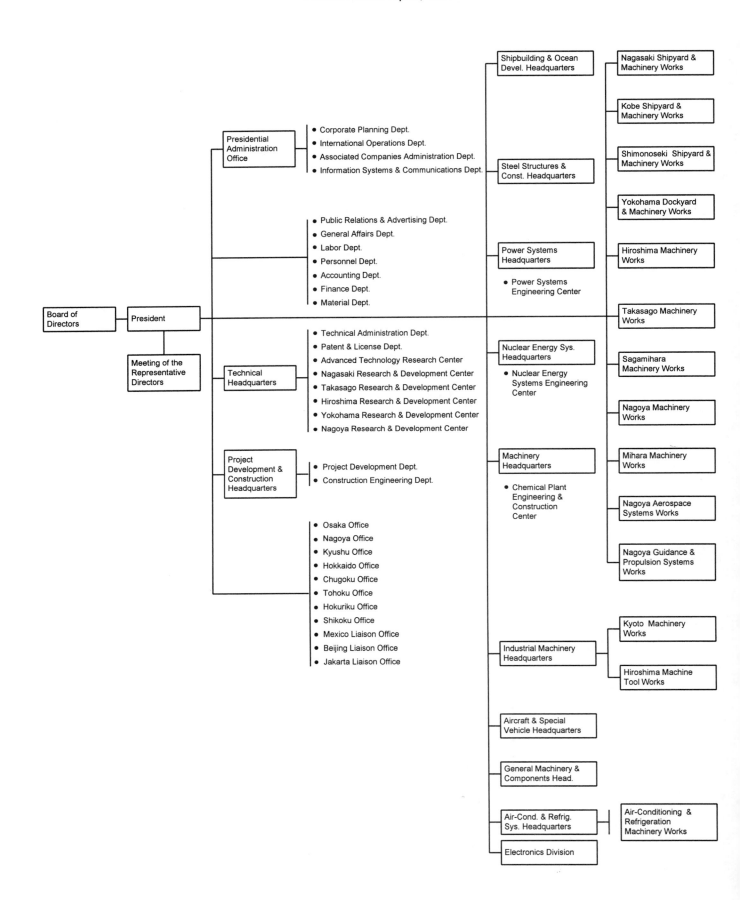

Mitsubishi Oil Company, Ltd. (Japan)

Source: Mitsubishi Oil Company, Ltd., 1996

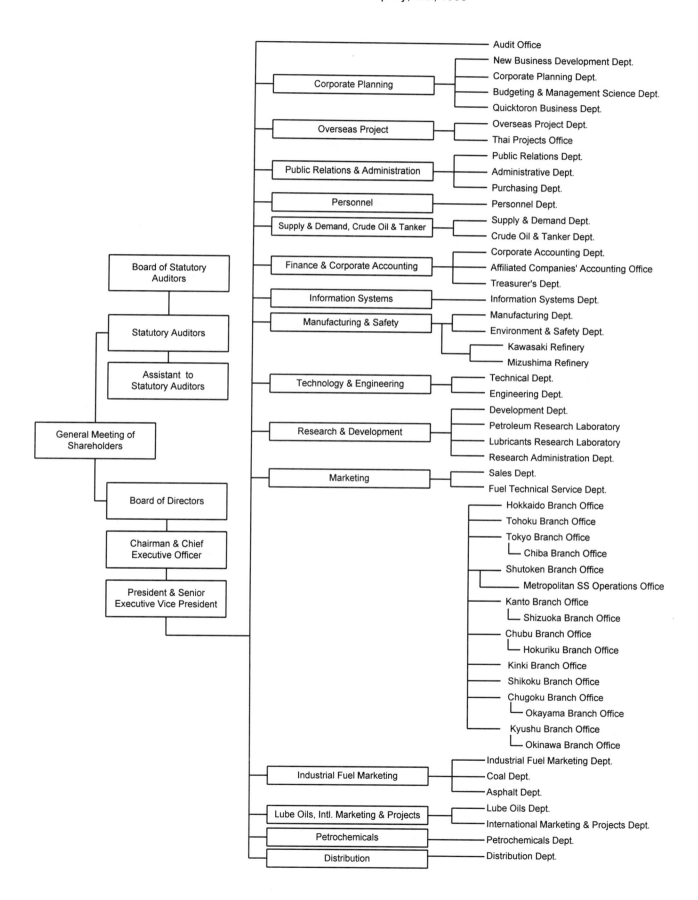

Mitsubishi Trust & Banking Corp. (Japan)

Source: Mitsubishi Trust & Banking Corp., 1996

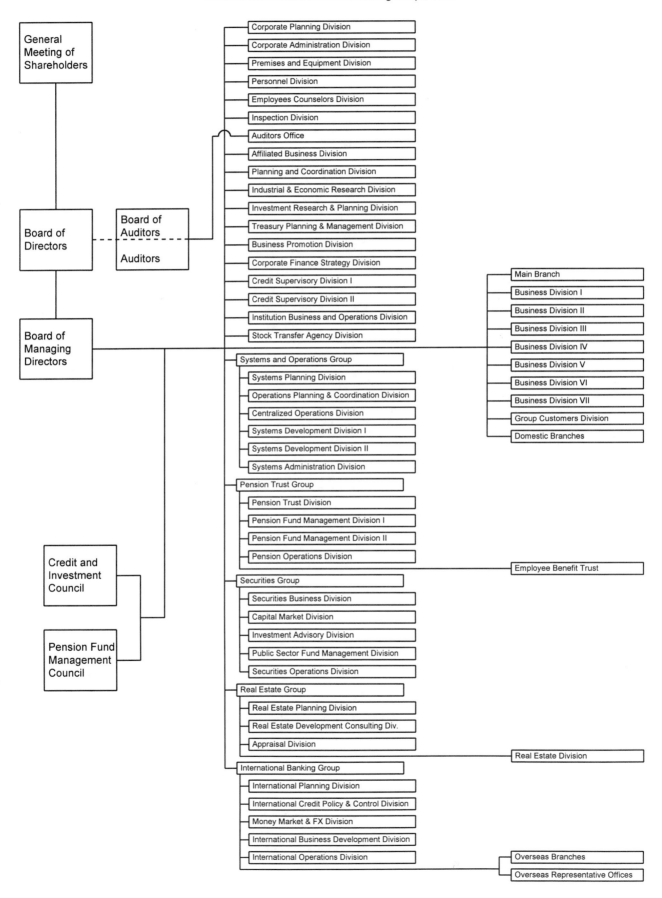

Mitsui & Co., Ltd. (Japan)

Source: Mitsui & Co., Ltd., 1996

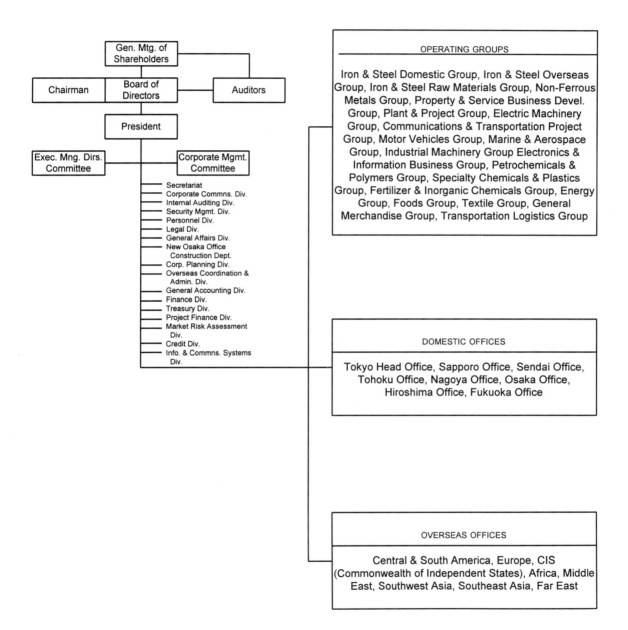

OPERATING GROUPS

Iron & Steel Domestic Group, Iron & Steel Overseas Group, Iron & Steel Raw Materials Group, Non-Ferrous Metals Group, Property & Service Business Devel. Group, Plant & Project Group, Electric Machinery Group, Communications & Transportation Project Group, Motor Vehicles Group, Marine & Aerospace Group, Industrial Machinery Group Electronics & Information Business Group, Petrochemicals & Polymers Group, Specialty Chemicals & Plastics Group, Fertilizer & Inorganic Chemicals Group, Energy Group, Foods Group, Textile Group, General Merchandise Group, Transportation Logistics Group

DOMESTIC OFFICES

Tokyo Head Office, Sapporo Office, Sendai Office, Tohoku Office, Nagoya Office, Osaka Office, Hiroshima Office, Fukuoka Office

OVERSEAS OFFICES

Central & South America, Europe, CIS (Commonwealth of Independent States), Africa, Middle East, Southwest Asia, Southeast Asia, Far East

Gen. Mtg. of Shareholders

Chairman

Board of Directors

Auditors

President

Exec. Mng. Dirs. Committee

Corporate Mgmt. Committee

Secretariat
Corporate Commns. Div.
Internal Auditing Div.
Security Mgmt. Div.
Personnel Div.
Legal Div.
General Affairs Div.
New Osaka Office Construction Dept.
Corp. Planning Div.
Overseas Coordination & Admin. Div.
General Accounting Div.
Finance Div.
Treasury Div.
Project Finance Div.
Market Risk Assessment Div.
Credit Div.
Info. & Commns. Systems Div.

Mitsui Mutual Life Insurance Co. (Japan)

Source: Mitsui Mutual Life Ins. Co., 1996

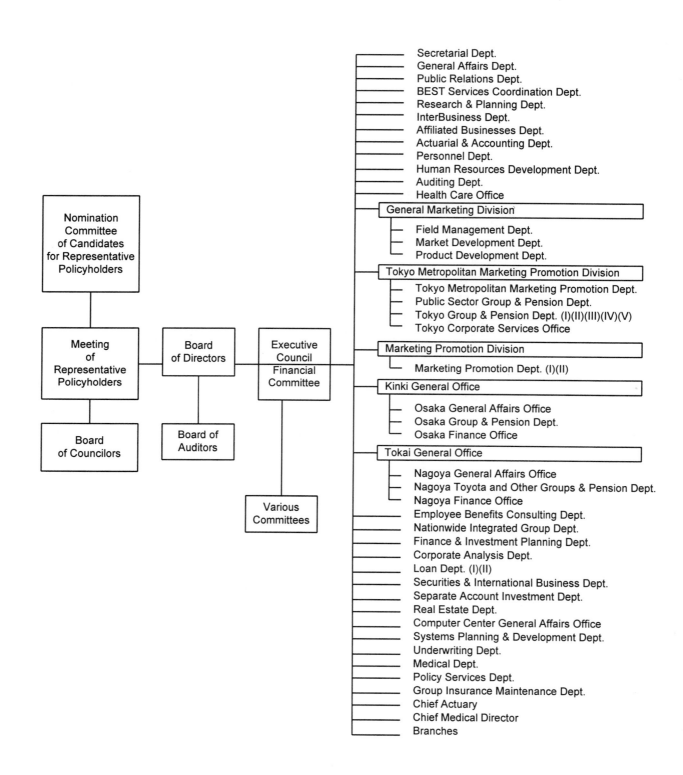

Monsanto Company
Source: Monsanto Company, 1996

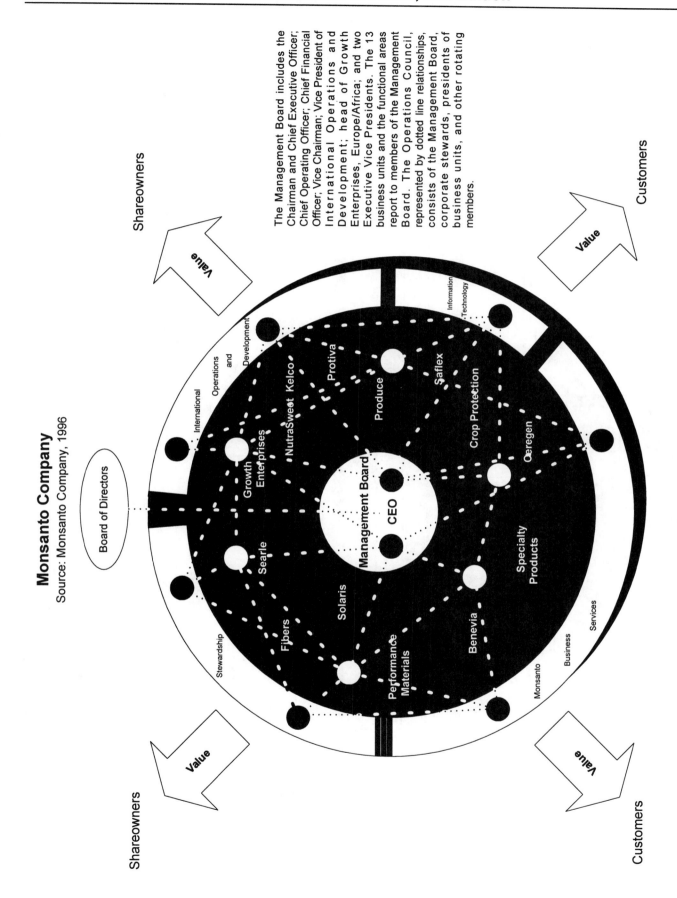

The Management Board includes the Chairman and Chief Executive Officer; Chief Operating Officer; Chief Financial Officer; Vice Chairman; Vice President of International Operations and Development; head of Growth Enterprises, Europe/Africa; and two Executive Vice Presidents. The 13 business units and the functional areas report to members of the Management Board. The Operations Council, represented by dotted line relationships, consists of the Management Board, corporate stewards, presidents of business units, and other rotating members.

Shareowners

Customers

Value

Value

Board of Directors

Management Board

CEO

International Operations and Development

Protiva

NutraSweet Kelco

Growth Enterprises

Produce

Saflex

Information Technology

Crop Protection

Ceregen

Searle

Solaris

Specialty Products

Fibers

Performance Materials

Benevia

Stewardship

Business Services

Monsanto

Shareowners

Customers

Value

Value

National City Corporation

Source: National City Corporation, 1996

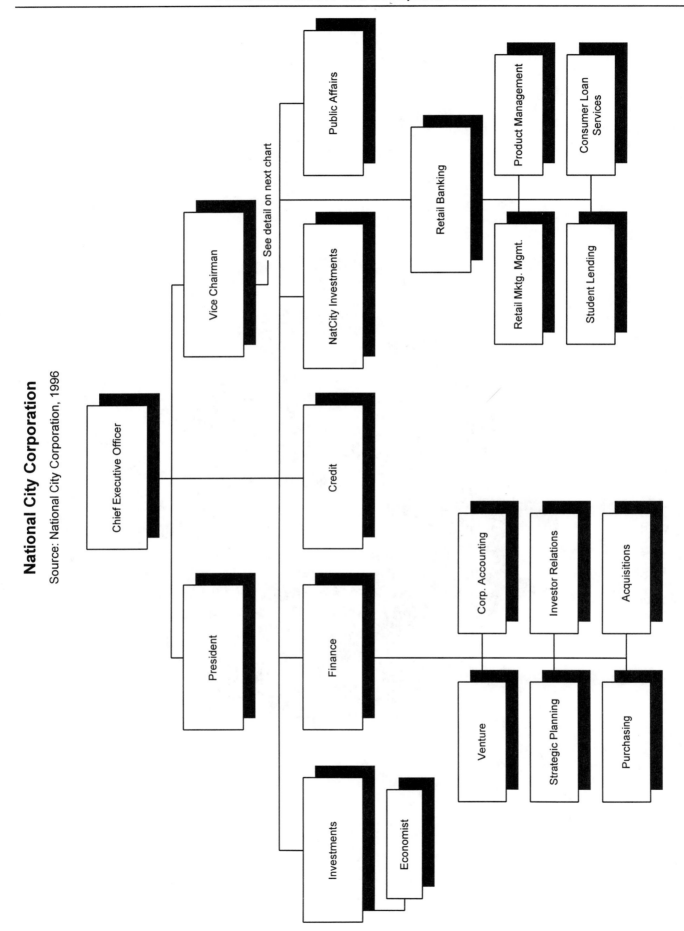

National City Corporation
Continued from previous page

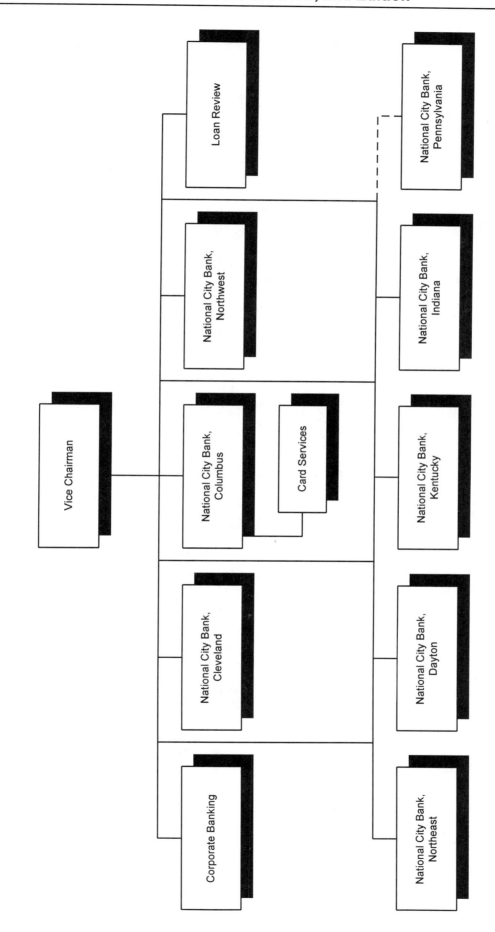

Nationwide Insurance Enterprise

Source: Nationwide Insurance Enterprise, 1996

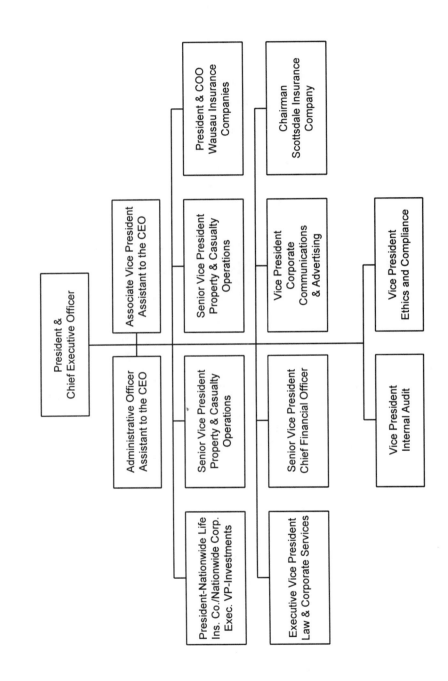

Nationwide Insurance Enterprise
Life & Investments

Source: Nationwide Insurance Enterprise, 1996

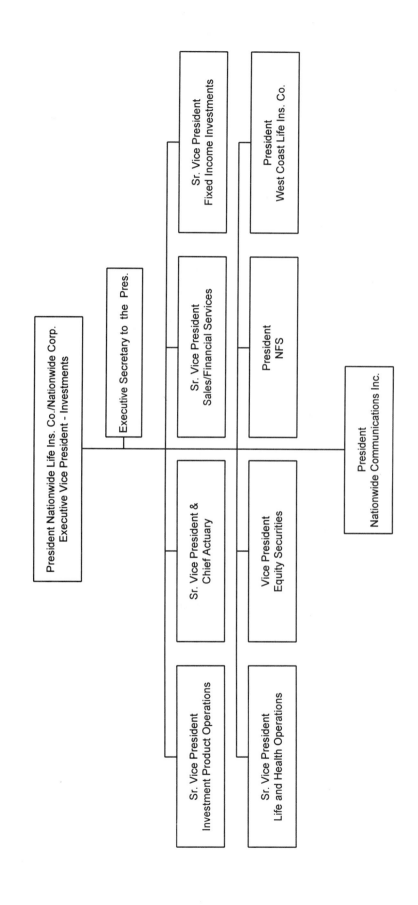

Nationwide Insurance Enterprise
Property/Casualty Operations

Source: Nationwide Insurance Enterprise, 1996

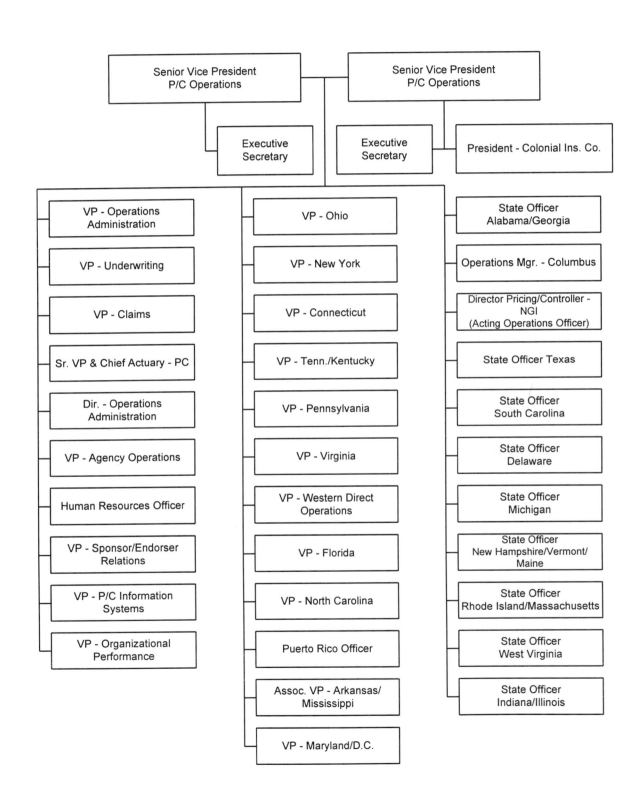

NEC Corporation (Japan)

Source: NEC Corporation, 1996

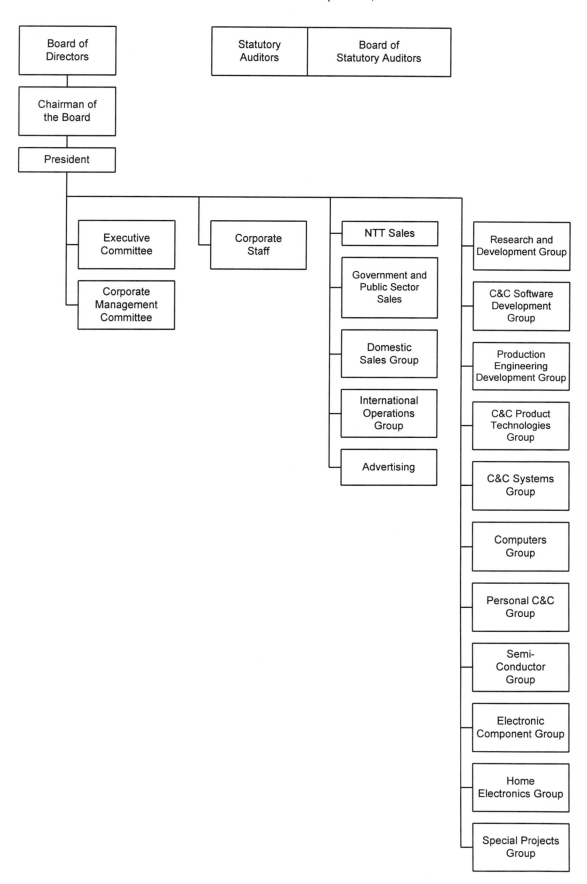

Nestlé S.A. (Switzerland)

Source: Nestlé S.A., 1996

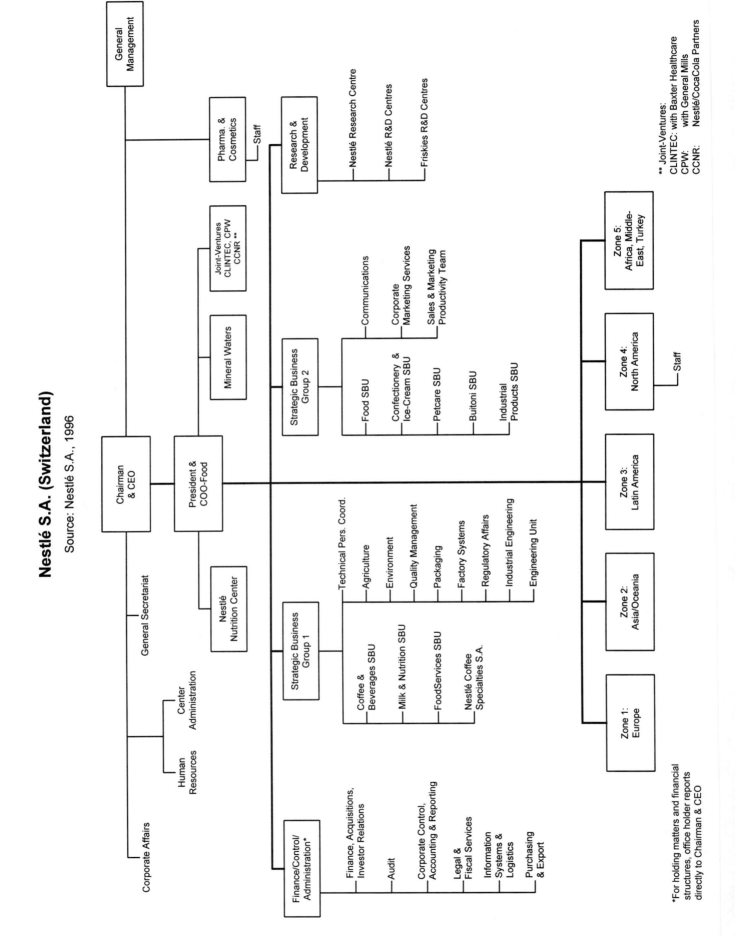

** Joint-Ventures:
CLINTEC: with Baxter Healthcare
CPW: with General Mills
CCNR: Nestlé/CocaCola Partners

*For holding matters and financial structures, office holder reports directly to Chairman & CEO

New Oji Paper Co., Ltd. (Japan)

Source: New Oji Paper Co., Ltd., 1996

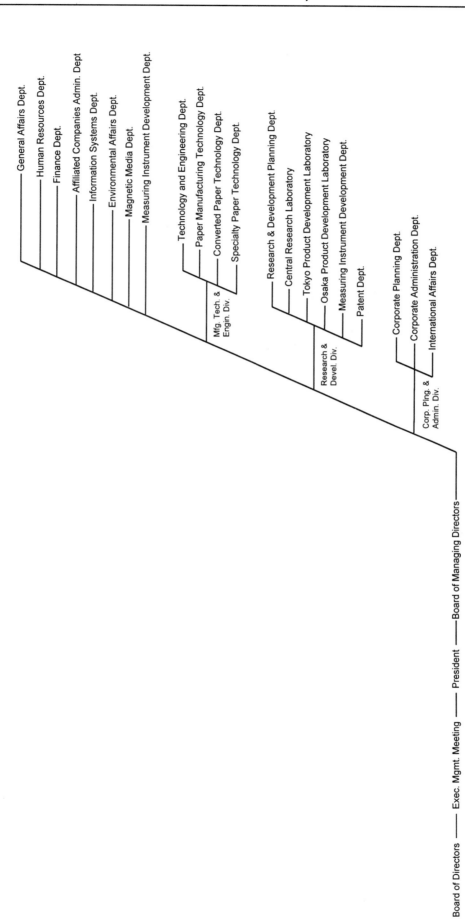

Continued on next page

New Oji Paper Co., Ltd. (Japan)

Continued from previous page

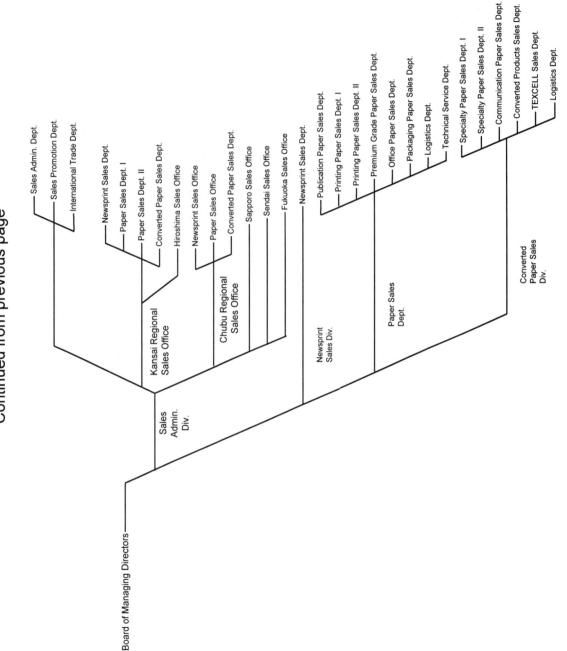

Board of Managing Directors

Sales Admin. Div.
- Sales Admin. Dept.
- Sales Promotion Dept.
- International Trade Dept.
- Kansai Regional Sales Office
  - Newsprint Sales Dept.
  - Paper Sales Dept. I
  - Paper Sales Dept. II
  - Converted Paper Sales Dept.
  - Hiroshima Sales Office
- Chubu Regional Sales Office
  - Newsprint Sales Office
  - Paper Sales Office
  - Converted Paper Sales Dept.
  - Sapporo Sales Office
  - Sendai Sales Office
  - Fukuoka Sales Office

Newsprint Sales Div.
- Newsprint Sales Dept.

Paper Sales Dept.
- Publication Paper Sales Dept.
- Printing Paper Sales Dept. I
- Printing Paper Sales Dept. II
- Premium Grade Paper Sales Dept.
- Office Paper Sales Dept.
- Packaging Paper Sales Dept.
- Logistics Dept.
- Technical Service Dept.

Converted Paper Sales Div.
- Specialty Paper Sales Dept. I
- Specialty Paper Sales Dept. II
- Communication Paper Sales Dept.
- Converted Products Sales Dept.
- TEXCELL Sales Dept.
- Logistics Dept.

Continued on next page

New Oji Paper Co., Ltd. (Japan)
Continued from previous page

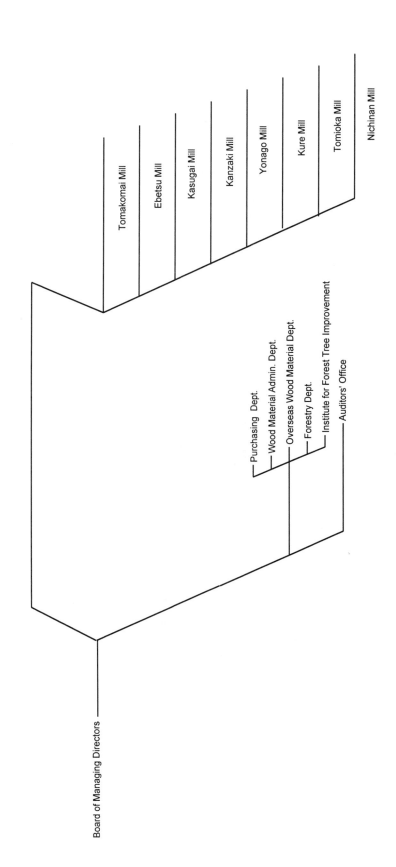

Board of Managing Directors

Tomakomai Mill
Ebetsu Mill
Kasugai Mill
Kanzaki Mill
Yonago Mill
Kure Mill
Tomioka Mill
Nichinan Mill

Purchasing Dept.
Wood Material Admin. Dept.
Overseas Wood Material Dept.
Forestry Dept.
Institute for Forest Tree Improvement
Auditors' Office

Nippon Paper Industries Co., Ltd. (Japan)

Source: Nippon Paper Industries Co., Ltd., 1996

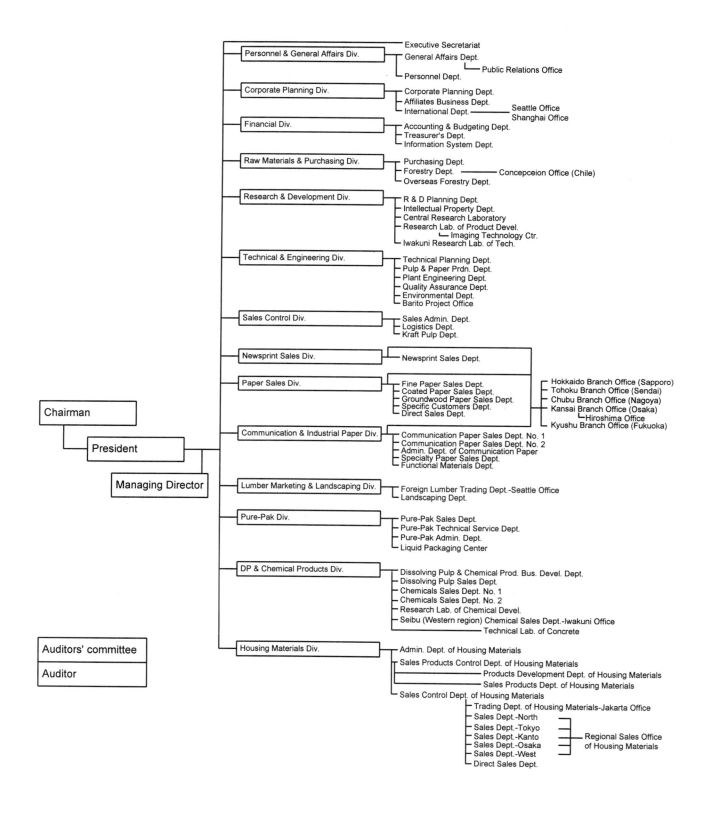

Nippon Steel Corporation (Japan)

Source: Nippon Steel Corporation, 1996

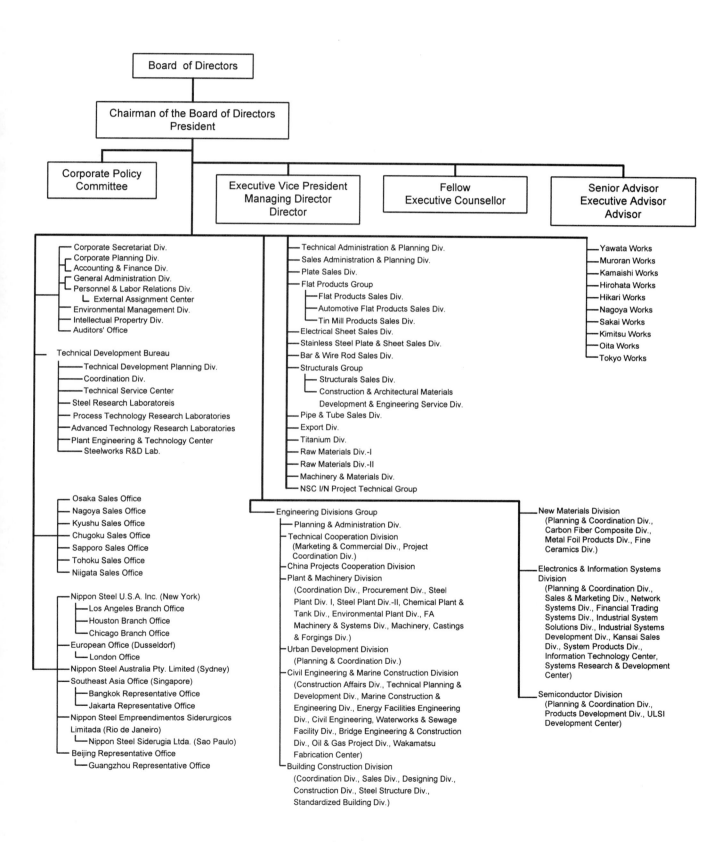

Nippon Telegraph and Telephone Corp. (Japan)
Source: Nippon Telegraph and Telephone Corp., 1996

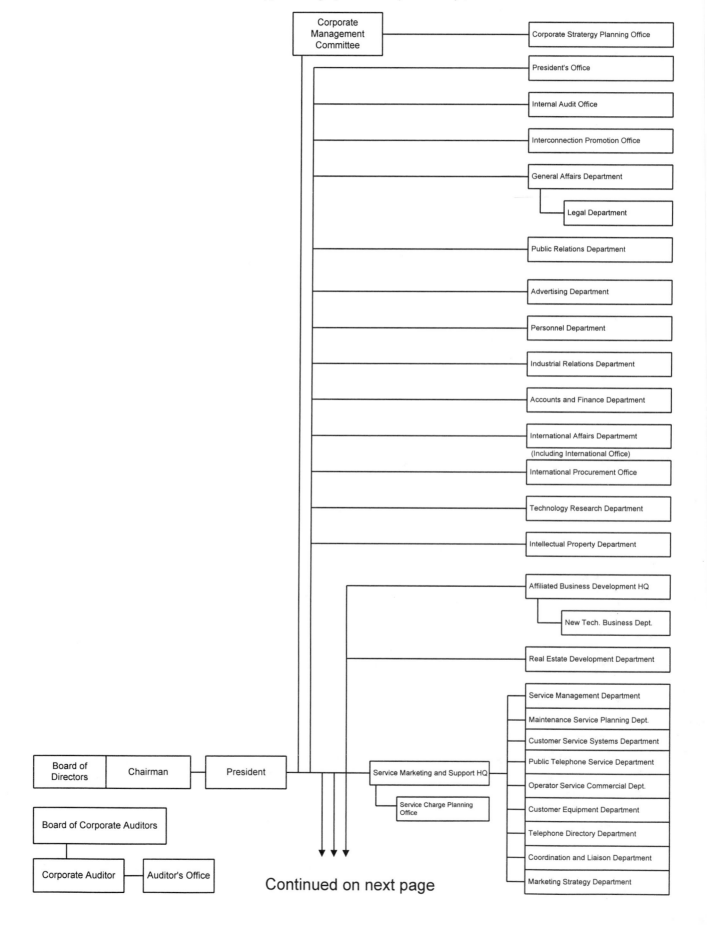

Continued on next page

Nippon Telegraph and Telephone Corp. (Japan)

Continued from previous page

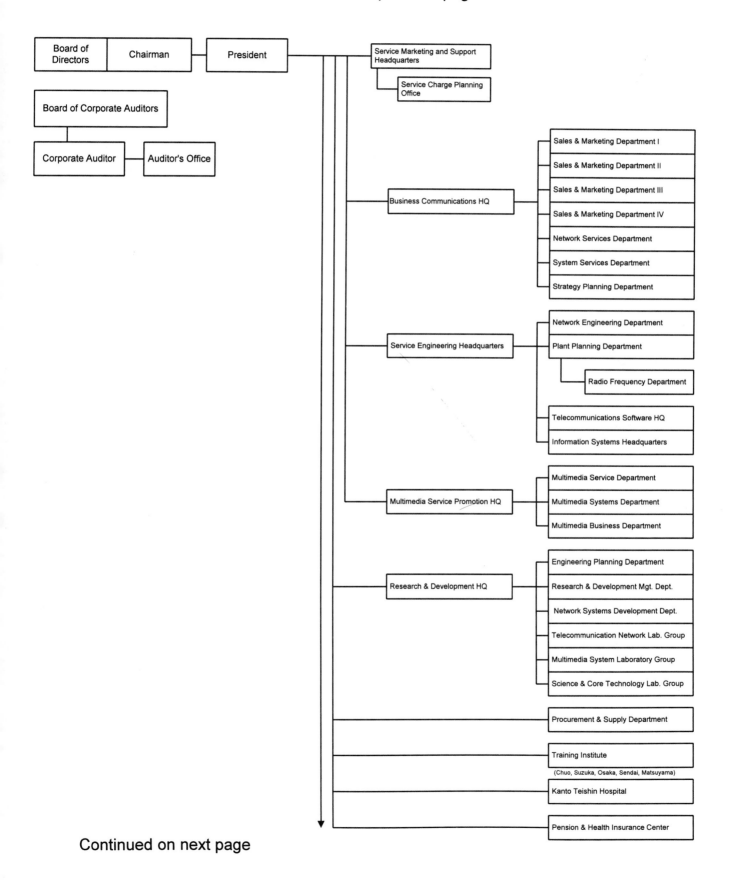

Continued on next page

Nippon Telephone and Telegraph Corp. (Japan)
Continued from previous page

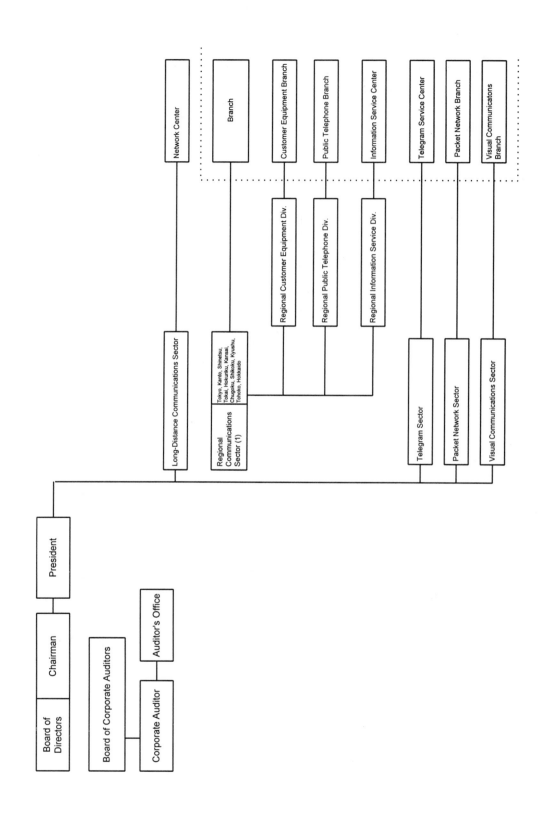

Nippondenso Co., Ltd. (Japan)

Source: Nippondenso Co., Ltd., 1996

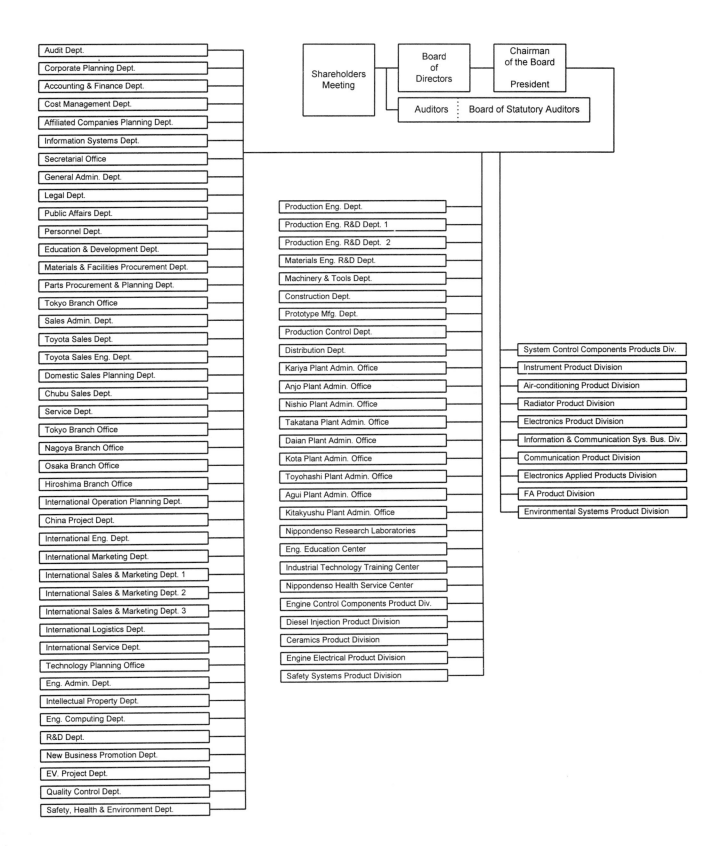

Audit Dept.
Corporate Planning Dept.
Accounting & Finance Dept.
Cost Management Dept.
Affiliated Companies Planning Dept.
Information Systems Dept.
Secretarial Office
General Admin. Dept.
Legal Dept.
Public Affairs Dept.
Personnel Dept.
Education & Development Dept.
Materials & Facilities Procurement Dept.
Parts Procurement & Planning Dept.
Tokyo Branch Office
Sales Admin. Dept.
Toyota Sales Dept.
Toyota Sales Eng. Dept.
Domestic Sales Planning Dept.
Chubu Sales Dept.
Service Dept.
Tokyo Branch Office
Nagoya Branch Office
Osaka Branch Office
Hiroshima Branch Office
International Operation Planning Dept.
China Project Dept.
International Eng. Dept.
International Marketing Dept.
International Sales & Marketing Dept. 1
International Sales & Marketing Dept. 2
International Sales & Marketing Dept. 3
International Logistics Dept.
International Service Dept.
Technology Planning Office
Eng. Admin. Dept.
Intellectual Property Dept.
Eng. Computing Dept.
R&D Dept.
New Business Promotion Dept.
EV. Project Dept.
Quality Control Dept.
Safety, Health & Environment Dept.

Shareholders Meeting
Board of Directors
Chairman of the Board
President
Auditors : Board of Statutory Auditors

Production Eng. Dept.
Production Eng. R&D Dept. 1
Production Eng. R&D Dept. 2
Materials Eng. R&D Dept.
Machinery & Tools Dept.
Construction Dept.
Prototype Mfg. Dept.
Production Control Dept.
Distribution Dept.
Kariya Plant Admin. Office
Anjo Plant Admin. Office
Nishio Plant Admin. Office
Takatana Plant Admin. Office
Daian Plant Admin. Office
Kota Plant Admin. Office
Toyohashi Plant Admin. Office
Agui Plant Admin. Office
Kitakyushu Plant Admin. Office
Nippondenso Research Laboratories
Eng. Education Center
Industrial Technology Training Center
Nippondenso Health Service Center
Engine Control Components Product Div.
Diesel Injection Product Division
Ceramics Product Division
Engine Electrical Product Division
Safety Systems Product Division

System Control Components Products Div.
Instrument Product Division
Air-conditioning Product Division
Radiator Product Division
Electronics Product Division
Information & Communication Sys. Bus. Div.
Communication Product Division
Electronics Applied Products Division
FA Product Division
Environmental Systems Product Division

Nissho Iwai Corporation (Japan)

Source: Nissho Iwai Corporation, 1996

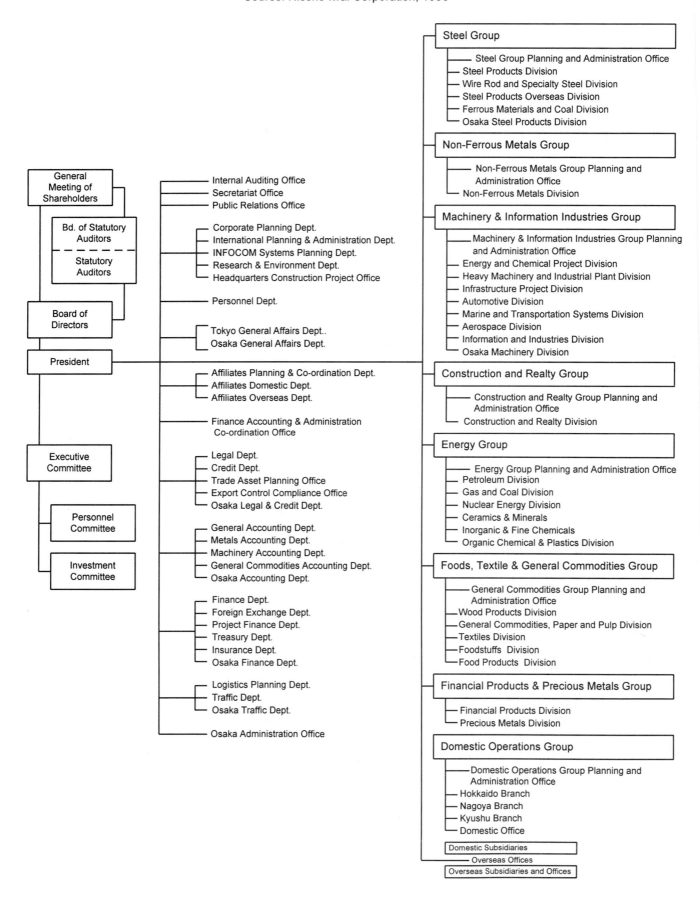

North Limited (Australia)

Source: Company update, 1996

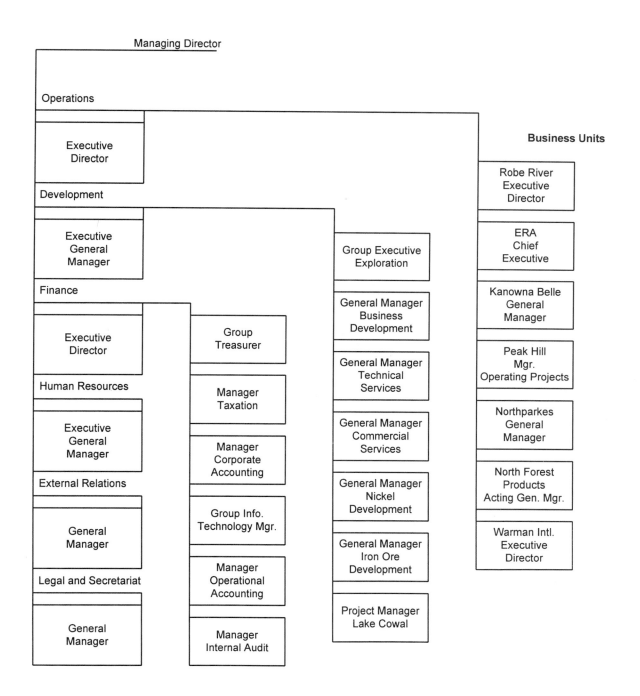

Managing Director

Operations

Executive Director

Development

Executive General Manager

Finance

Executive Director

Human Resources

Executive General Manager

External Relations

General Manager

Legal and Secretariat

General Manager

Group Treasurer

Manager Taxation

Manager Corporate Accounting

Group Info. Technology Mgr.

Manager Operational Accounting

Manager Internal Audit

Group Executive Exploration

General Manager Business Development

General Manager Technical Services

General Manager Commercial Services

General Manager Nickel Development

General Manager Iron Ore Development

Project Manager Lake Cowal

Business Units

Robe River Executive Director

ERA Chief Executive

Kanowna Belle General Manager

Peak Hill Mgr. Operating Projects

Northparkes General Manager

North Forest Products Acting Gen. Mgr.

Warman Intl. Executive Director

Orbital Sciences Corp.

Source: Orbital Sciences Corp., 1996

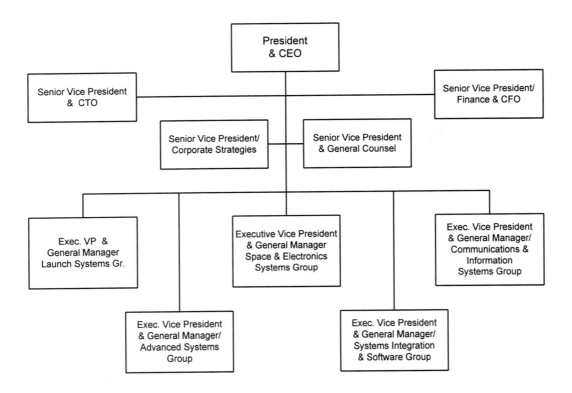

Oriental Scientific Instruments Import and Export Corp. (People's Republic of China)

Source: Oriental Scientific Instruments Import and Export Corporation, 1996

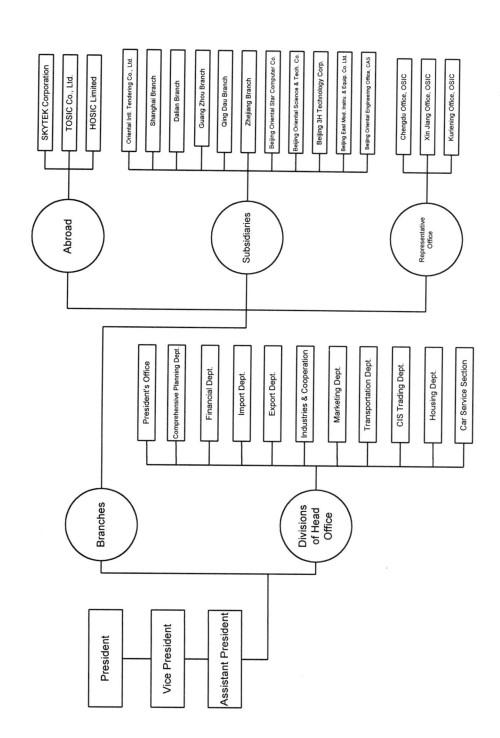

Orlando Regional Healthcare System

Source: Orlando Regional Healthcare System, 1996

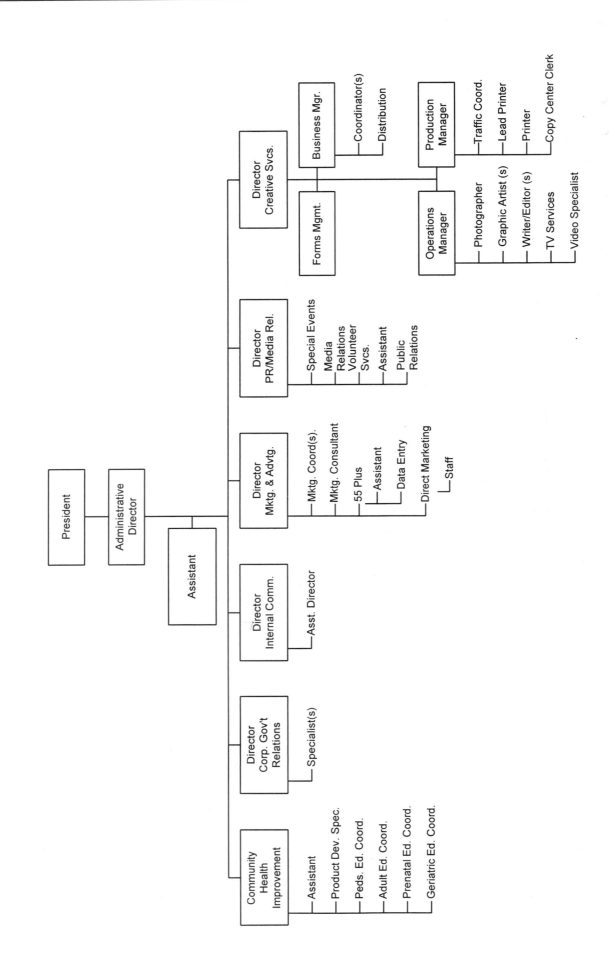

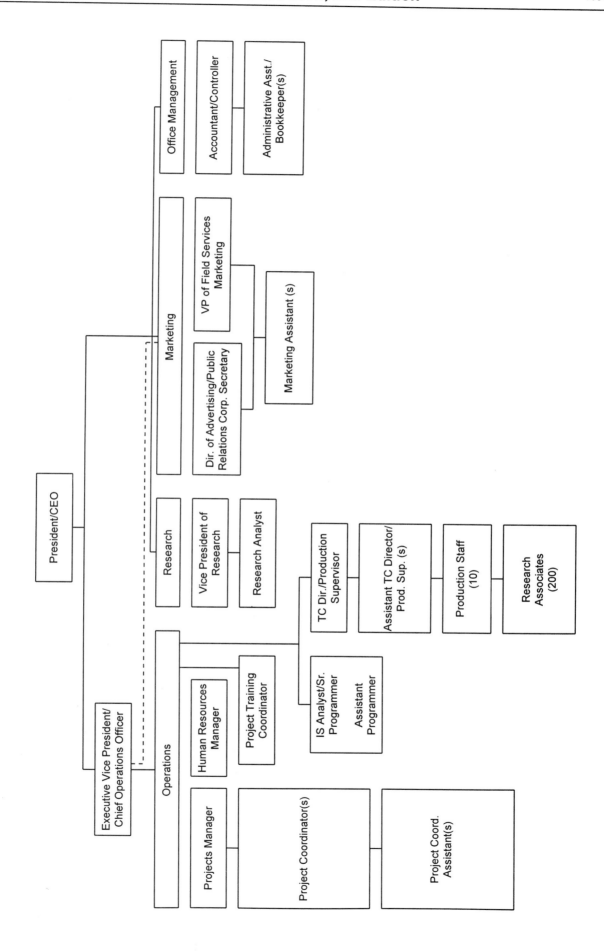

Paria Group, Inc.

Source: Paria Group, Inc., 1996

Parker Hannifin Corp.

Source: Parker Hannifin Corp., 1996

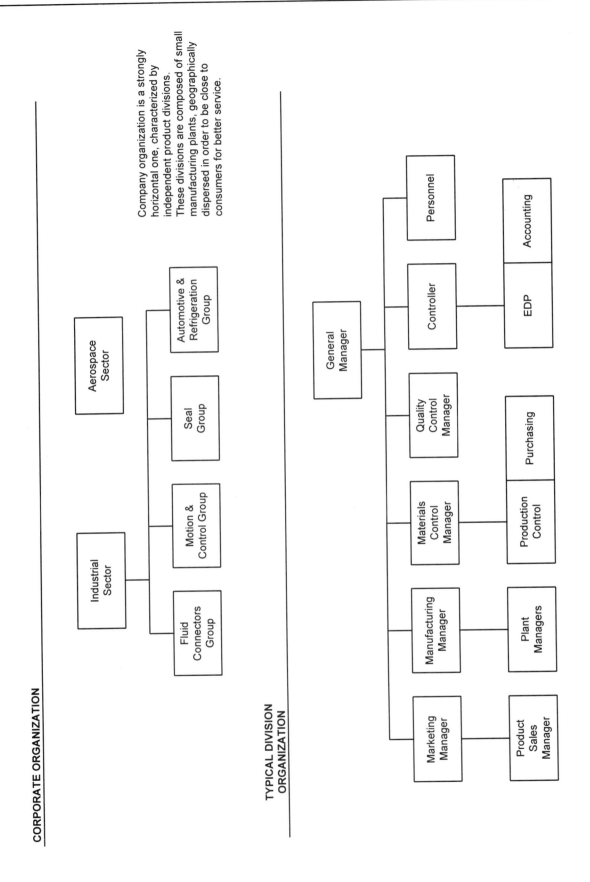

CORPORATE ORGANIZATION

Company organization is a strongly horizontal one, characterized by independent product divisions. These divisions are composed of small manufacturing plants, geographically dispersed in order to be close to consumers for better service.

Industrial Sector

Aerospace Sector

Fluid Connectors Group

Motion & Control Group

Seal Group

Automotive & Refrigeration Group

TYPICAL DIVISION ORGANIZATION

General Manager

Marketing Manager

Manufacturing Manager

Materials Control Manager

Quality Control Manager

Controller

Personnel

Product Sales Manager

Plant Managers

Production Control

Purchasing

EDP

Accounting

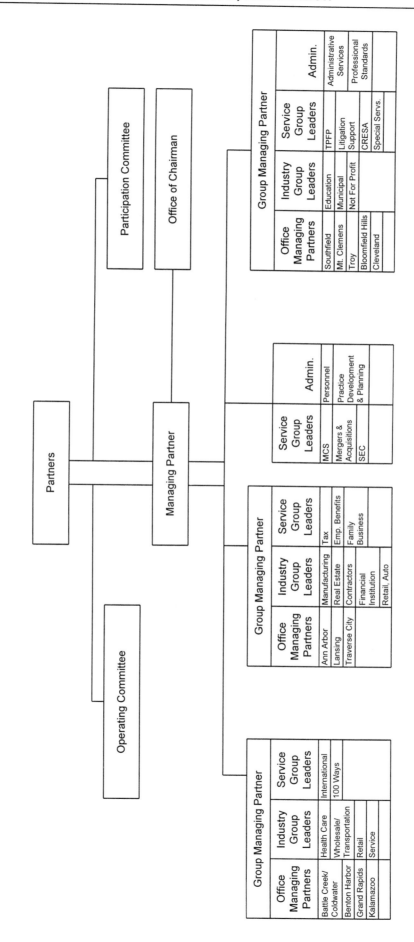

Plante & Moran, LLP

Source: Plante & Moran, LLP, 1996

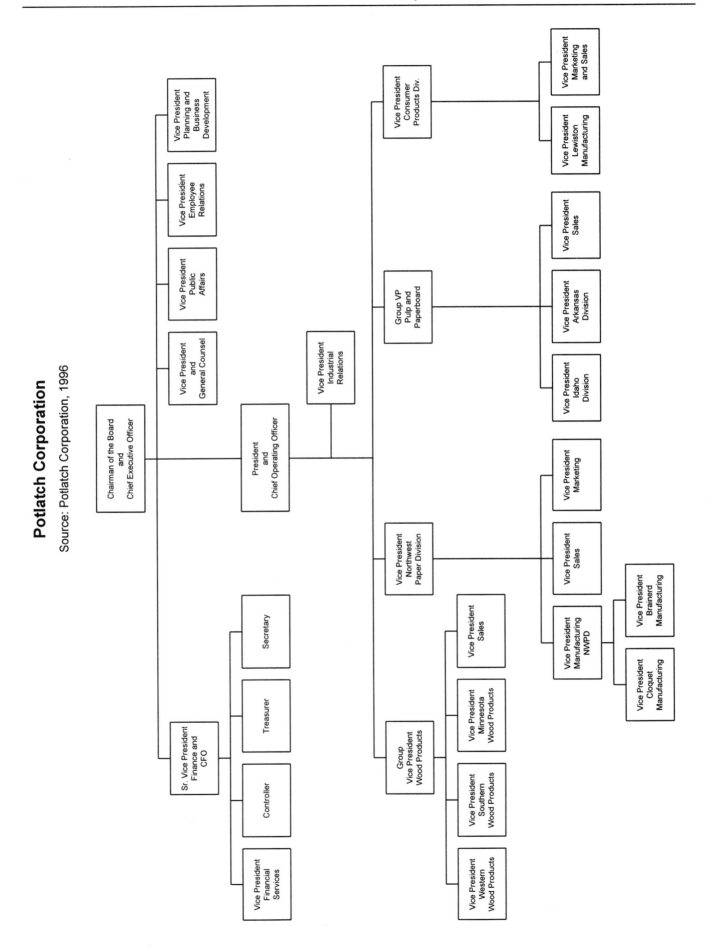

Potlatch Corporation

Source: Potlatch Corporation, 1996

PPG Industries, Inc.

Source: PPG Industries, Inc., 1996

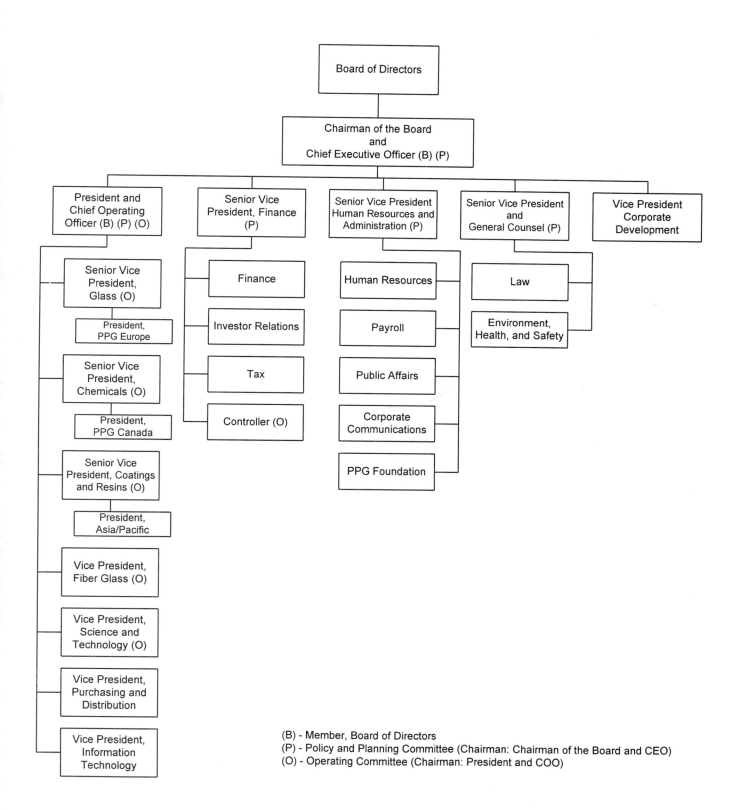

(B) - Member, Board of Directors
(P) - Policy and Planning Committee (Chairman: Chairman of the Board and CEO)
(O) - Operating Committee (Chairman: President and COO)

Proffitt's, Inc.

Source: Proffitt's, Inc., 1996

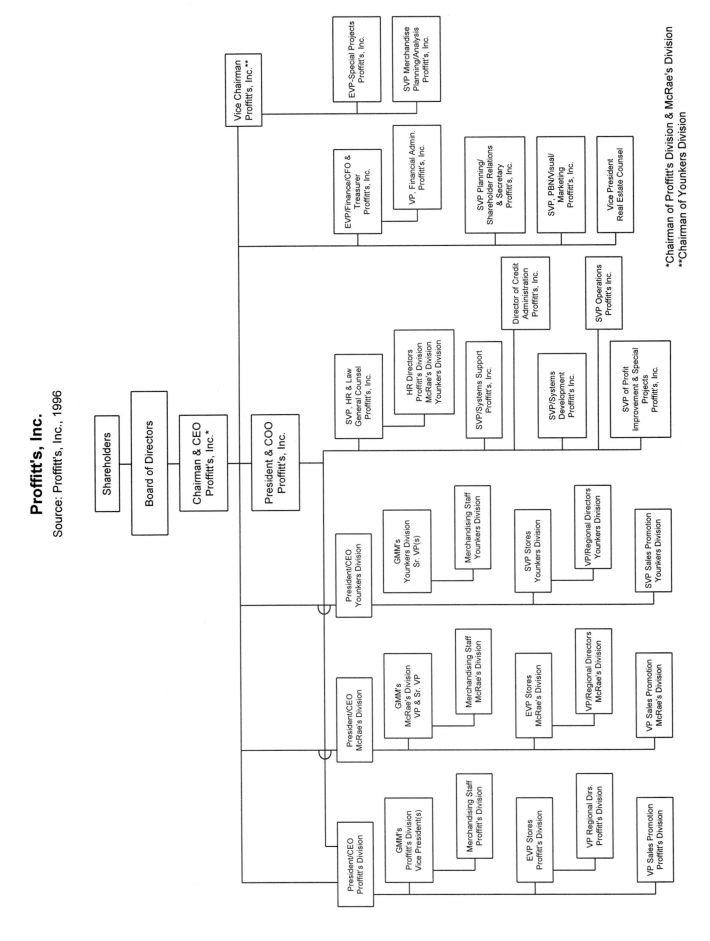

*Chairman of Proffitt's Division & McRae's Division
**Chairman of Younkers Division

ProMark One Marketing Services, Inc.

Source: ProMark One Marketing Services Inc., 1996

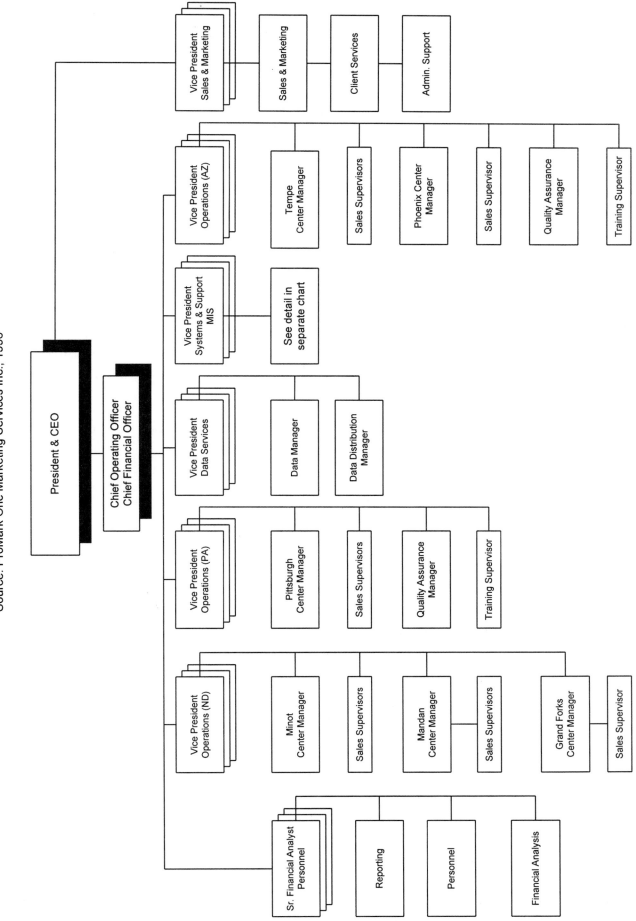

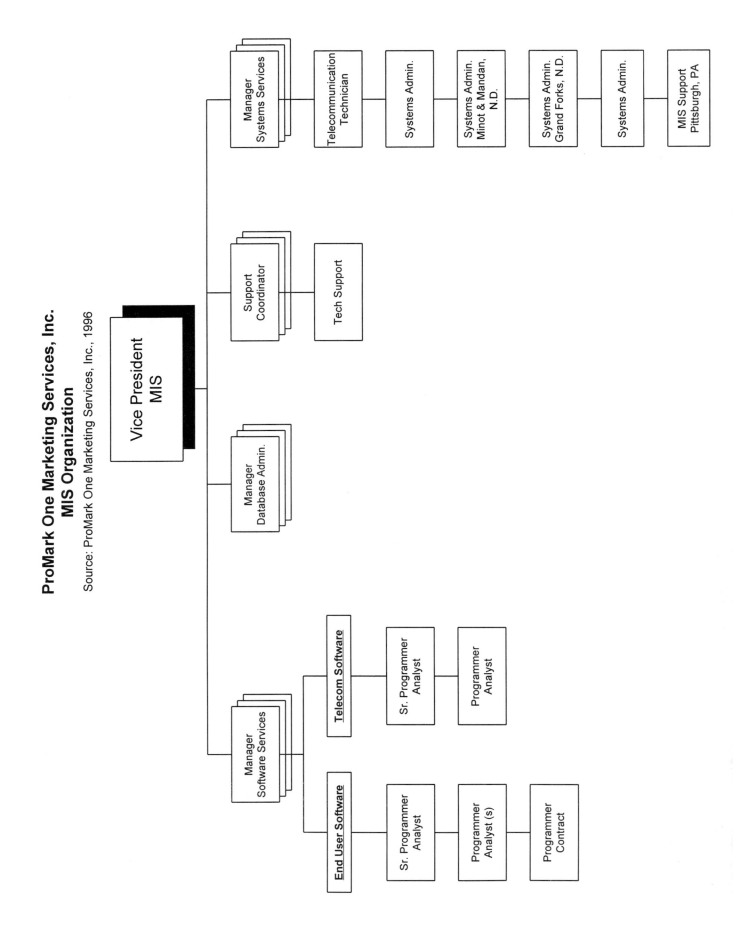

ProMark One Marketing Services, Inc.
MIS Organization

Source: ProMark One Marketing Services, Inc., 1996

Vice President MIS

- Manager Software Services
  - Telecom Software
    - Sr. Programmer Analyst
      - Programmer Analyst
  - End User Software
    - Sr. Programmer Analyst
      - Programmer Analyst (s)
        - Programmer Contract
- Manager Database Admin.
- Support Coordinator
  - Tech Support
- Manager Systems Services
  - Telecommunication Technician
  - Systems Admin.
  - Systems Admin. Minot & Mandan, N.D.
  - Systems Admin. Grand Forks, N.D.
  - Systems Admin.
  - MIS Support Pittsburgh, PA

Rabobank Nederland (The Netherlands)

Source: Rabobank Nederland, 1996

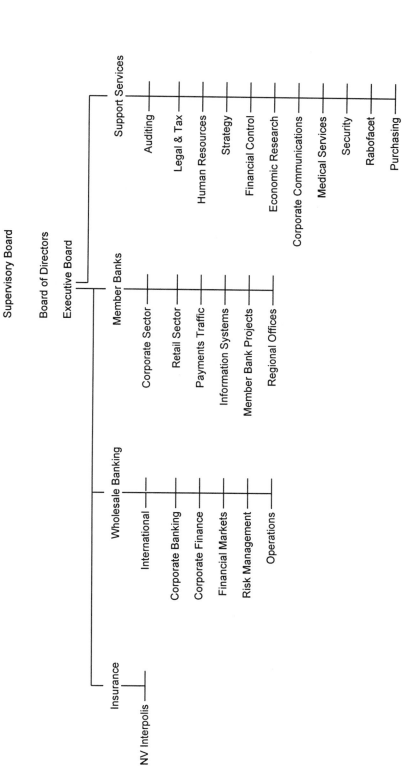

Republican National Committee

Source: Republican National Committee, 1996

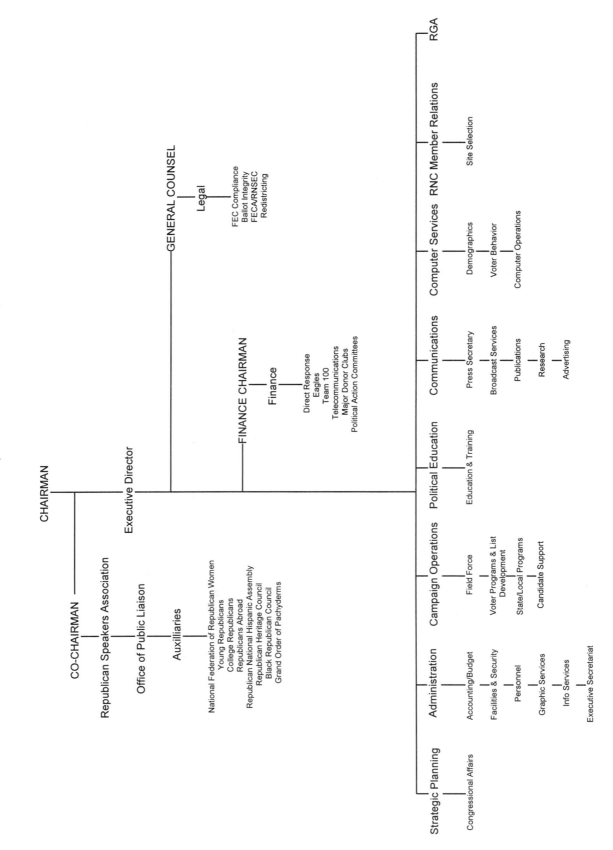

Royal Ahold nv (The Netherlands)

Source: Royal Ahold nv, 1996

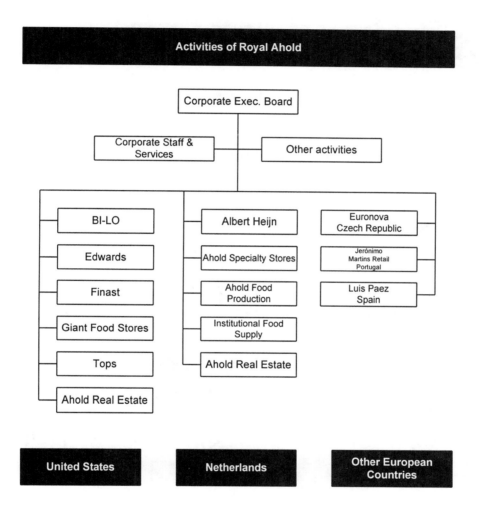

Royal PTT Nederland NV (The Netherlands)

Source: Royal PTT Nederland NV, 1996

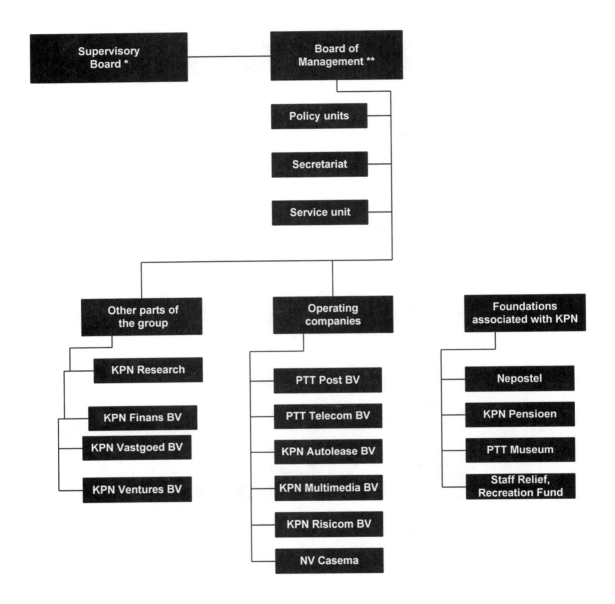

* Comprised of a chairman, deputy chairman, secretary, other members
** Comprised of a chairman, secretary, other members

RWE Energie AG (Germany)

Source: RWE Energie AG, 1996

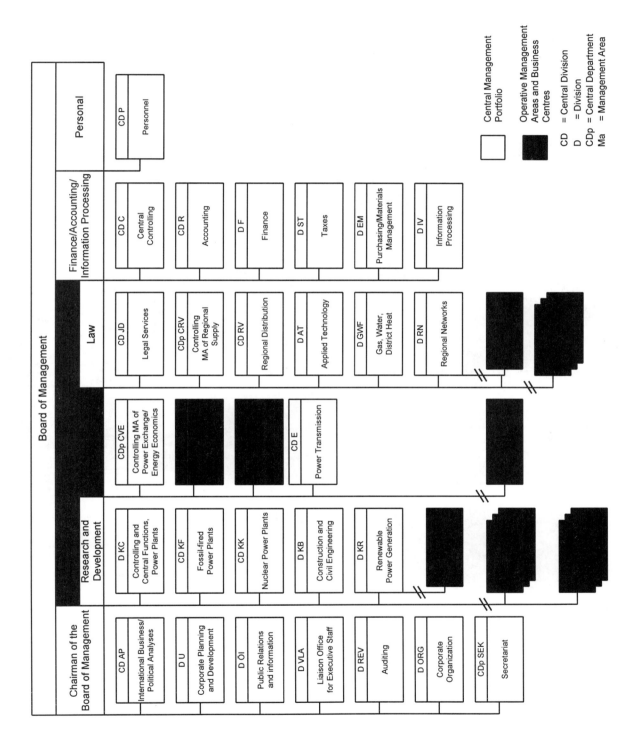

Legend:

☐	Central Management Portfolio
■	Operative Management Areas and Business Centres

CD = Central Division
D = Division
CDp = Central Department
Ma = Management Area

Board of Management

Personal — Personnel (CD P)

Finance/Accounting/Information Processing:
- CD C — Central Controlling
- CD R — Accounting
- D F — Finance
- D ST — Taxes
- D EM — Purchasing/Materials Management
- D IV — Information Processing

Law:
- CD JD — Legal Services
- CDp CRV — Controlling MA of Regional Supply
- CD RV — Regional Distribution
- D AT — Applied Technology
- D GWF — Gas, Water, District Heat
- D RN — Regional Networks

- CDp CVE — Controlling MA of Power Exchange/Energy Economics
- CD E — Power Transmission

Research and Development:
- D KC — Controlling and Central Functions, Power Plants
- CD KF — Fossil-fired Power Plants
- CD KK — Nuclear Power Plants
- D KB — Construction and Civil Engineering
- D KR — Renewable Power Generation

Chairman of the Board of Management:
- CD AP — International Business/Political Analyses
- D U — Corporate Planning and Development
- D ÖI — Public Relations and Information
- D VLA — Liaison Office for Executive Staff
- D REV — Auditing
- D ORG — Corporate Organization
- CDp SEK — Secretariat

Sanyo Electric Co., Ltd. (Japan)

Source: Sanyo Electric Co., Ltd., 1996

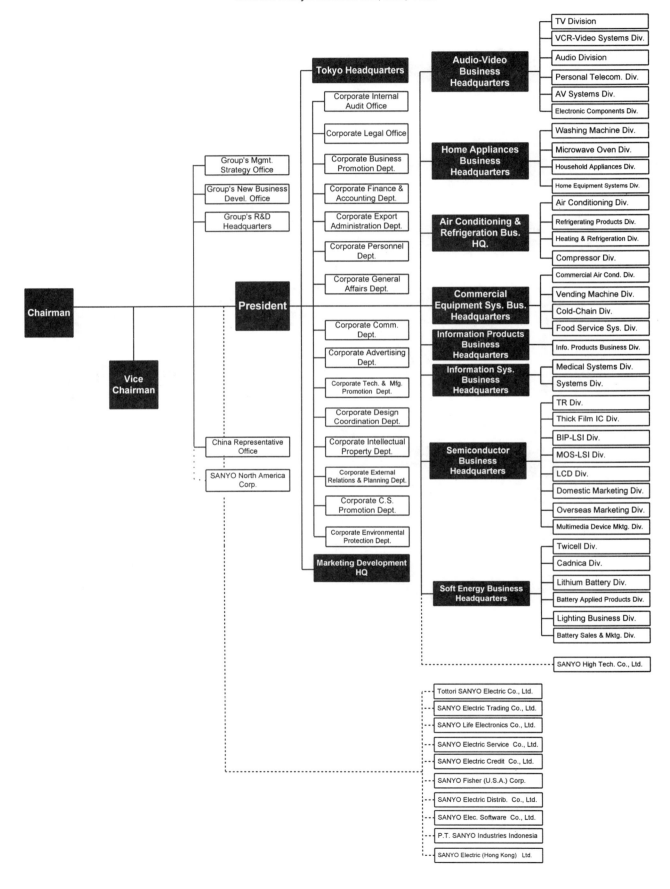

Saturn Corporation

Source: Saturn Corporation, 1996

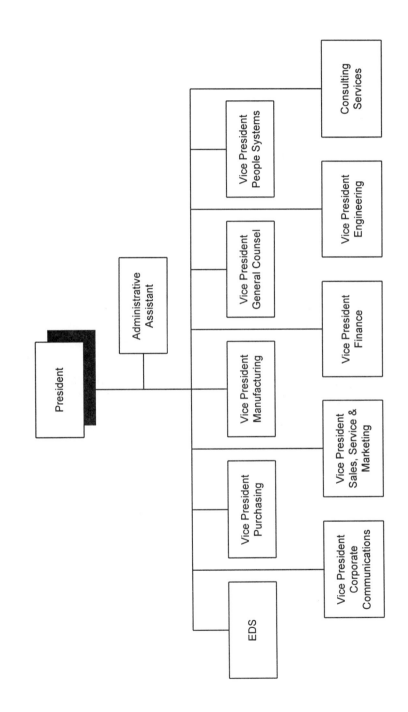

SBC Communications Inc.

Source: SBC Communications Inc., 1996

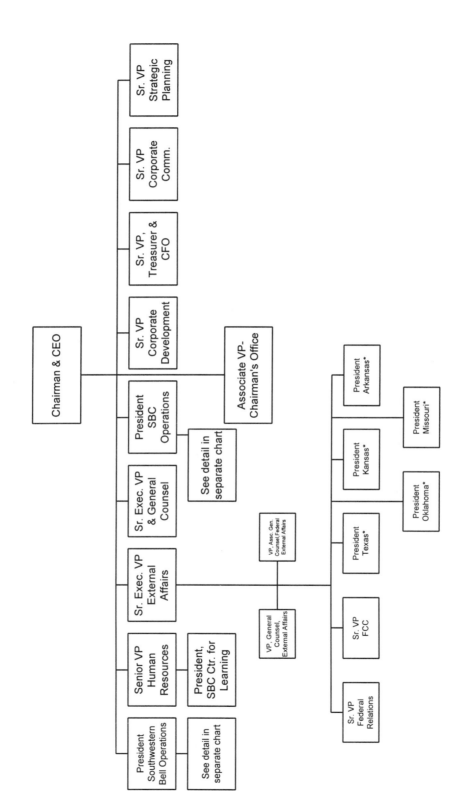

*Southwestern Bell Telephone

SBC Communications Inc.
SBC Operations

Source: SBC Communications Inc., 1996

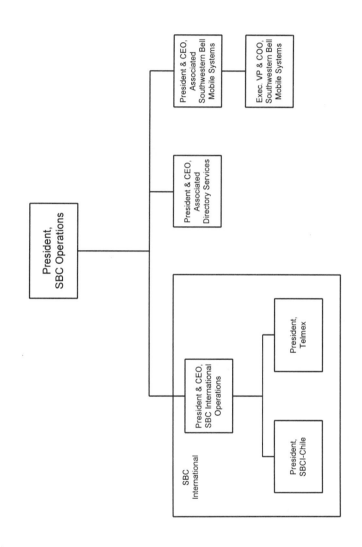

SBC Communications Inc.
Southwestern Bell Operations

Source: SBC Communications Inc., 1996

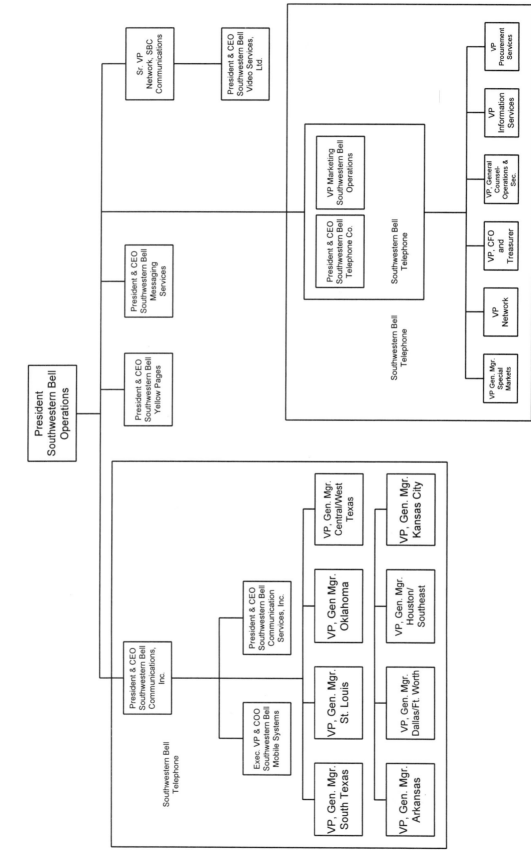

Sheetz, Inc.

Source: Sheetz, Inc., 1996

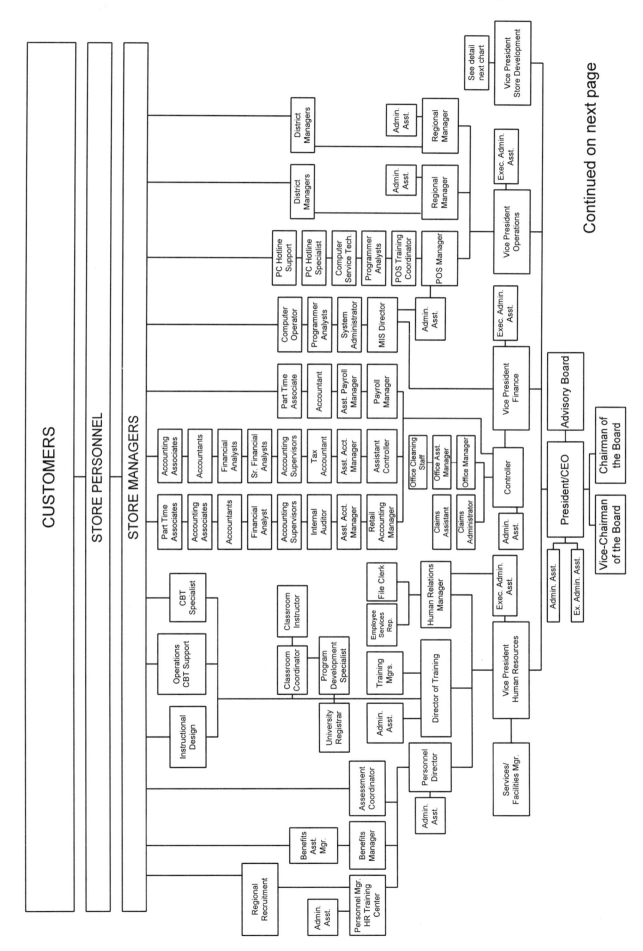

CUSTOMERS

STORE PERSONNEL

STORE MANAGERS

Continued on next page

Sheetz, Inc.

Continued from previous page

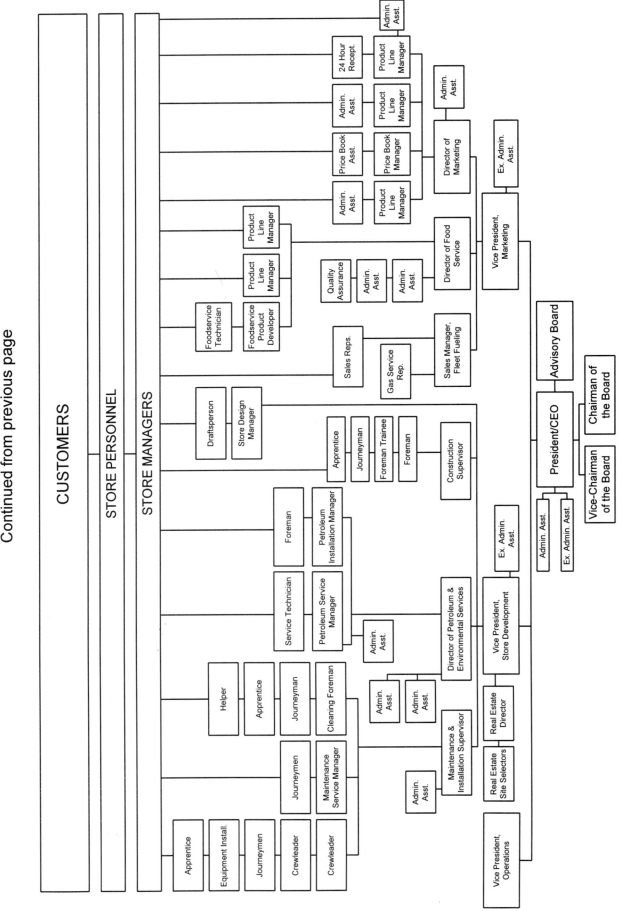

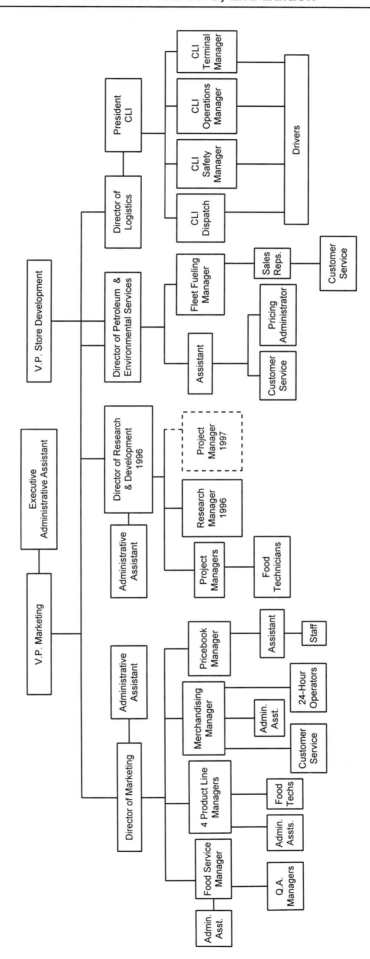

Sheetz, Inc.
Marketing
Source: Sheetz, Inc., 1996

SHL Systemhouse Inc.

Source: SHL Systemhouse Inc., 1996

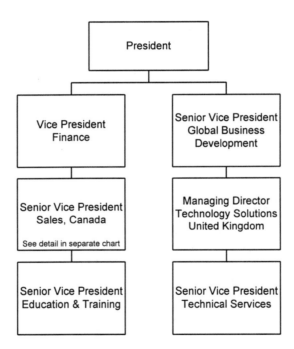

SHL Systemhouse Inc.
Sales, Canada

Source: SHL Systemhouse Inc., 1996

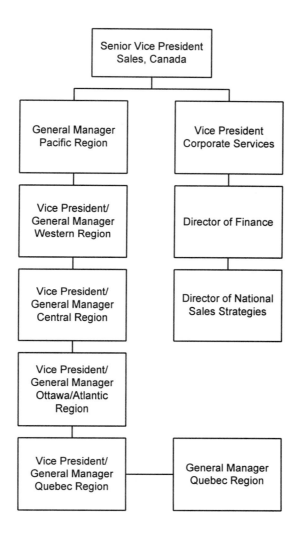

Siemens Nixdorf Informationssysteme AG (Germany)

Source: Siemens Nixdorf Informationssysteme AG, 1996

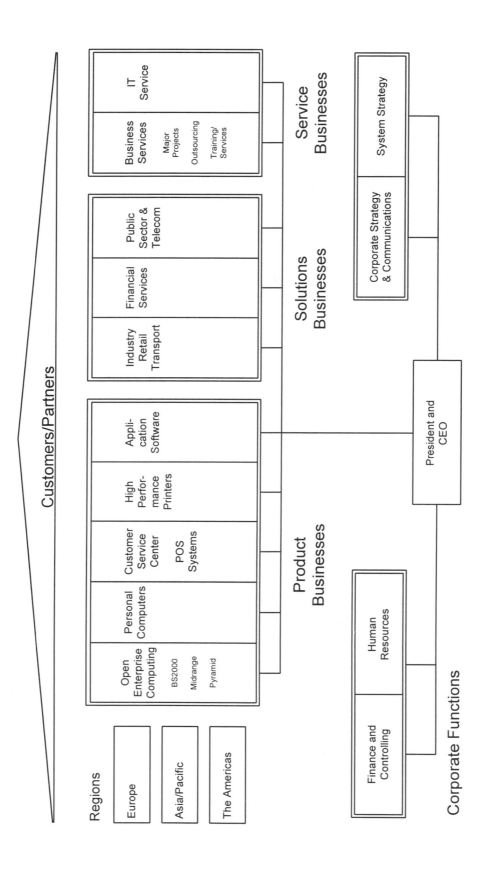

Sinochem (People's Republic of China)

Source: Sinochem, 1996

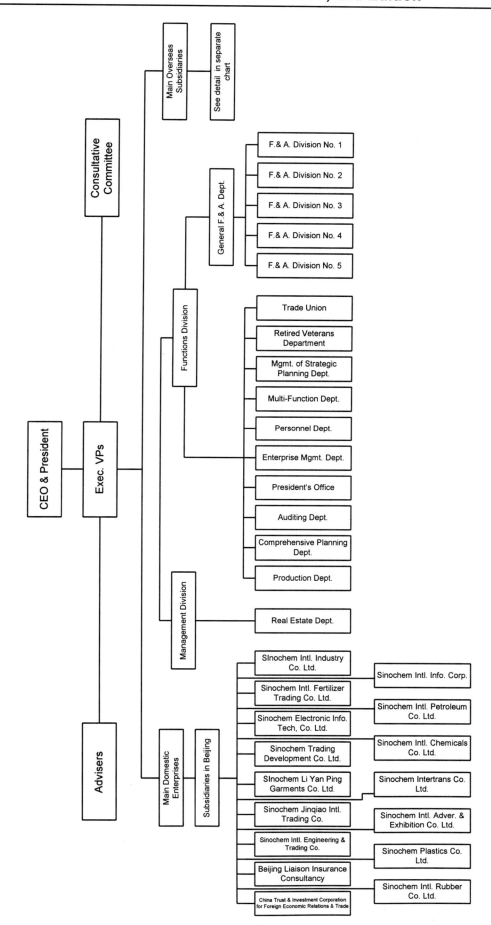

Continued on next page

Sinochem (People's Republic of China)
Continued from previous page

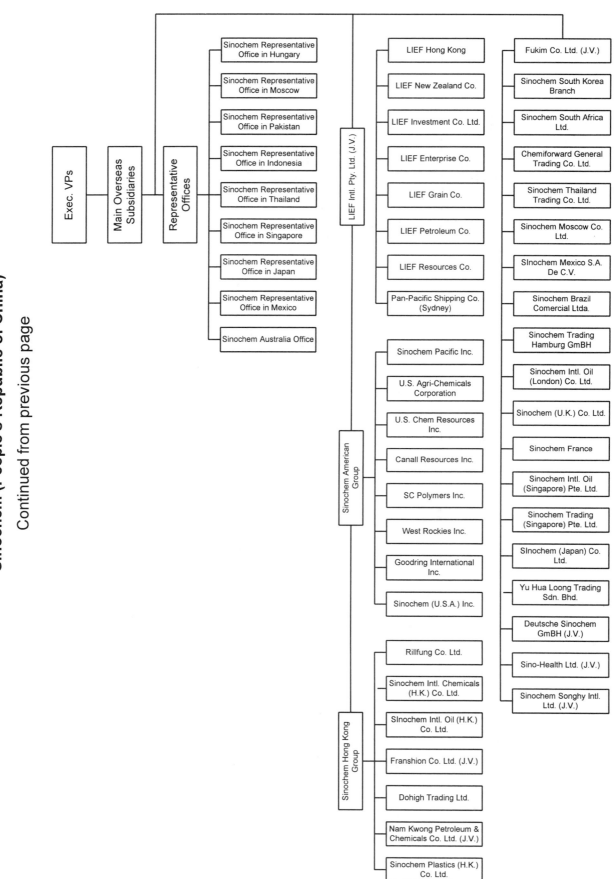

Exec. VPs

Main Overseas Subsidiaries

Representative Offices
- Sinochem Representative Office in Hungary
- Sinochem Representative Office in Moscow
- Sinochem Representative Office in Pakistan
- Sinochem Representative Office in Indonesia
- Sinochem Representative Office in Thailand
- Sinochem Representative Office in Singapore
- Sinochem Representative Office in Japan
- Sinochem Representative Office in Mexico
- Sinochem Australia Office

LIEF Intl. Pty. Ltd. (J.V.)
- LIEF Hong Kong
- LIEF New Zealand Co.
- LIEF Investment Co. Ltd.
- LIEF Enterprise Co.
- LIEF Grain Co.
- LIEF Petroleum Co.
- LIEF Resources Co.
- Pan-Pacific Shipping Co. (Sydney)

Sinochem American Group
- Sinochem Pacific Inc.
- U.S. Agri-Chemicals Corporation
- U.S. Chem Resources Inc.
- Canall Resources Inc.
- SC Polymers Inc.
- West Rockies Inc.
- Goodring International Inc.
- Sinochem (U.S.A.) Inc.

Sinochem Hong Kong Group
- Rillfung Co. Ltd.
- Sinochem Intl. Chemicals (H.K.) Co. Ltd.
- Sinochem Intl. Oil (H.K.) Co. Ltd.
- Franshion Co. Ltd. (J.V.)
- Dohigh Trading Ltd.
- Nam Kwong Petroleum & Chemicals Co. Ltd. (J.V.)
- Sinochem Plastics (H.K.) Co. Ltd.

- Fukim Co. Ltd. (J.V.)
- Sinochem South Korea Branch
- Sinochem South Africa Ltd.
- Chemiforward General Trading Co. Ltd.
- Sinochem Thailand Trading Co. Ltd.
- Sinochem Moscow Co. Ltd.
- Sinochem Mexico S.A. De C.V.
- Sinochem Brazil Comercial Ltda.
- Sinochem Trading Hamburg GmBH
- Sinochem Intl. Oil (London) Co. Ltd.
- Sinochem (U.K.) Co. Ltd.
- Sinochem France
- Sinochem Intl. Oil (Singapore) Pte. Ltd.
- Sinochem Trading (Singapore) Pte. Ltd.
- Sinochem (Japan) Co. Ltd.
- Yu Hua Loong Trading Sdn. Bhd.
- Deutsche Sinochem GmBH (J.V.)
- Sino-Health Ltd. (J.V.)
- Sinochem Songhy Intl. Ltd. (J.V.)

Continued on next page

Sinochem (People's Republic of China)
Continued from previous page

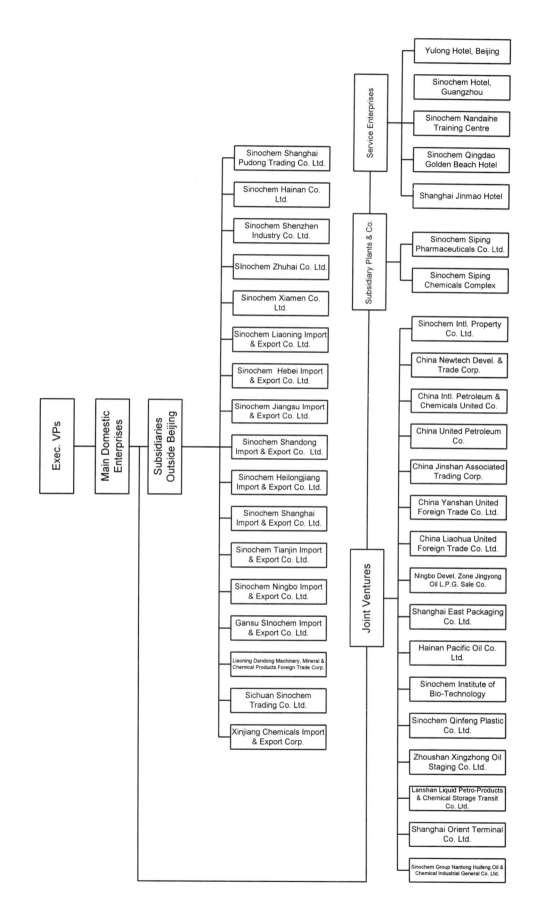

Exec. VPs

Main Domestic Enterprises

Subsidiaries Outside Beijing
- Sinochem Shanghai Pudong Trading Co. Ltd.
- Sinochem Hainan Co. Ltd.
- Sinochem Shenzhen Industry Co. Ltd.
- SInochem Zhuhai Co. Ltd.
- Sinochem Xiamen Co. Ltd.
- Sinochem Liaoning Import & Export Co. Ltd.
- Sinochem Hebei Import & Export Co. Ltd.
- Sinochem Jiangsu Import & Export Co. Ltd.
- Sinochem Shandong Import & Export Co. Ltd.
- Sinochem Heilongjiang Import & Export Ltd.
- Sinochem Shanghai Import & Export Co. Ltd.
- Sinochem Tianjin Import & Export Co. Ltd.
- Sinochem Ningbo Import & Export Co. Ltd.
- Gansu SInochem Import & Export Co. Ltd.
- Liaoning Dandong Machinery, Mineral & Chemical Products Foreign Trade Corp.
- Sichuan Sinochem Trading Co. Ltd.
- Xinjiang Chemicals Import & Export Corp.

Service Enterprises
- Yulong Hotel, Beijing
- Sinochem Hotel, Guangzhou
- Sinochem Nandaihe Training Centre
- Sinochem Qingdao Golden Beach Hotel
- Shanghai Jinmao Hotel

Subsidiary Plants & Co.
- Sinochem Siping Pharmaceuticals Co. Ltd.
- Sinochem Siping Chemicals Complex

Joint Ventures
- Sinochem Intl. Property Co. Ltd.
- China Newtech Devel. & Trade Corp.
- China Intl. Petroleum & Chemicals United Co.
- China United Petroleum Co.
- China Jinshan Associated Trading Corp.
- China Yanshan United Foreign Trade Co. Ltd.
- China Liaohua United Foreign Trade Co. Ltd.
- Ningbo Devel. Zone Jingyong Oil L.P.G. Sale Co.
- Shanghai East Packaging Co. Ltd.
- Hainan Pacific Oil Co. Ltd.
- Sinochem Institute of Bio-Technology
- Sinochem Qinfeng Plastic Co. Ltd.
- Zhoushan Xingzhong Oil Staging Co. Ltd.
- Lanshan Liquid Petro-Products & Chemical Storage Transit Co. Ltd.
- Shanghai Orient Terminal Co. Ltd.
- Sinochem Group Nantong Huifeng Oil & Chemical Industrial General Co. Ltd.

Sisu Corporation (Finland)

Source: Sisu Corporation, 1996

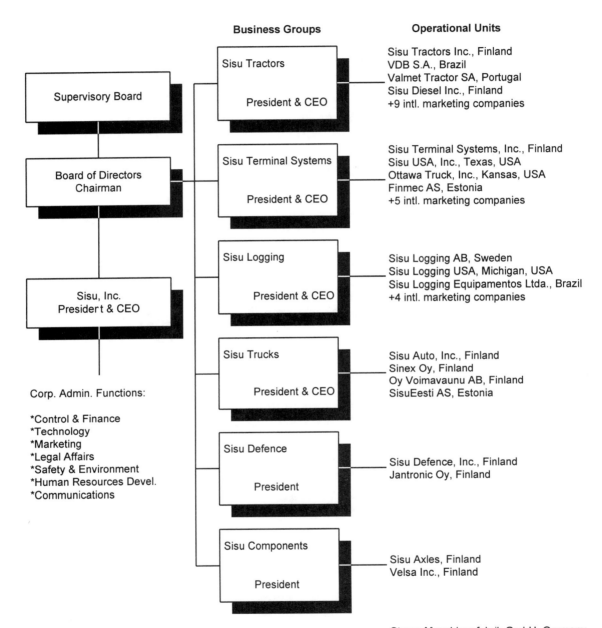

Business Groups

Operational Units

Supervisory Board

Board of Directors
Chairman

Sisu, Inc.
President & CEO

Corp. Admin. Functions:

*Control & Finance
*Technology
*Marketing
*Legal Affairs
*Safety & Environment
*Human Resources Devel.
*Communications

Sisu Tractors

President & CEO

Sisu Tractors Inc., Finland
VDB S.A., Brazil
Valmet Tractor SA, Portugal
Sisu Diesel Inc., Finland
+9 intl. marketing companies

Sisu Terminal Systems

President & CEO

Sisu Terminal Systems, Inc., Finland
Sisu USA, Inc., Texas, USA
Ottawa Truck, Inc., Kansas, USA
Finmec AS, Estonia
+5 intl. marketing companies

Sisu Logging

President & CEO

Sisu Logging AB, Sweden
Sisu Logging USA, Michigan, USA
Sisu Logging Equipamentos Ltda., Brazil
+4 intl. marketing companies

Sisu Trucks

President & CEO

Sisu Auto, Inc., Finland
Sinex Oy, Finland
Oy Voimavaunu AB, Finland
SisuEesti AS, Estonia

Sisu Defence

President

Sisu Defence, Inc., Finland
Jantronic Oy, Finland

Sisu Components

President

Sisu Axles, Finland
Velsa Inc., Finland

Stama Maschinenfabrik GmbH, Germany

Smithsonian Institution

Source: Smithsonian Institution, 1996

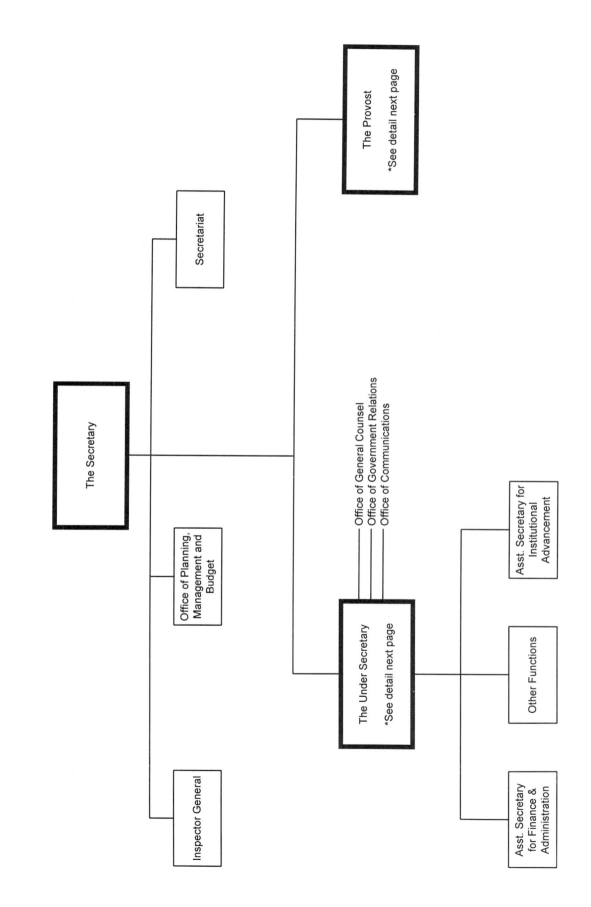

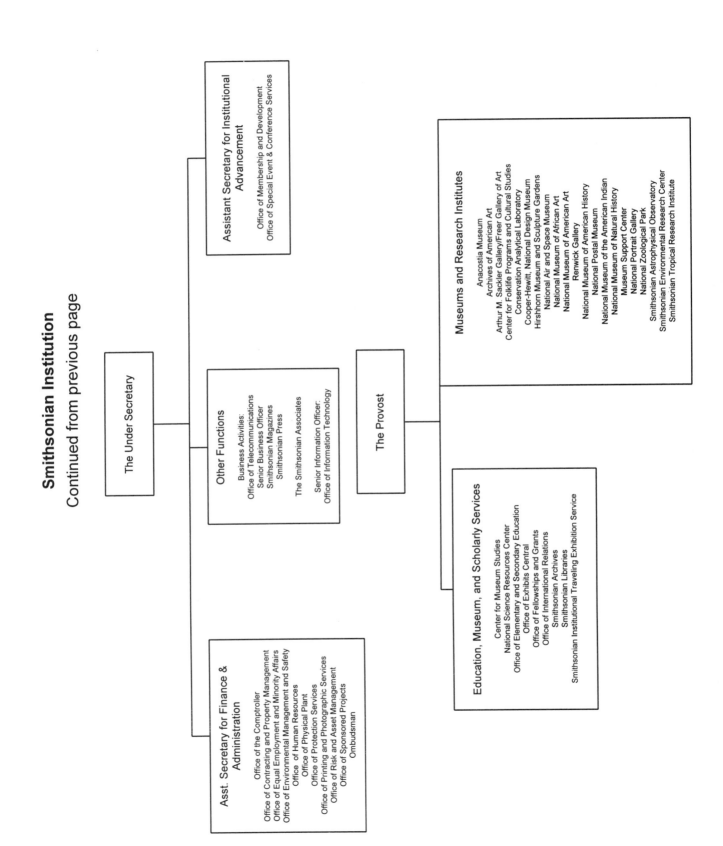

Smithsonian Institution
Continued from previous page

The Under Secretary

Assistant Secretary for Institutional Advancement

Office of Membership and Development
Office of Special Event & Conference Services

Asst. Secretary for Finance & Administration

Office of the Comptroller
Office of Contracting and Property Management
Office of Equal Employment and Minority Affairs
Office of Environmental Management and Safety
Office of Human Resources
Office of Physical Plant
Office of Protection Services
Office of Printing and Photographic Services
Office of Risk and Asset Management
Office of Sponsored Projects
Ombudsman

Other Functions

Business Activities:
Office of Telecommunications
Senior Business Officer
Smithsonian Magazines
Smithsonian Press

The Smithsonian Associates

Senior Information Officer:
Office of Information Technology

The Provost

Museums and Research Institutes

Anacostia Museum
Archives of American Art
Arthur M. Sackler Gallery/Freer Gallery of Art
Center for Folklife Programs and Cultural Studies
Conservation Analytical Laboratory
Cooper-Hewitt, National Design Museum
Hirshhorn Museum and Sculpture Gardens
National Air and Space Museum
National Museum of African Art
National Museum of American Art
Renwick Gallery
National Museum of American History
National Postal Museum
National Museum of the American Indian
National Museum of Natural History
Museum Support Center
National Portrait Gallery
National Zoological Park
Smithsonian Astrophysical Observatory
Smithsonian Environmental Research Center
Smithsonian Tropical Research Institute

Education, Museum, and Scholarly Services

Center for Museum Studies
National Science Resources Center
Office of Elementary and Secondary Education
Office of Exhibits Central
Office of Fellowships and Grants
Office of International Relations
Smithsonian Archives
Smithsonian Libraries
Smithsonian Institutional Traveling Exhibition Service

Sony Corp. (Japan)

Source: Sony Corp., 1996

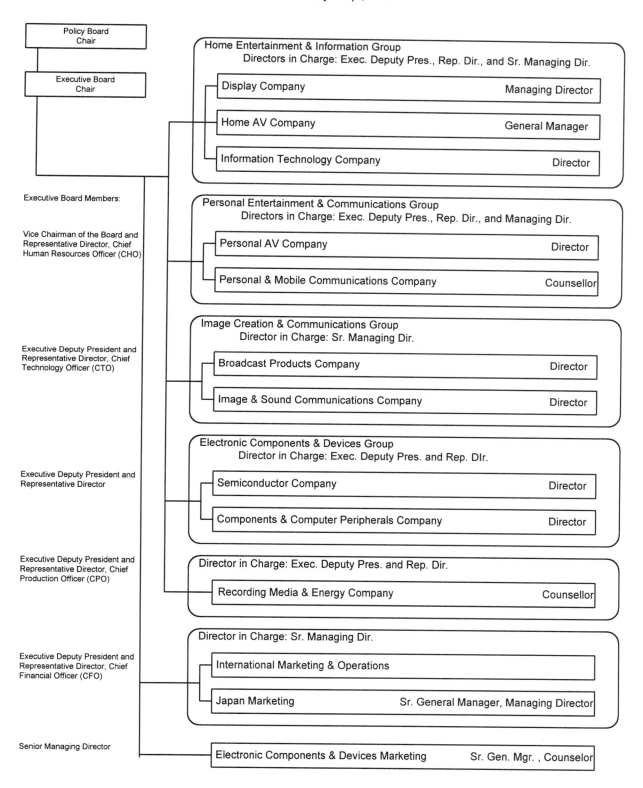

Continued on next page

Sony Corp. (Japan)

Continued from previous page

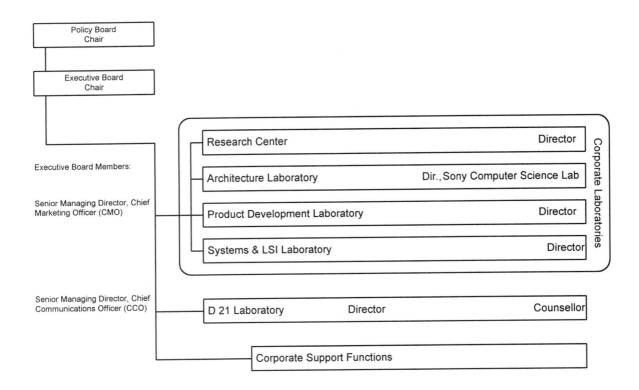

Staple Cotton Cooperative Association

Source: Staple Cotton Cooperative Association, 1996

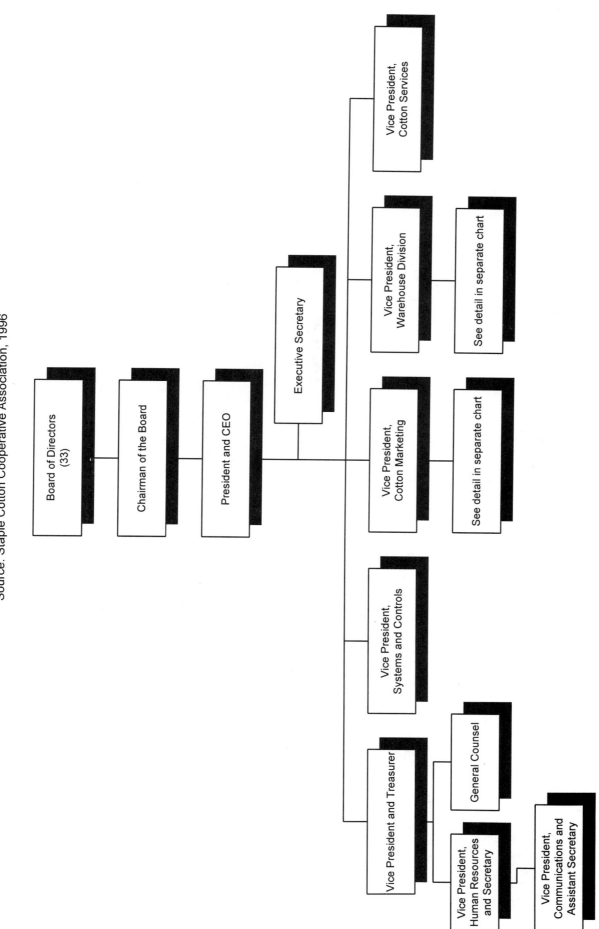

Staple Cotton Cooperative Association Cotton Marketing

Source: Staple Cotton Cooperative Association, 1996

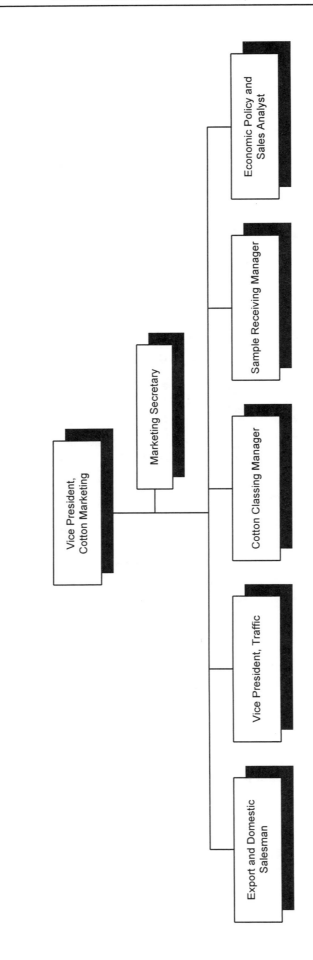

**Staple Cotton Cooperative Association
Warehouse Division**

Source: Staple Cotton Cooperative Association, 1996

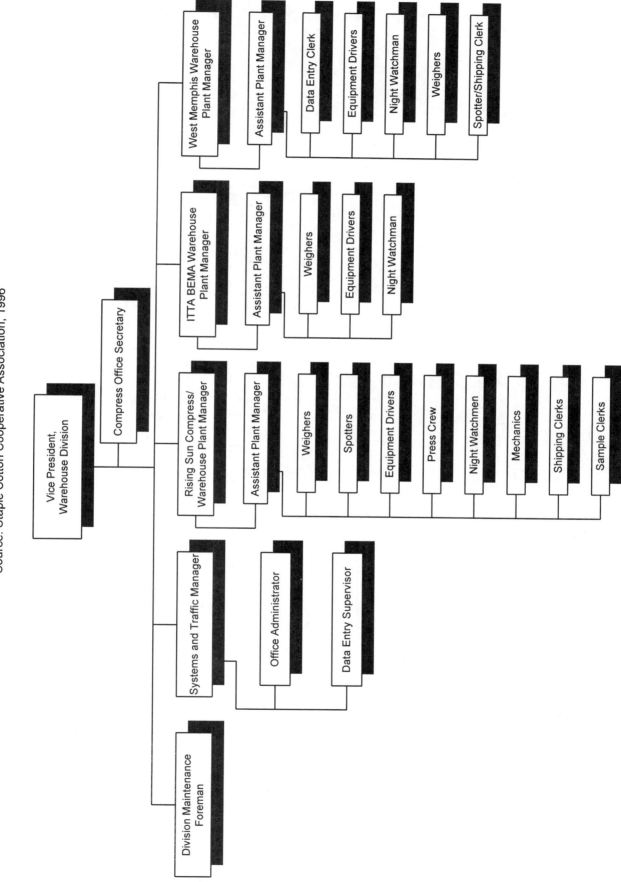

Stora Kopparbergs Bergslags AB (Sweden)

Source: Stora Kopparbergs Bergslags AB, 1996

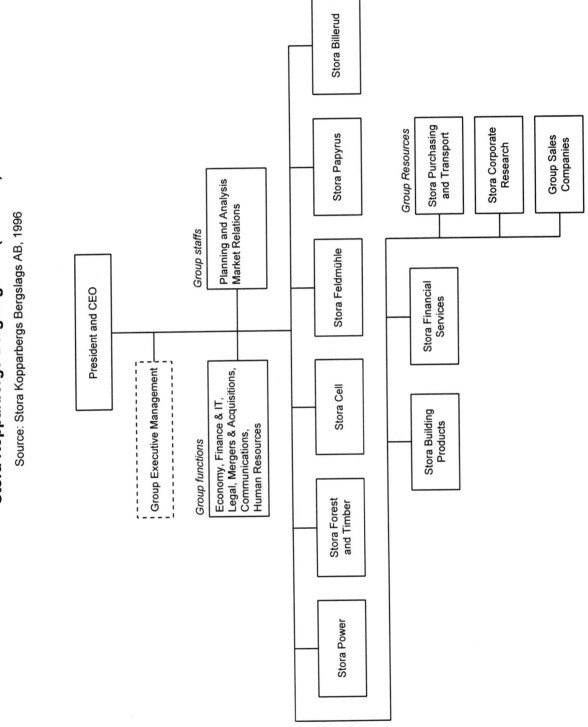

Sumitomo Chemical Company, Limited (Japan)

Source: Annual report, 1996

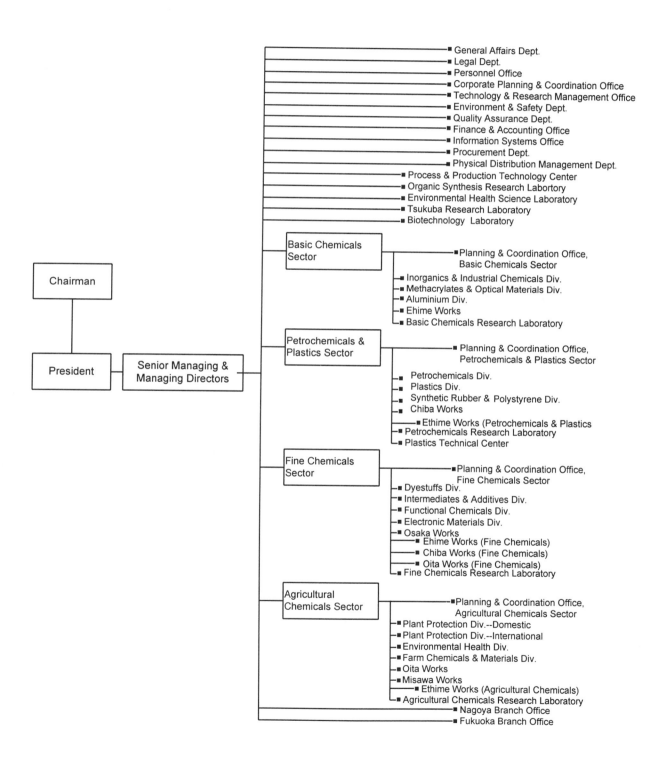

Sumitomo Heavy Industries, Ltd. (Japan)

Source: Sumitomo Heavy Industries , Ltd., 1996

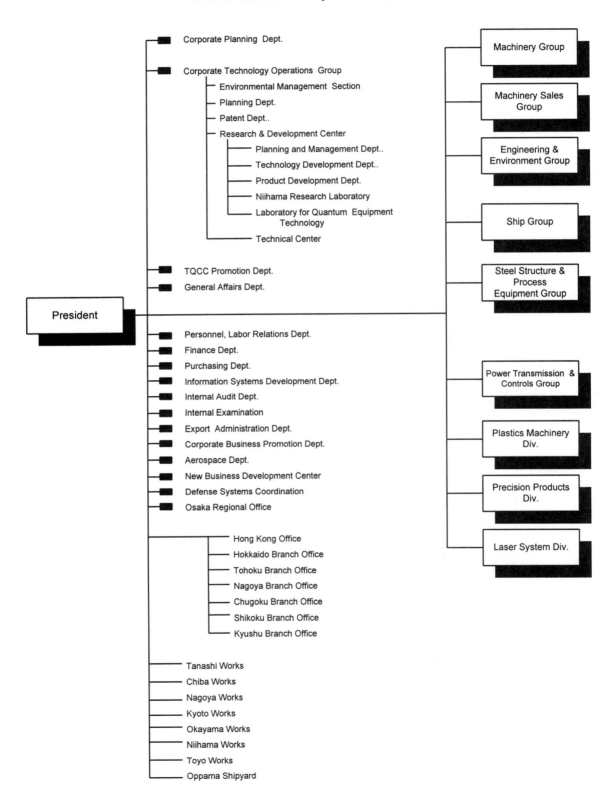

President

- Corporate Planning Dept.
- Corporate Technology Operations Group
  - Environmental Management Section
  - Planning Dept.
  - Patent Dept..
  - Research & Development Center
    - Planning and Management Dept..
    - Technology Development Dept..
    - Product Development Dept.
    - Niihama Research Laboratory
    - Laboratory for Quantum Equipment Technology
  - Technical Center
- TQCC Promotion Dept.
- General Affairs Dept.
- Personnel, Labor Relations Dept.
- Finance Dept.
- Purchasing Dept.
- Information Systems Development Dept.
- Internal Audit Dept.
- Internal Examination
- Export Administration Dept.
- Corporate Business Promotion Dept.
- Aerospace Dept.
- New Business Development Center
- Defense Systems Coordination
- Osaka Regional Office
  - Hong Kong Office
  - Hokkaido Branch Office
  - Tohoku Branch Office
  - Nagoya Branch Office
  - Chugoku Branch Office
  - Shikoku Branch Office
  - Kyushu Branch Office
- Tanashi Works
- Chiba Works
- Nagoya Works
- Kyoto Works
- Okayama Works
- Niihama Works
- Toyo Works
- Oppama Shipyard

- Machinery Group
- Machinery Sales Group
- Engineering & Environment Group
- Ship Group
- Steel Structure & Process Equipment Group
- Power Transmission & Controls Group
- Plastics Machinery Div.
- Precision Products Div.
- Laser System Div.

Sun Healthcare Group, Inc.

Source: Sun Healthcare Group, Inc., 1996

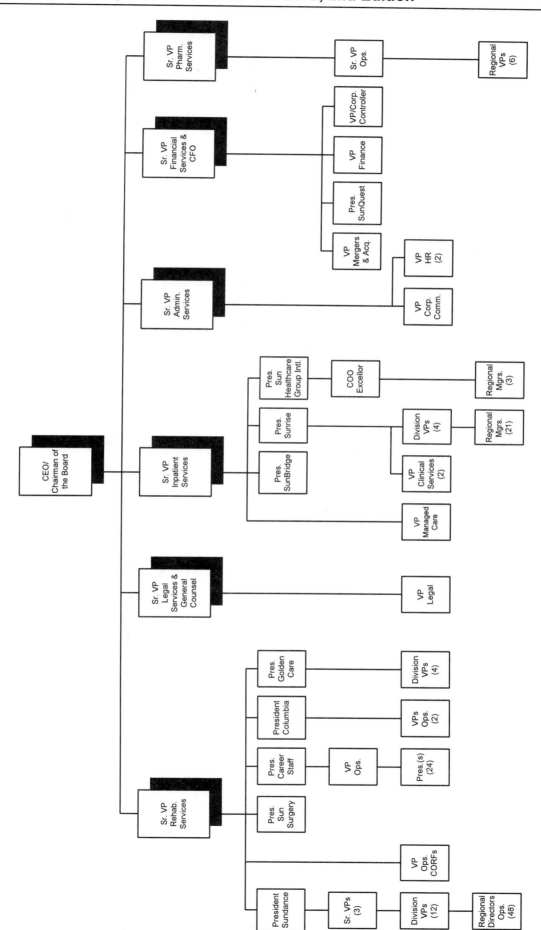

Swiss Bank Corp. (Switzerland)

Source: Swiss Bank Corp., 1996

Group Chief Executive Officer		
Domestic Division	**Corporate Center**	**SBC Warburg Division**
Head, "Domestic Division"* Head, "Corporates & Institutionals" Head, "Private Investors & Asset Mgt.* Deputy Head "Private Investors & Asset Management Head, "Retail" Head, "Logistics" Regional Head, Zurich, Eastern Switzerland and Ticino Regional Head, Western Switzerland Regional Head, Central and North- Western Switzerland	Deputy Group Chief Financial Officer* Chief Financial Officer* Chief Credit Officer*	Chief Executive, "SBC Warburg"* Chief Operating Officer Head, "Global Institutional Asset Management" Head, "Investment Banking Operations" Corporate Finance Head, "Equities" Head, "Foreign Exchange" Head, "Rates" Regional Chairman, North America Regional Chairman, Asia/Pacific Regional Chairman, Switzerland and Latin America

*Members of the Group Executive Committee

Additional members of the SBC Warburg
Executive Board include staff from
Equities; Customer Services; Corporate
Finance; the President and Chief
Executive Officer, SBC Capital Markets
Inc., USA; Operations & Controls;
Information Technology; Equity Capital
Markets; and Human Resources

Swiss Life Insurance and Pension Company (Switzerland)

Source: Swiss Life Insurance and Pension Company, 1996

Chairman of the Supervisory Board	

Chairman of the Executive Board	
President	

Presidential Functions	Finances	Management Services
CEO	Co-President	Deputy Co-President

Actuarial Services/Accounting
Deputy Co-President

General Secretarial/Legal & Taxation Svcs.	Staff Finances	Corporate Development Corporate Planning & Controlling IT Coordination
Executive Vice President Senior Vice President Vice President	Exec. Vice President	Deputy Co-President

Actuarial Services/Annual Accounts
Senior Vice President

Advertising & Sponsoring	Mortgages/Loans	Human Resources
Executive Vice President	Vice President	Exec. Vice President

Actuarial Services Development
Senior Vice President

PR & Information	Securities	Data Centers
Vice President	Vice President	Senior Vice President

Reinsurance
Vice President

Corporate Internal Auditing	Real Estate	Internal Services
Vice President	Executive Vice President Vice President(s)	Vice President

Accounting
Senior Vice President Vice President

Portfolio Manager
Vice President

Taisei Corporation (Japan)

Source: Taisei Corporation, 1996

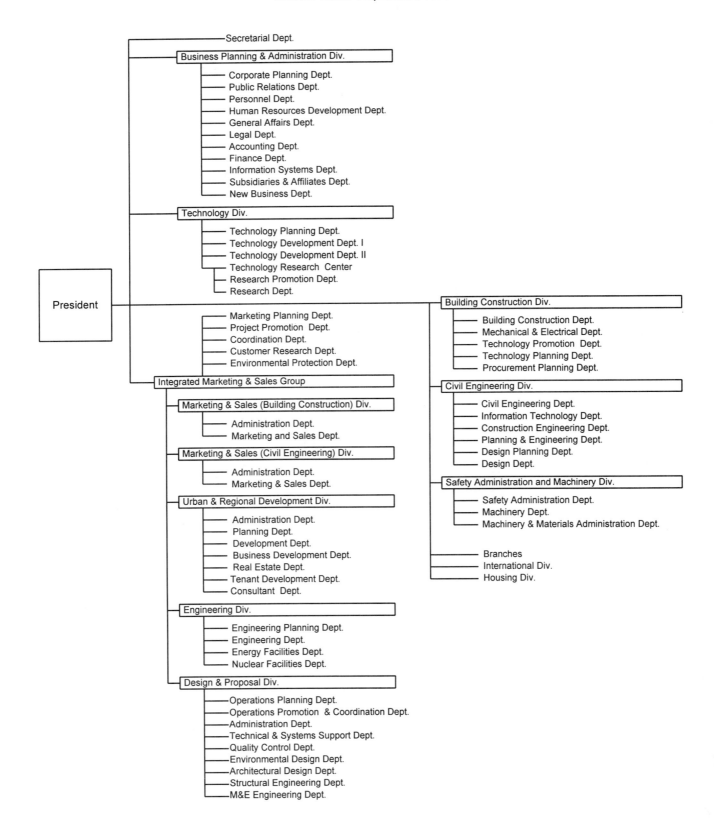

Taiwan Power Company (Taipower)

Source: Taiwan Power Company (Taipower), 1996

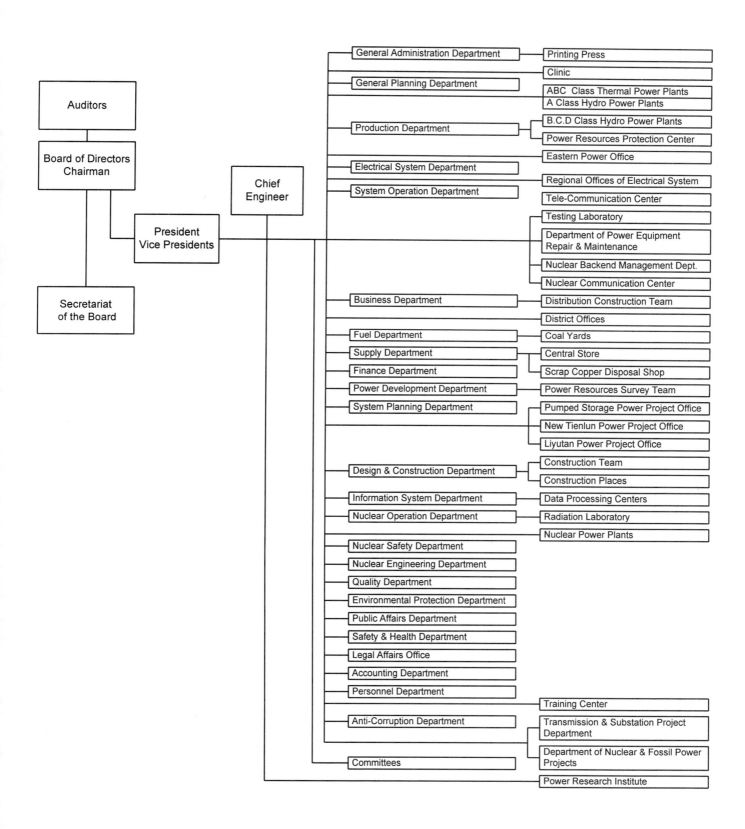

Taiyo Mutual Life Insurance Co. (Japan)

Source: Taiyo Mutual Life Insurance Co., 1996

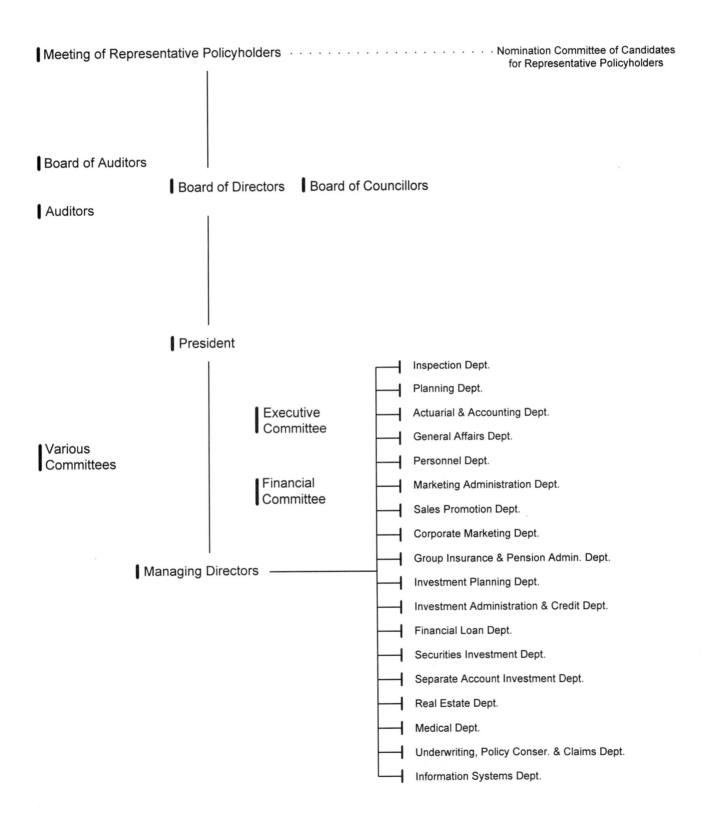

Meeting of Representative Policyholders · Nomination Committee of Candidates for Representative Policyholders

Board of Auditors

Board of Directors   Board of Councillors

Auditors

President

Various Committees

Executive Committee

Financial Committee

Managing Directors

- Inspection Dept.
- Planning Dept.
- Actuarial & Accounting Dept.
- General Affairs Dept.
- Personnel Dept.
- Marketing Administration Dept.
- Sales Promotion Dept.
- Corporate Marketing Dept.
- Group Insurance & Pension Admin. Dept.
- Investment Planning Dept.
- Investment Administration & Credit Dept.
- Financial Loan Dept.
- Securities Investment Dept.
- Separate Account Investment Dept.
- Real Estate Dept.
- Medical Dept.
- Underwriting, Policy Conser. & Claims Dept.
- Information Systems Dept.

Tatham EURO RSCG

Source: Tatham EURO RSCG, 1996

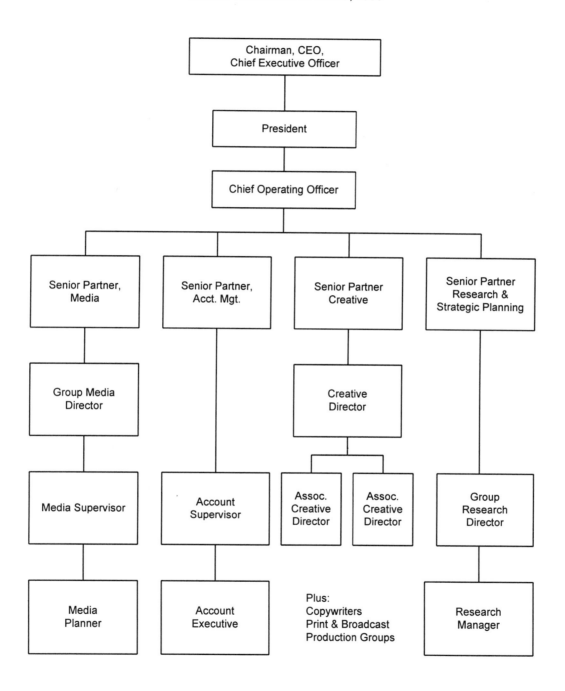

Plus:
Spot Broadcast Group
Media Information Group

Techmatics Inc.

Source: Techmatics Inc., 1996

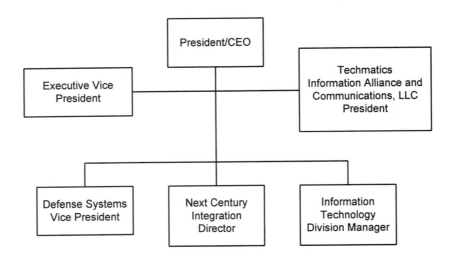

Teledyne Brown Engineering Co.

Source: Teledyne Brown Engineering Co., 1996

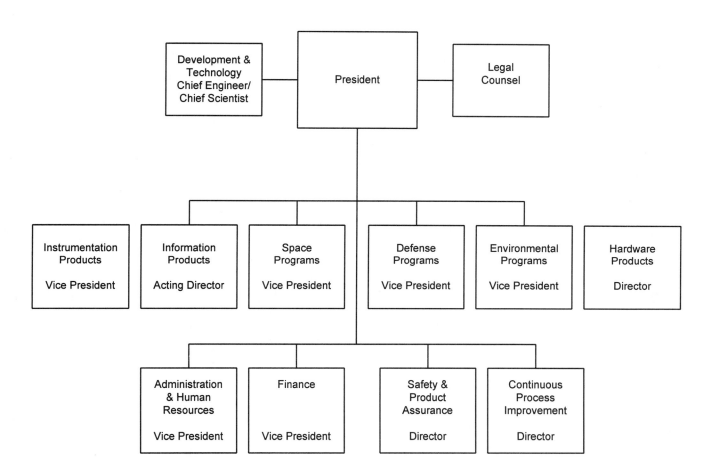

Tenet Healthcare Corporation

Source: Tenet Healthcare Corporation, 1996

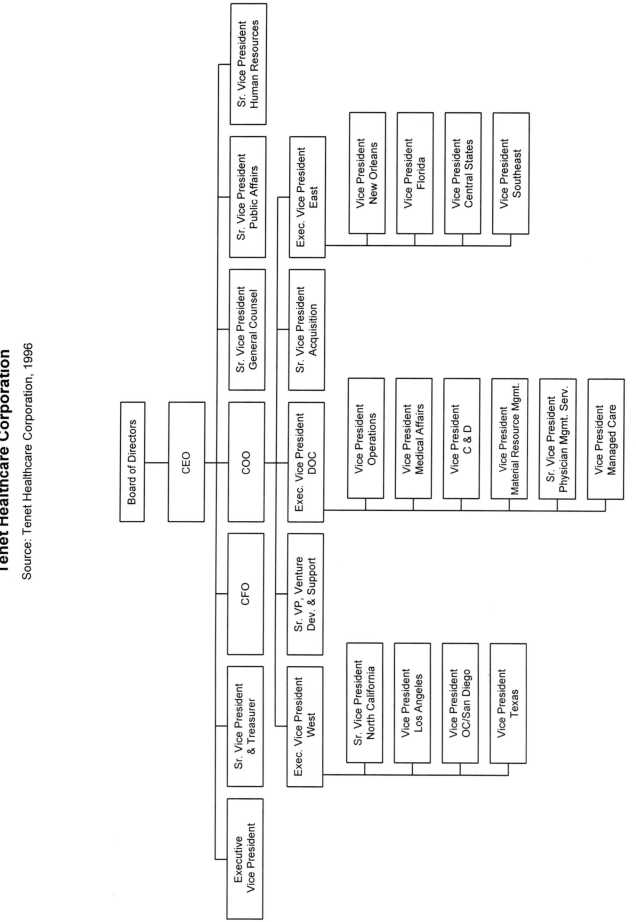

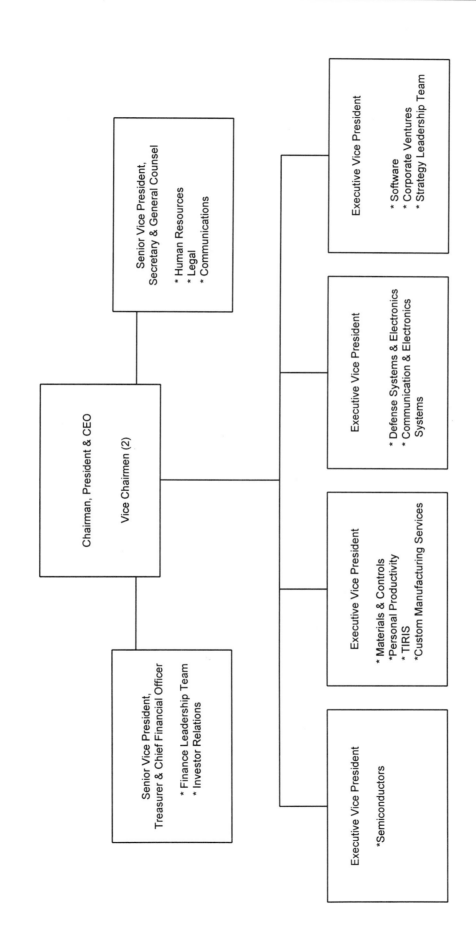

Texas Instruments, Inc.

Source: Texas Instruments, Inc., 1996

Chairman, President & CEO

Vice Chairmen (2)

Senior Vice President,
Secretary & General Counsel

* Human Resources
* Legal
* Communications

Senior Vice President,
Treasurer & Chief Financial Officer

* Finance Leadership Team
* Investor Relations

Executive Vice President

*Semiconductors

Executive Vice President

* Materials & Controls
*Personal Productivity
* TIRIS
*Custom Manufacturing Services

Executive Vice President

* Defense Systems & Electronics
* Communication & Electronics
  Systems

Executive Vice President

* Software
* Corporate Ventures
* Strategy Leadership Team

Tohoku Electric Power Co., Inc. (Japan)

Source: Tohoku Electric Power Co., Inc., 1996

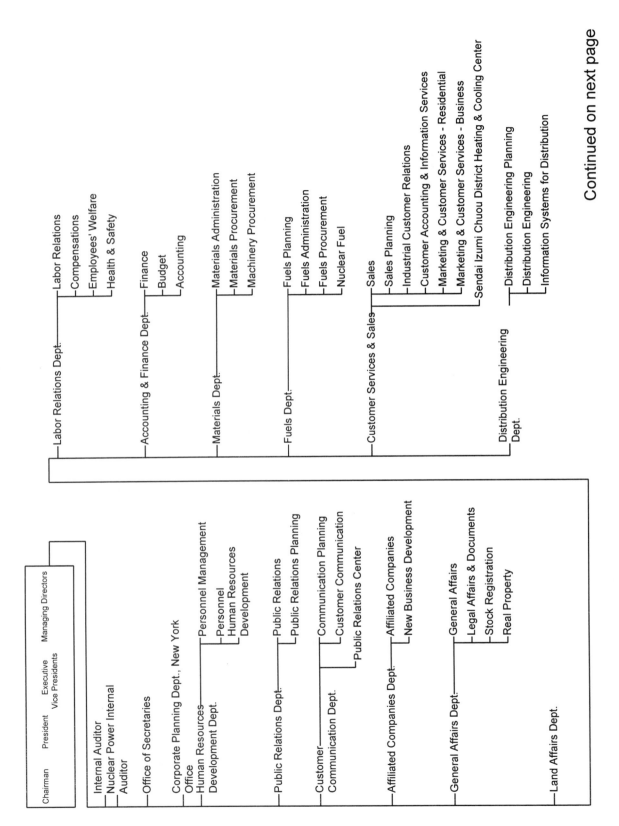

Continued on next page

Tohoku Electric Power Co., Inc.
Continued from previous page

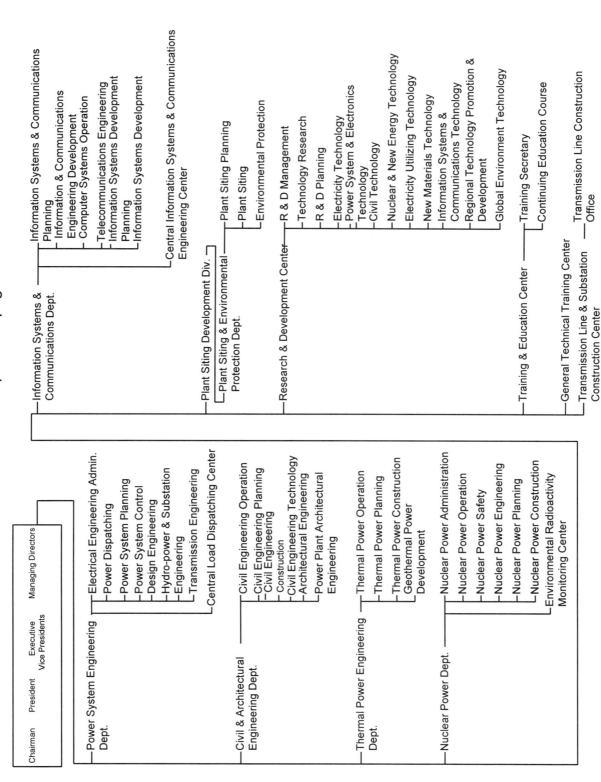

Tokio Marine and Fire Insurance Co., Ltd. (Japan)

Source: Tokio Marine and Fire Insurance Co., Ltd., 1996

Internal Auditing Dept.

Corporate Planning Dept.

Corporate Management Dept.

Business Research & Planning Dept.

Business Development Dept.

Personnel Planning Dept.

Corporate Administration Dept.

Corporate Communications Dept.

Real Estate Dept.

General Accounts Dept.

Intl. Accounting & Financial Planning Dept.

Financial Planning Dept.

Financial Planning Dept. I, II

Global Investments Dept.

Savings-Type Insurance Investment Dept.

Information Systems Management Dept.

Information Systems Development Dept.

Information Systems Service Dept.

Office Procedures & Accounting Dept.

CS Distribution System Dept.

Hull Underwriting Dept.

Cargo Underwriting Dept.

Non-Marine Underwriting Dept.

Guarantee & Credit Underwriting Dept.

Accident, Health & Savings-Type Insur. Dept.

Engineering & Loss Control Dept.

Board of "Jomukai" Directors   Automobile Underwriting Dept.

Aviation Dept.

Marketing & Planning Dept.

Marketing Promotion Dept. (Commercial)

Marketing Promotion Dept.

Marketing Promotion Dept. (Trainee & Professional Agent)

Marketing Promotion Dept. (Automobile Industry)

Overseas Management Dept.

Marine Claims Dept.

Claims Management Dept.

Continued on next page

Tokio Marine and Fire Insurance Co., Ltd. (Japan)

Continued from previous page

Non-Marine Claims Dept.

Hull Production Dept., I, II

General Production Dept. I-II

Production Dept. I-VII

Financial Institutions Dept.

Travel & Tourism Production Dept.

Distribution Industry Production Dept.

Marketing Promotion Dept. (Governmental)

Government Sector Dept.

Public Organization Dept.

Automobile Industry Production Dept. I-IV

Tokyo Regional Headquarters

      Tokyo Metropolitan Gvt. & Public Org. Dept.

      Marunouchi Branch

      Ueno Branch

Board of "Jomukai" Directors

      Ikebukuro Branch

      Shinjuku Branch

      Shibuya Branch

      Musashino Branch

      Nishitokyo Branch

      Tokyo Claims Service Dept. II

Overseas Dept. I

      Shanghai Branch

Overseas Dept. II

International Reinsurance Dept.

Tokyo Claims Service Dept. I

Tokyo Automobile Claims Service Dept.

Hokkaido Regional Headquarters

Aomori Branch

Morioka Branch

Akita Branch

Miyagi Regional Headquarters

Yamagata Branch

Fukushima Branch

Niigata Branch

Continued on next page

Tokio Marine and Fire Insurance Co., Ltd. (Japan)

Continued from previous page

Board of "Jomukai" Directors

- Nagano Branch
- Gunma Branch
- Tochigi Branch
- Ibaraki Regional Headquarters
- Chiba Regional Headquarters
- Saitama Regional Headquarters
- Kanagawa Regional Headquarters
- Yamanashi Branch
- Shizuoka Regional Headquarters
- Toyama Branch
- Kanazawa Branch
- Fukui Branch
- Nagoya Branch
- Gifu Branch
- Mie Branch
- Kyoto Regional Headquarters
- Shiga Branch
- Osaka Branch
- Nara Branch
- Wakayama Branch
- Kobe Branch
- Okayama Branch
- Sanin Branch
- Hiroshima Regional Headquarters
- Yamaguchi Branch
- Takamatsu Branch
- Tokushima Branch
- Ehime Branch
- Kochi Branch
- Kyushu Branch
- Saga Branch
- Nagasaki Branch
- Kumamoto Branch
- Oita Branch
- Miyazaki Branch
- Kagoshima Branch
- Okinawa Branch
- United States Branch

Tokyo Gas Co., Ltd. (Japan)

Source: Tokyo Gas Co., Ltd., 1996

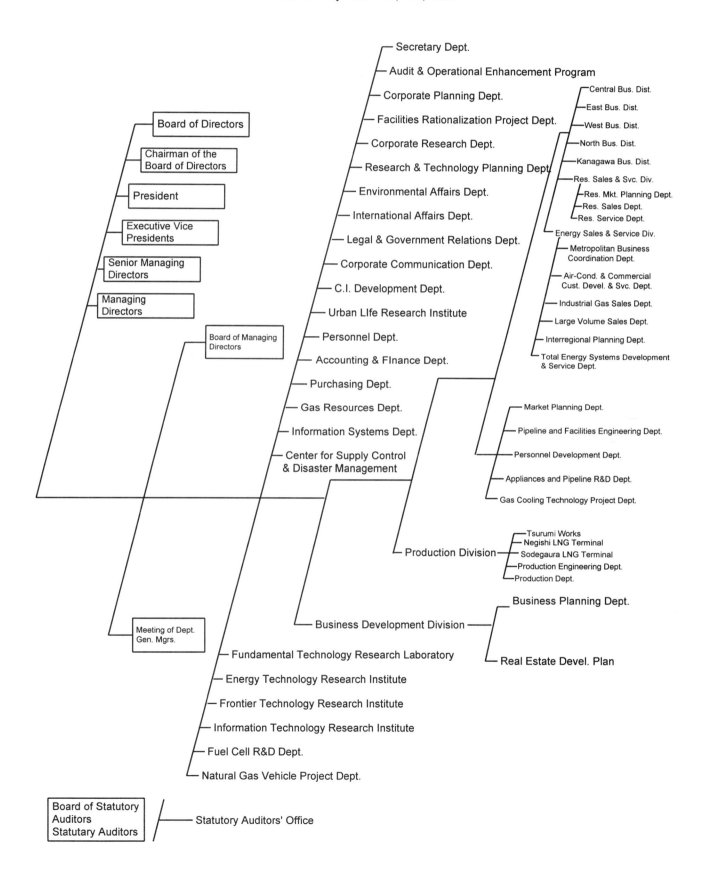

Toray Industries, Inc. (Japan)

Source: Toray Industries, Inc., 1996

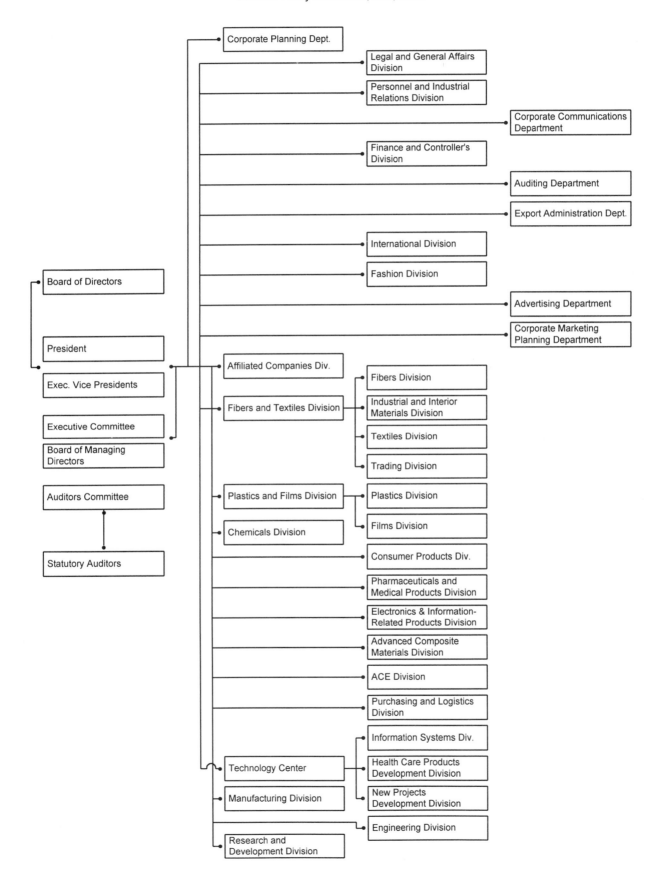

**Total System Services, Inc.
Client Relations**

Source: Total System Services, Inc., 1996

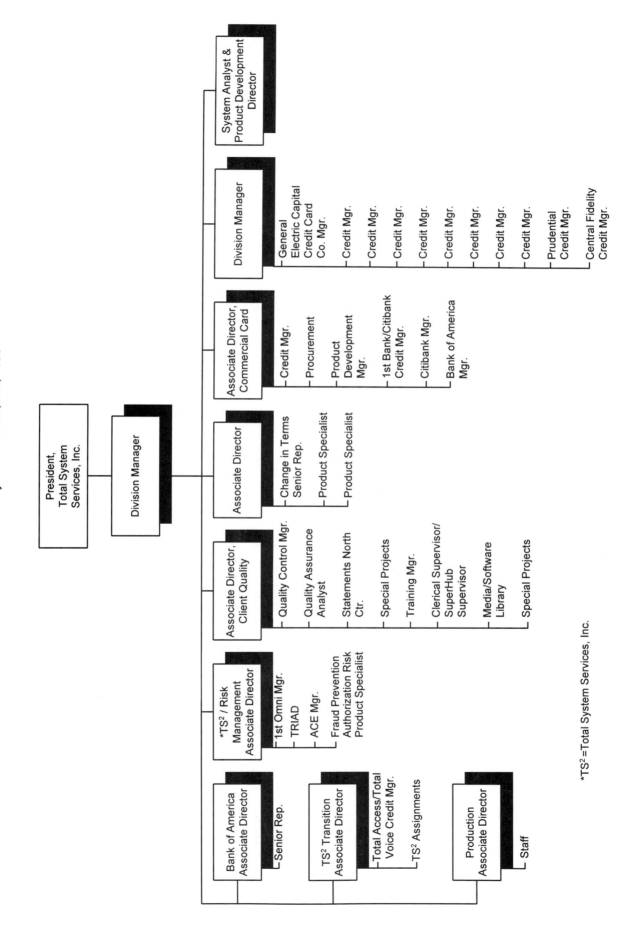

*TS² = Total System Services, Inc.

Total System Services, Inc.
Marketing and Business Development Departments

Source: Total System Services, Inc., 1996

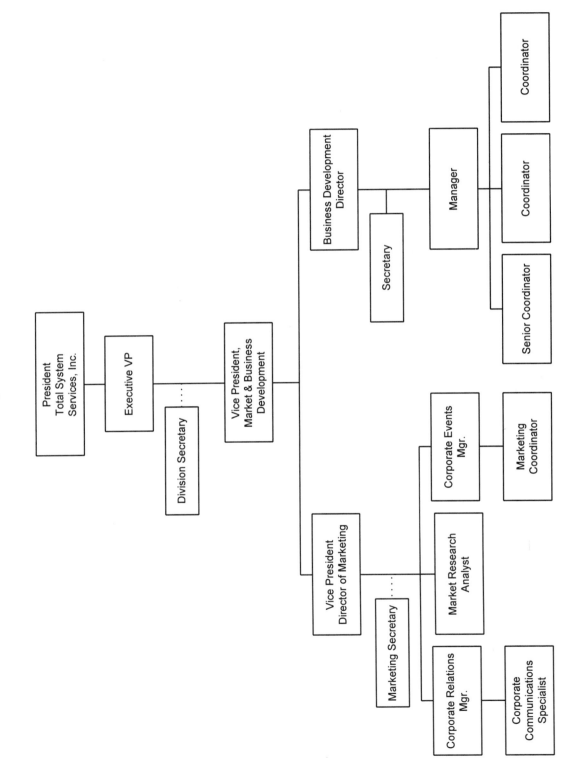

**Total System Services, Inc.
Sales Organization**

Source: Total System Services, Inc., 1996

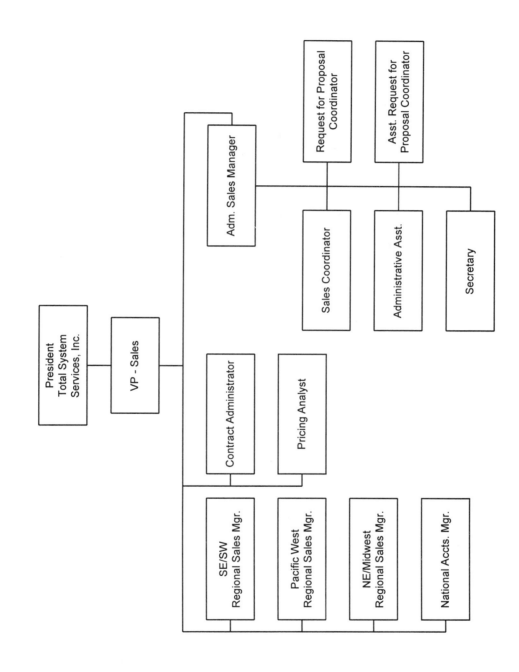

University of California
Governance

Source: The University of California, 1996

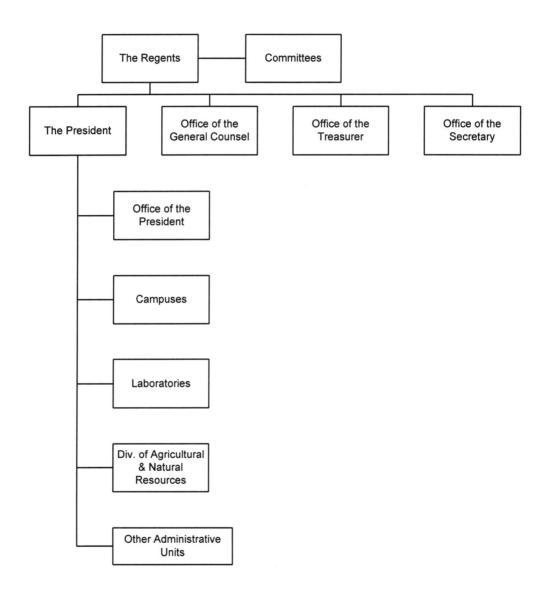

Unocal Corporation

Source: Annual report, 1994

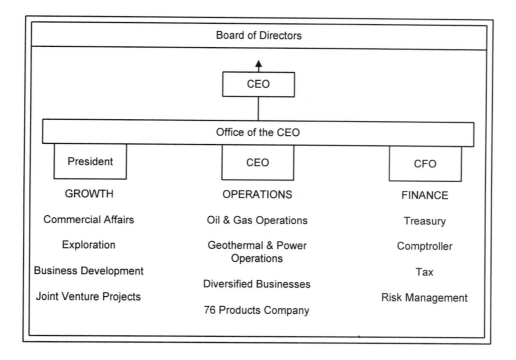

Board of Directors		
	CEO	
Office of the CEO		
President	CEO	CFO
GROWTH	OPERATIONS	FINANCE
Commercial Affairs	Oil & Gas Operations	Treasury
Exploration	Geothermal & Power Operations	Comptroller
Business Development	Diversified Businesses	Tax
Joint Venture Projects	76 Products Company	Risk Management

USoft: The Server/Client Software Company

Source: USoft: The Server/Client Software Company, 1996

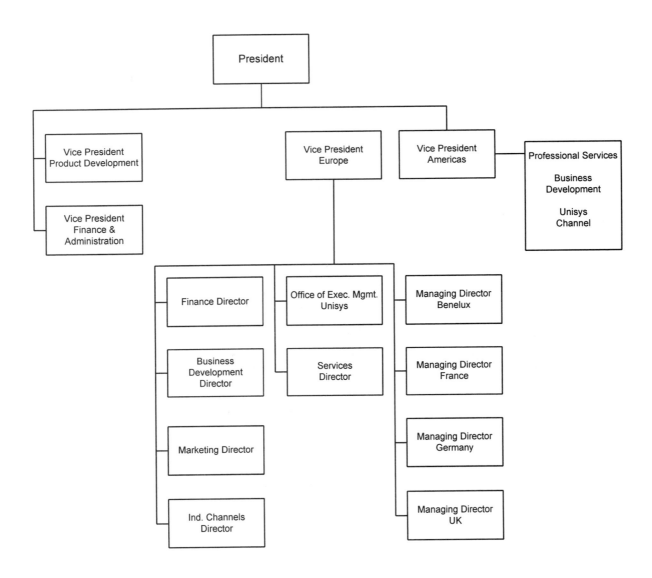

VF Corporation

Source: VF Corporation, 1996

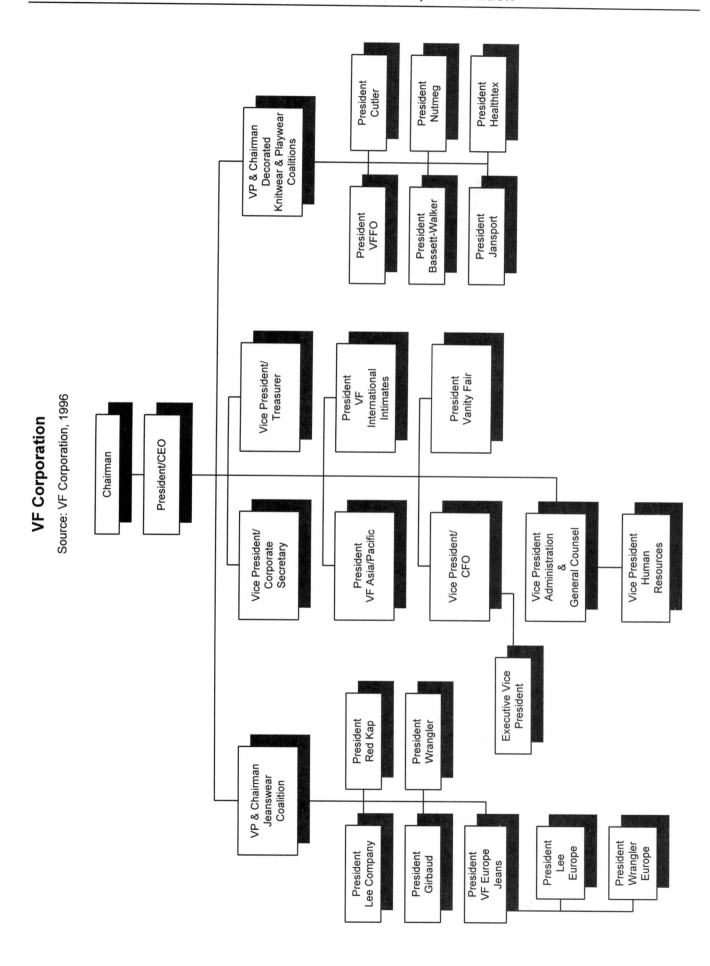

Volvo Truck Parts Gent (Belgium)

Source: Volvo Truck Parts Gent, 1996

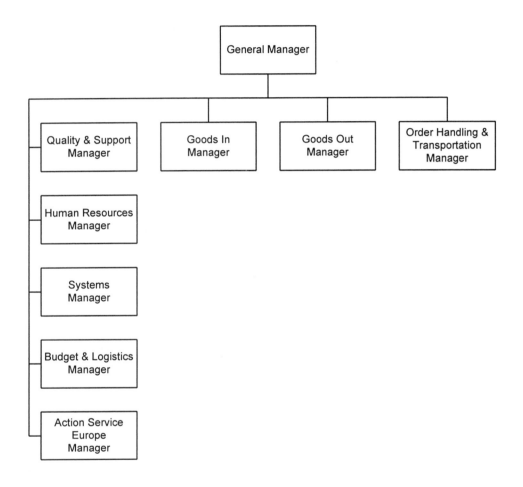

Vulcan Materials Company

Source: Vulcan Materials Company, 1996

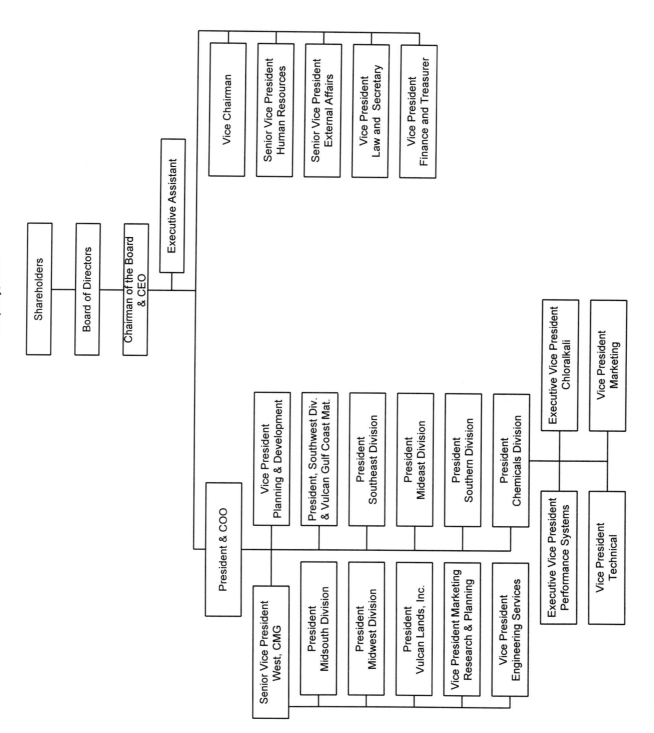

West Japan Railway Co. (Japan)

Source: West Japan Railway Co., 1996

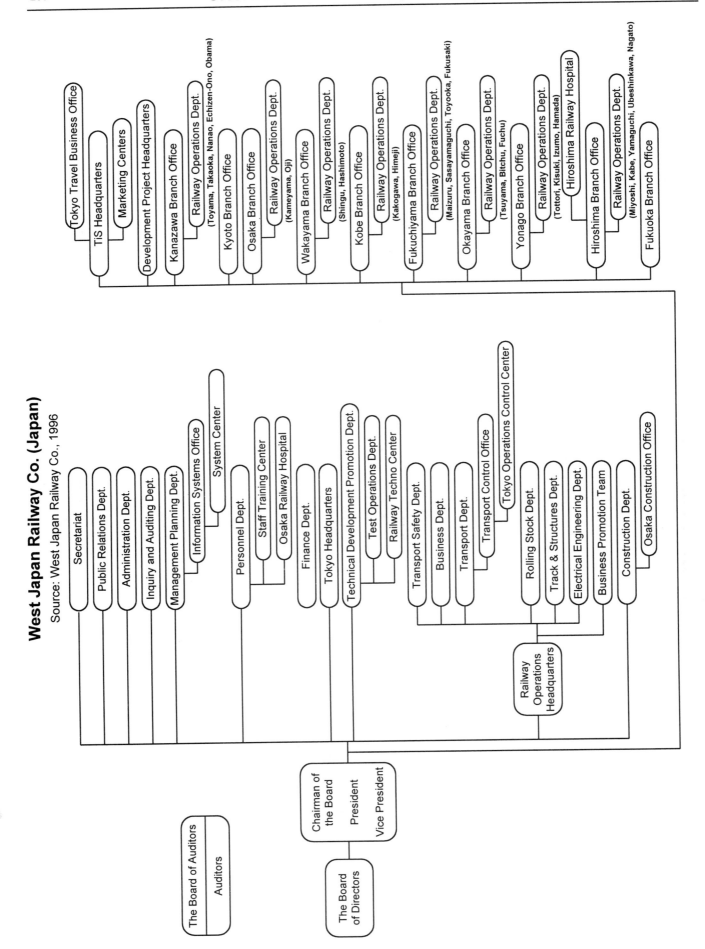

Woodward-Clyde Companies

Source: Woodward-Clyde Group, Inc., 1996

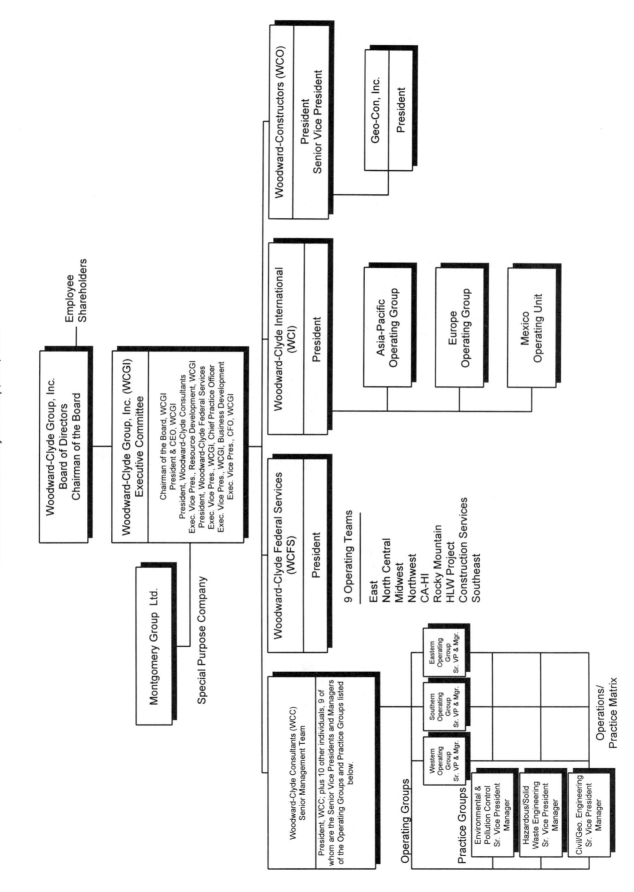

Xerox Corp.

Source: Xerox Corp., 1996

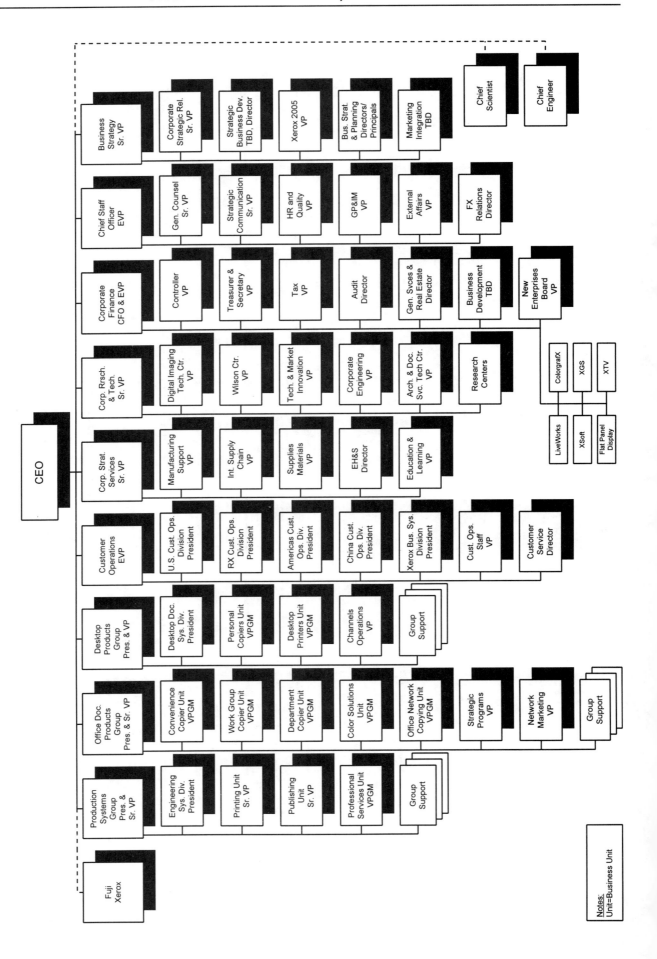

Notes:
Unit=Business Unit

Zendex Corp.

Source: Zendex Corp., 1996

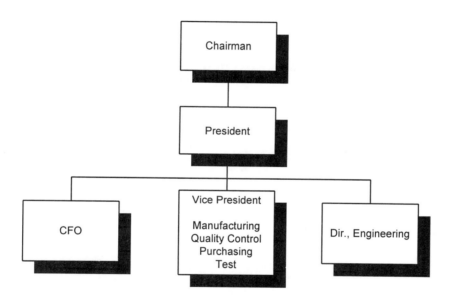

Zenith Media Services Inc.

Source: Zenith Media Services Inc., 1996

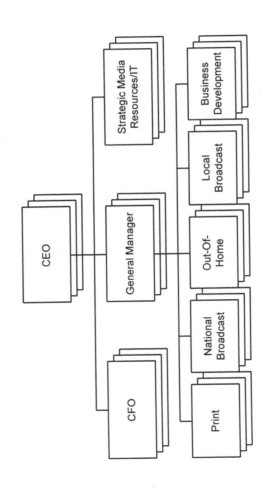

Appendix

ABB Asea Brown Boveri Ltd.
P.O. Box 8131
CH-8050 Zurich, Switzerland
1 3177334
Fax: 1 3177958

Adventist Health System/West
P.O. Box 619002
Roseville, CA 95661
(916)781-2000

Aerospace Corp.
2350 E. El Segundo Blvd.
El Segundo, CA 90245-4691
(310)336-5000
Fax: (310)336-8249

All Nippon Airways Co., Ltd.
3-2-5 Kasumigaseki
Chiyoda-ku
Tokyo 100, Japan
81-3-3592-3065

All Nippon Airways Co., Ltd.
Tokyo International Airport
 Public Relations Office
3-3-2 Haneda Kuko
Ota-ku
Tokyo 144, Japan
3 57575548
Fax: 3 57575550

Alliant Health System Inc.
P.O. Box 35070
Louisville, KY 40232
(502)629-6000

Allianz AG Holdings
Köningstraße 28
D-80802 Munich, Germany
89 38000
Fax: 89 349941

AlliedSignal Aerospace
2525 W. 190th St.
Torrance, CA 90504-6099
(310)512-1656
Fax: (310)512-2490
URL: http://www.alliedsignal.com

Asahi Chemical Industry Co., Ltd.
1-1-2 Yuraku-cho
Chiyoda-ku
Tokyo 100, Japan
81-3-3507-2730

Atlanta Falcons
2745 Burnette Rd.
Suwanee, GA 30174
(770)945-1111
Fax: (770)271-1221

Atlanta Gas Light Co.
P.O. Box 4569
303 Peachtree St., N.E.
Atlanta, GA 30302
(404)584-4000
Fax: (404)584-3958

Atmosphere Processing Inc.
100 N. Fairbanks
Holland, MI 49423
(616)392-7017

Austrian Postal and Telegraph Administration
Postgasse 8-10
A-1011 Vienna, Austria
1 515515040
Fax: 1 5134052

Autoliv AB
Box 70381
S-107 244 Stockholm, Sweden
8 4020600
Fax: 8 244479

Avalon Natural Cosmetics Inc.
1129 Industrial Ave.
Petaluma, CA 94952
(707)769-5120
Fax: (707)769-0868

Avon Products Inc.
Nine W. 57th St.
New York, NY 10019
(212)546-6015
Fax: (212)546-6136

Babcock & Wilcox Co.
120 S. Van Buren Ave.
Barberton, OH 44203-0351
(216)753-4511
Fax: (216)860-1886

Bangkok Bank PCL
333 Silom Rd.
Bangkok 10500, Thailand
2 2343333
Fax: 2 2365913

Bass PLC
20 North Audley St.
London W1Y 1WE, England
171 4098103
Fax: 171 4098502

Battelle Memorial Institute Corp.
505 King Ave.
Columbus, OH 43201-2693
(614)424-6424
Fax: (614)424-5263

Bay View Federal Bank F.S.B.
2121 S. El Camino Real
San Mateo, CA 94403
(415)573-7300

BellSouth Corp.
1155 Peachtree St., NE
Atlanta, GA 30367
(404)249-2000
URL: http://www.bis.com
E-Mail: mike.richard@bellsouth.com

Beth Israel Hospital
330 Brookline Ave.
Boston, MA 02215
(617)735-3531

Bethlehem Steel Corp.
1170 Eighth Ave.
Bethlehem, PA 18016-7699
(610)694-2424
Fax: (610)694-5743

Blount International, Inc.
4520 Executive Park Dr.
Montgomery, AL 36116
(334)272-8020
Fax: (334)271-8177

Bob Evans Farms, Inc.
3776 S. High St.
P.O. Box 07863-0863
Columbus, OH 43207
(614)491-2225
Fax: (614)492-4949

Bob Evans Farms, Inc.
Xenia Plant
P.O. Box 44
Xenia, OH 45385
(513)372-4493
Fax: (513)372-4176

Boise Cascade Corp.
P.O. Box 50
Boise, ID 83728
(208)384-6161
URL: http://www.bc.com
E-Mail: bcweb@bc.com

Brasfield and Gorrie General Contractors Inc.
P.O. Box 10383
Birmingham, AL 35202
(205)328-4000
Fax: (205)251-1304

British Steel PLC
9 Albert Embankment
London SE1 7SN, England
171 7357654
Fax: 171 5871142

Bronner's Christmas Wonderland
25 Christmas Ln.
P.O. Box 176
Frankenmuth, MI 48734-0176
(517)652-9931
Fax: (517)652-3466

Campbell Soup Co.
Campbell Pl.
Camden, NJ 08103
(609)342-4800
URL: http://www.campbellsoups.com
E-Mail: campbell@campbellsoups.com

Caterpillar Inc.
100 N.E. Adams St.
Peoria, IL 61629
(309)675-1000

Centerior Energy Corp.
P.O. Box 94661
Cleveland, OH 44101-4661
(216)447-3100
Fax: (214)447-3240
URL: http://www.centerior.com
E-Mail: webmaster@commercepark.com

Chinese Petroleum Corp.
83 Chung Hwa Rd., Sec. 1
Taipei 10031, Taiwan
2 3610221

Chrysler Corp.
12000 Chrysler Dr.
Highland Park, MI 48288
(313)956-5741

Chubu Electric Power Co., Inc.
1 Higashi-Shincho
Higashi-ku
Nagoya 461-91, Japan
52 9518211

Chugoku Electric Power Co., Inc.
4-33 Komachi
Naka-ku
Hiroshima 730-91, Japan
82 2410211

Consumers Power Co.
212 W. Michigan Ave.
Jackson, MI 49201
(517)788-0550
Fax: (517)788-0940

Credit Suisse
Paradeplatz 8
CH-8070 Zurich, Switzerland
1 3331111
Fax: 1 3325555

Dai-Ichi Mutual Life Insurance Company
13-1 Yurako-Cho 1-chome
Chiyoda-ku
Tokyo 100, Japan
3 32161211
Fax: 3 52213255

The Daiei, Inc.
4-1-1, Minatojima-Nakamachi
Chuo-ku
Kobe 105, Japan
78 3025001
Fax: 78 3205572

Daimler-Benz AG
Postfach 800230
D-70322 Stuttgart, Germany
711 1793283
Fax: 711 1794022

Dana Corp.
P.O. Box 1000
Toledo, OH 43697
(419)535-4500
Fax: (419)535-4643
URL: http://www.dana.com

Dana World Trade Corp.
P.O. Box 405
Toledo, OH 43697
(419)867-2105
Fax: (419)657-2118

Degussa AG
Weissfrauenstrasse 9
D-60311 Frankfurt am Main, Germany
69 21801
Fax: 69 2183218

Deutsche Bundespost Postdienst
Heinrich-von-Stephan-Str. 1
Robert-Schuman-Platz
D-53105 Bonn, Germany
228 1829988
Fax: 228 1827099

Douglas Aircraft Co.
3855 Lakewood Blvd.
Long Beach, CA 90846
(310)593-5511
Fax: (310)593-0097

Edeka Zentrale AG
New York Ring 6
D-2297 Düsseldorf, Germany
40 63772505
Fax: 40 63772231

Elf Aquitaine
2, place de la Coupole
Tour Elf - La Defense 6
F-92078 Paris la Defense, France
1 47444546
Fax: 1 47447878

Eskom
PO Box 1091
Johannesburg 2000, Republic of South Africa
11 8008111
Fax: 11 8005684

Ethyl Corporation
330 South St.
Richmond, VA 23219-4304
(804)788-5000
Fax: (804)788-5618

European Union
20, rue de la Lois
B-1049 Brussels, Belgium
2 2991111
Fax: 2 2950138

Exxon Corp.
225 E. John W. Carpenter Fwy.
Irving, TX 75062-2298
(214)444-1000
Fax: (214)444-1348

Fina Oil & Chemical Co., Inc.
8350 N. Central Expwy.
Dallas, TX 75206
(214)750-2400
Fax: (214)750-2891

Fortis
Archimedeslaan 10
NL-3584 BA Utrecht, The Netherlands
30 579111
Fax: 30 522394

Fuji Electric Co., Ltd.
12-1, Yurakucho 1-chome
Chiyoda-ku
Tokyo 100, Japan
3 32117103
Fax: 3 32117971

Fuji Heavy Industries Ltd.
1-7-2 Nishi-Shinjuku
Shinjuku-ku
Tokyo 160, Japan
3 33472111

Gebroeders De Rycke n.v.
Vesten 57
B-9120 Beveren, Belgium
3 7551609
Fax: 3 7550524
URL: http://www.autoctrl.rug.ac/
    bkir94/derycke/index.html
E-mail: kdrijcke@eduserve.rug.ac.be

General Electric Co.
3135 Easton Tpk.
Fairfield, CT 06431
(203)373-2211
Fax: (203)373-2884
URL: http://www.ge.com
E-Mail: geinfo@www.ge.com

General Motors Corp.
3044 W. Grand Blvd.
Detroit, MI 48202
(313)556-5000

Green Bay Packers
1265 Lombardi Ave.
Green Bay, WI 54304
(414)496-5700
Fax: (414)496-5738
URL: http://nflhome.com

Harrah's Entertainment, Inc.
1023 Cherry Rd.
Memphis, TN 38117-5423
(901)762-8629
Fax: (901)762-8637

Henry Ford Health System
One Ford Place
Detroit, MI 48202-3450
(313)872-8100

Henry Ford Museum & Greenfield Village
20900 Oakwood Blvd.
Dearborn, MI 48121
(313)271-1620
Fax: (313)271-7753

Hewlett-Packard Co.
3000 Hanover St.
Palo Alto, CA 94304-1185
(415)857-1501
Fax: (415)857-3258
URL: http://www.hp.com

Hitachi, Ltd.
6, Kandasurugadai 4-chome
Chiyoda-ku
Tokyo 101, Japan
3 32581111
Fax: 3 32585480

International Lottery and Totalizator Systems, Inc.
2131 Faraday Ave.
Carlsbad, CA 92008
(619)931-4000
Fax: (619)931-1789

Invetech Co.
1400 Howard St.
Detroit, MI 48216
(313)963-6011
Fax: (313)963-5427

Ishikawajima-HarimaHeavy Industries Co., Ltd.
2-2-1, Ohtemachi
Chiyoda-ku
Tokyo 100, Japan
3 32445111
Fax: 2 32445131

Ito-Yokado Co., Ltd.
1-4, Shibakoen 4-chome
Minato-ku
Tokyo 105, Japan
3 34592111
Fax: 3 34596872

Kansai Electric Power Co. Inc.
3-22, Nakanoshima 3-chome
Kita-ku
Osaka 530-70, Japan
6 4418821
Fax: 6 4418598

Kawasaki Steel Corp.
2-3, Uchi Saiwaicho, 2-chome
Chiyoda-ku
Tokyo 100, Japan
2 35973111
Fax: 3 35974868

Kirin Brewery Co., Ltd.
10-1, Shinkawa 2-chome
Chou-ku
Tokyo 104, Japan
3 55403424
Fax: 3 55403550

Komatsu Ltd.
2-3-6 Akasaka
Minato-ku
Tokyo 107, Japan
3 55612616
Fax: 3 35059662

K.P.R. Sports International, Inc.
555 S. Henderson Rd.
King of Prussia, PA 19406
(610)768-0900
Fax: (610)768-0753

Kubota Corp.
2-47, Shikitsuhigashi 1-chome
Naniwa-ku
Osaka 556, Japan
6 6482111
Fax: 6 6483862

Kyoei Life Insurance Co., Ltd.
4-4-1 Nihonbashi Hongo Kucho
Chuo-ku
Tokyo 103, Japan
3 32708511
Fax: 3 32410822

La-Z-Boy Chair Co.
1284 N. Telegraph Rd.
Monroe, MI 48162-3390
(313)242-1444
Fax: (313)457-2005

Landis & Gyr AG
Gubelstrasse 22
CH-6301 Zug, Switzerland
42 241124
Fax: 42 243522

Livonia Historcial Society
20501 Newburgh
Livonia, MI 48152

Long John Silver's, Inc.
P.O. Box 11988
Lexington, KY 40579
(606)263-6000
Fax: (606)263-6509

Long-Term Credit Bank of Japan, Ltd.
1-8 Uchisaiwaicho 2-chome
Chiyoda-ku
Tokyo 100, Japan
3 55115111
Fax: 3 53538716

MagneTek, Inc.
P.O. Box 290159
Nashville, TN 37229
(615)316-5100
Fax: (615)316-5188

Maruha Corp.
P.O. Box 475
1-2, Ohtemachi 1-chome
Chiyoda-ku
Tokyo 100, Japan
3 32160821
Fax: 3 32160342

Matsushita Electric Works, Ltd.
1048 Kadoma
Osaka 571, Japan
6 9097187
Fax: 6 9063770

Mazda Motor Corp.
3-1 Shinchi, Fuchu-cho, Aki-gun
Hiroshima 730-91, Japan
82 2821111
Fax: 82 2875190

McDermott International, Inc.
1450 Poydras St.
New Orleans, LA 70112-6050
(504)587-5400
Fax: (504)587-6153

J. Ray McDermott S.A.
P.O. Box 188
Morgan City, LA 70381
(504)631-2561
Fax: (504)631-8542

McDonnell Douglas Aerospace
P.O. Box 516
St. Louis, MO 63166
(314)232-0232

McDonnell Douglas Corp.
P.O. Box 516
St. Louis, MO 63166-0516
(314)232-0232
Fax: (314)234-3826
URL: http://pat.mdc.com

Memorial Health System
800 N. Rutledge St.
Springfield, IL 62781
(217)788-3000
Fax: (217)788-5594

Methodist Health Systems Inc.
1211 Union Ave.
Memphis, TN 38104-6619
(901)726-2300
Fax: (901)726-2393

Methodist Hospitals of Memphis
1265 Union Ave.
Memphis, TN 38104
(901)726-7000

MicroHelp, Inc.
4211 J.V.L. Industrial Park Dr., NE
Marietta, GA 30086
(770)516-0899
Fax: (770)516-1099

Micron Technology Inc.
8000 S. Federal Way
Boise, ID 83707-0006
(208)368-4000
Fax: (208)368-2536
URL: http://www.micron.com
E-Mail: webmaster@micron.com

Mid-America Dairymen, Inc.
3253 E. Chestnut Expressway
Springfield, MO 65802
(417)865-7100
Fax: (417)865-9176

Migros Cooperative
P.O. Box 266
CH-8031 Zurich, Switzerland
1 2772063
Fax:1 2773333

Ministry of Posts and Telecommunications, Japan
3-2, Kasumigaseki 1-chome
Chiyoda-ku
Tokyo 100-90, Japan
3 35044411

Minnesota Mining and Manufacturing Co.
3M Ctr.
St. Paul, MN 55144
(612)733-1110
URL: http://www.mmm.com

Mitsubishi Corp.
6-3, Marunouchi 2-chome
Chiyoda-ku
Tokyo 100-86, Japan
3 32102121
Fax: 3 32788051

Mitsubishi Heavy Industries, Ltd.
5-1 Marunouchi, 2-chome
Chiyoda-ku
Tokyo 100, Japan
3 32123111
Fax: 3 32129860

Mitsubishi Oil Co., Ltd.
6-41 Konan 1-chome
Minato-Ku
Tokyo 108, Japan
3 34727500
Fax: 3 34500251

Mitsubishi Trust & Banking Corp.
4-5 Marunouchi 1-chome
Chiyoda-ku
Tokyo 100, Japan
3 32121211
Fax: 3 32841326

Mitsui & Co., Ltd.
2-1 Ohtemachi 1-chome
Chiyoda-ku
Tokyo 100, Japan
3 32851111
Fax: 3 32859800

Mitsui Mutual Life Insurance Co.
2-3, Ohtemachi 1-chome
Chiyoda-ku
Tokyo 100, Japan
3 32116111
Fax: 3 32870874

Monsanto Co.
800 N. Lindbergh Blvd.
St. Louis, MO 63167
(314)694-1000
Fax: (314)694-7625
URL: http://www.monsanto.com

National City Corp.
1900 E. Ninth St.
Cleveland, OH 44114
(216)575-2000
Fax: (216)575-2983

Nationwide Insurance Enterprise
1 Nationwide Plaza
Columbus, OH 43215-2220
(614)249-7111
Fax: (614)249-7705
URL: http://nationwide.com

NEC Corp.
7-1, Shiba 5-chome
Minato-ku
Tokyo 108, Japan
3 3454111
Fax: 3 37981510
URL:http: //130.34.82.51/nec/english

Nestlé SA
Ave. Nestlé 55
CH-1800 Vevey, Switzerland
21 9242111
Fax: 21 9226334

New Oji Paper Co., Ltd.
7-5 Ginza, 4-chome
Chuo-ku
Tokyo 104, Japan
3 35631111
Fax: 3 35631135

Nippon Paper Industries Co., Ltd.
1-12-1, Yuraku-cho
Chiyoda-ku
Tokyo 100, Japan
3 32188000
Fax: 3 32136791

Nippon Steel Corp.
2-6-3, Ohtemachi
Chiyoda-ku
Tokyo 100-71, Japan
3 32424111
Fax: 3 32755611
E-mail: sasafuch@syspro.ei.nsc.co.jp

Nippon Telegraph and Telephone Corp.
1-1-6 Uchisaiwai-cho, Chiyoda-ku
Tokyo 100-19, Japan
3 35093101
Fax: 3 35094290
E-mail: a-kato@hibiya.hqs.ntt.jp

Nippondenso Co., Ltd.
1-1, Showa-cho, Kariya
Aichi 448, Japan
566 255511
Fax: 566 220620

Nissho Iwai Corp.
4-5, Akasaka 2-chome
Minato-ku
Tokyo 107, Japan
3 35883829
Fax: 3 35884240

North Limited
476 St. Kilda Rd.
Melbourne
Victoria 3004, Australia
3 92075111
Fax: 3 98200528

Orbital Sciences Corp.
217000 Atlantic Blvd.
Dulles, VA 20166
(703)406-5000
Fax: (703)406-3502
URL: http://www.orbital.com
E-mail: webmaster@www.orbital.com

Oriental Scientific Instruments Import and
    Export Corp. (OSIC)
52 Sahlihe Rd.
Beijing 100864, People's Republic of China
1 3297611
Fax: 1 8512412

Orlando Regional Healthcare System Inc.
1414 Kuhl Ave.
Orlando, FL 32806
(407)841-5111

Paria Group Inc.
390 W. 800 N.
Orem, UT 84057
(801)226-8200
Fax: (801)226-4819

Parker Hannifin Corp.
17325 Euclid Ave.
Cleveland, OH 44112-1219
(216)531-3000
Fax: (216)486-8785

Plante and Moran, LLP
27400 Northwestern Hwy.
P.O. Box 307
Southfield, MI 48037-0307
(810)352-2500
Fax: (810)352-0018

Potlatch Corp.
One Maritime Plaza
San Francisco, CA 94111-3576
(415)576-8800
Fax: (415)576-8832

PPG Industries, Inc.
1 PPG Place
Pittsburgh, PA 15272
(412)434-3131
Fax: (412)434-2545

Proffitt's, Inc.
P.O. Box 388
Alcoa, TN 37701
(615)983-7000
Fax: (615)983-7000

ProMark One Marketing Services Inc.
14040 N. Cave Creek Rd.
Phoenix, AZ 85022
(602)867-0233
Fax: (602)493-8506

Rabobank Nederland
Croeselaan 18, Utrecht
The Netherlands
302 161854
Fax: 302 161916

Republican National Committee
310 First St., SE
Washington, DC 20003
(202)863-8500
Fax: (202)863-8820

Royal Ahold
Albert Heijnweg 1
NL-1507 EH Zaandam,The Netherlands
317 5595720
Fax: 317 56598360

Royal PTT Nederland NV
P.O. Box 15000
NL-9700 CD Groningen,The Netherlands
31 50822822
Fax: 31 50822688

RWE Energie AG
Kruppstrasse 5
D-45128 Essen, Germany
201 1224258
Fax: 201 1223427

SANYO Electric Co., Ltd.
5-5, Keihan Hondori 2-chome
Moriguchi
Osaka 570, Japan
6 9911181
Fax: 6 9916566
URL: http://www.sanyo.co.jp
E-mail: www-admin@sanyo.co.jp

Saturn Corp.
1420 Stephenson Hwy.
Troy, MI 48007
(810)524-5000
Fax: (810)528-6125
URL: http://www.saturncars.com

SBC Communications Inc.
P.O. Box 2933
175 E. Houston, 6th Fl.
San Antonio, TX 78299-2933
(210)351-2161
Fax: (210)351-2198
URL: http://www.sbc.com/swbell

Sheetz, Inc.
5700 Sixth Ave.
Altoona, PA 16602
(814)941-5502
Fax: (814)941-5139

SHL Systemhouse Inc.
13155 Noel Rd.
Dallas, TX 75240
(214)383-2700

Siemens Nixdorf Informationssysteme AG
Otto-Hahn-Ring 6
D-81739 Munich, Germany
89 63601
Fax: 89 63652

Sinochem
Erligou Xijiao
Beijing 100044, People's Republic of China
1 8494210
Fax:1 8021280

Sisu Corp.
Lentokonetehtaantie
P.O. Box 696
SF-33101 Tampere, Finland
312 658311
Fax: 312 658324
URL: http://www.sisucorp.com/kons.htm
E-Mail: Sisu@nedecon.fi

Smithsonian Institution
1000 Jefferson Dr., SW
Washington, D.C. 20560
(202)357-2627
202)786-2515
URL: http://www.si.edu

Sony Corp.
6-7-35 Kitashinagawa
Shingawa-ku
Tokyo 141, Japan
3 54482200
Fax: 3 54483061

Staple Cotton Cooperative Association
P.O. Box 547
Greenwood, MS 38935
(601)453-6231
Fax: (601)453-6274

Stora Kopparbergs Bergslags AB
S-791 80 Falun, Sweden
23 782162
Fax: 23 25329

Sumitomo Chemical Co., Ltd.
Tokyo Sumitomo Twin Bldg.
27-1, Shinkawa 2-chome
Chuo-ku
Tokyo 104, Japan
3 55435152
Fax: 3 55435901

Sumitomo Heavy Industries, Ltd.
9-11, Kitashinagawa 5-chome
Shinagawa
Tokyo 141, Japan
3 54888219
Fax: 3 54888056

Sun Healthcare Group Inc.
5131 Masthead St. N.E.
Albuquerque, NM 87109
(505)858-4572
Fax: (505)823-4108

Swiss Bank Corp.
Aeschenplatz 6
CH-4002 Basel, Switzerland
61 2882020
Fax: 61 2884576

Swiss Life Insurance and Pension Co.
General Guisan-Quai 40
CH-8022 Zurich, Switzerland
1 2843311
Fax: 1 2812080

Taisei Corp.
1-25-1, Nishi-Shinjuku
Shinjuku-ku
Tokyo 163-06, Japan
3 33481111
Fax: 3 33450481

Taiwan Power Co. (Taipower)
242 Roosevelt Rd.
Sec. 3
Taipei 100, Taiwan
2 3651234
Fax: 2 3650522

Taiyo Mutual Life Insurance Co.
11-2 Nihonbashi 2-chome
Chuo-ku
Tokyo 103, Japan
3 32726211

Tatham Euro RSCG
980 N. Michigan Ave.
Chicago , IL 60611-4592
(312)337-4400
Fax: (312)337-5930

Techmatics Inc.
12450 Fiar Lakes Circle
Fairfax, VA 22033
(703)802-8300
Fax: (703)802-0406
URL: http://www.techmatics.com
E-mail: Webmaster@techmatics.com

Teledyne Brown Engineering Co.
300 Sparkman Dr., N.W.
P.O. Box 070007
Huntsville, AL 35807-7007
(205)726-1000
Fax: (205)726-3434
URL: http://tbe.com
E-Mail: WebTrekker@nebula.tbe.com

Tenet Healthcare Corp.
P.O. Box 4070
Santa Monica, CA 90411
(310)998-8000

Texas Instruments Inc.
P.O. Box 655474
Dallas, TX 75265
(214)995-3333
Fax: (214)995-4360
URL: http://www.ti.com

Tohoku Electric Power Co., Inc.
3-7-1, Aobaku, Sendai
Miyagi 980, Japan
22 2252111

Tokio Marine & Fire Insurance Co., Ltd.
2-1, Marunouchi 1-chome
Chiyoda-ku
Tokyo 100, Japan
3 32126211
Fax: 3 52233100

Tokyo Gas Co., Ltd.
1-5-20, Kaigan
Minato-ku
Tokyo 105, Japan
3 34332111
Fax: 3 34379130

Toray Industries, Inc.
2-1 Nihonbashi-Muromachi 2-chome
Chuo-ku
Tokyo 103, Japan
3 32455111
Fax: 3 32455555

Total Systems Services, Inc.
P.O. Box 1755
Columbus, GA 31902
(706)649-2310
Fax: (706)649-4499

University of California
Office of the President
University Hall
Berkeley, CA 94720
(510)642-6000

USoft: The Server/Client Software Co.
1000 Marina Blvd.
Brisbane, CA 94005
(415)875-3300
Fax: (415)875-3333
URL: http://222.usoft.com
E-mail: info@usoft.com

VF Corporation
1047 N. Park Rd.
Wyomissing, PA 19610
(610)378-1151
Fax: (610)375-9371

Volvo Truck Parts Gent
Smalle Heerweg 29
B-9041 Oostakker, Belgium
9 2256240
Fax: 9 2515977

Vulcan Materials Co.
P.O. Box 530187
Birmingham, AL 35253
(205)877-3000
Fax: (205)877-3048

West Japan Railway Co.
4-24, Shibata 2-chome
Kita-ku
Osaka 530, Japan
063758939
Fax: 063758862

Woodward-Clyde Companies
Stanford Place 3, Suite 600
4582 S. Ulster St.
Denver, CO 80237-2637
(303)740-2600
Fax: (303)740-2650

Xerox Corp.
P.O. Box 1600
800 Long Ridge Rd.
Stamford, CT 06904
(203)968-3000
Fax: (203)968-3572
URL: http://www.xerox.com

Zendex Corp.
6780A Sierra Court
Dublin, CA 94568
(510)828-3000
Fax: (510)828-1574
URL: http://www.zendex.com
E-mail: zendex@worldnet.att.net

Zenith Media Services Inc.
299 W. Houston St.
New York, NY 10014
(212)859-5100
URL: http://www.zenithmedia-us.com
E-mail: info@zenithmedia.com

List of Companies in *Organization Charts*, 1st edition, 1992

Companies and associations asterisked (*) are represented
in *Organization Charts*, 2nd Edition

Acurex Corp.
Aerospace Corp.*
Aetna - Human Resources Dept.
AGRGXCO (Agricultural Export Corp. of Israel)
Airbus Industrie (France)
Allied-Signal Aerospace Co.*
Altana Industrie-Aktien Und Anlagen AG (Germany)
American Airlines Inc.
American Bar Association - Meetings & Travel Dept.
American Foundrymen's Society - Technical Council
American Petrofina, Inc.
Aoki Corp. (Japan)
Apogee Enterprises, Inc.
ARCO (Atlantic Richfield Co.)
Armstrong World Indsustries, Inc.
Asahi Brewery Ltd. (Japan)
AT&T Communications
AT&T Communications - American Transtech
Bacardi & Co. Ltd. (Bahamas)
Baltimore Gas and Electric Company - Corporate & Utility Organization
Bank of Thailand
Barlow Rand Ltd. (South Africa)
Bass PLC (United Kingdom)*
Baxter Healthcare Corp.
Bayer AG (Germany) - Corporate Structure
Bayer AG (Germany) - Major Affiliated Companies
BBDO - Media Department
Bell & Howell Co.
Bell Canada
BellSouth Corp. - BellSouth Enterprises*
BellSouth Corp. - BellSouth Telecommunications
Berol Nobel (Sweden)
Best Foods Baking Group
Bethlehem Steel Corp.*
Boeing Co.
Boise Cascade Corp.*
BSN Groupe (France)
BT North America Inc.
Carlson Hospitality Group
Caterpillar Inc.*
Chemed Corp.
Chevron U.S.A. Inc.
Chrysler Corp.*
Chrysler Corp. - Acustar Inc., Procurement and Supply
Chrysler Corp. - Chrysler Canada Ltd., Sales
Cilcorp Inc.
Cilcorp Inc. - Subsidiaries
Clark Equipment Co.
Comcast Sound Communications, Inc.
Compagnia Finanziaria de Benedetti Spa (Italy)

Consumers Power Co.*
Cooper Tire & Rubber Co.
Cray Research, Inc.
CSR Ltd. (Australia)
Daehan Life Insurance Co., Ltd. (Korea) - EDP Division
Daimler-Benz AG (Germany)*
Dana Corp.*
Drug Emporium
E.I. du Pont de Nemours
Eagle-Picher Industries, Inc. - Subsidiaries
Edper/Hess (Canada)
EG & G Inc.
Electric Arc Ltd. (Jamaica)
Elf Aquitaine (France)*
Equitable Resources, Inc.
Ethyl Corp.*
Exxon Corp.*
Fleetwood Enterprises, Inc.
Ford Motor Co.
Gannett
Gencorp
General Electric Co.*
General Motors Corp*.
General Motors - Buick, Oldsmobile, Cadillac Group, Cadillac Motor Car Div.
General Motors - Buick, Oldsmobile, Cadillac Group, Typical Manufacturing Structure
General Services Administration - Real Property Management, National Capital Region
Genesco Inc.
Gevaert Groupe (Belgium)
The Gitano Group, Inc.
GKN plc. (United Kingdom)
Gralla Publications
Hahnemann University - Hospital Laboratory
Harnischfeger Industries, Inc.
Hawker Siddeley Group (England)
Healthtrust Inc. - The Hospital Co.
Heil Co.
Henry Ford Health System*
Hewlett-Packard Co.*
Himont Inc.
Honda (Japan)
Hospital Corp. of America
IBM Corp.
International Monetary Fund
Inventive Packaging Corp.
Japan Fine Ceramics Center
Johns Hopkins Hospital
Kansallis-Osake-Pankki (Finland)

Kao Corp. - Production Division (Japan)
Kellwood Co.
Kemper Group
Knight-Ridder, Inc.
Leggett & Platt Inc.
Lex Service PLC (Great Britain)
Thomas J. Lipton Co.
Lone Star Technologies, Inc.
Longview Fibre Co.
LSI Logic Corp.
M.A. Hanna Co.
Mandarin Oriental Hotel Group (Hong Kong)
Mariner Hotel Corp.
Maxwell Online, Inc.
Maxxam Inc.
The May Institute
McCormick & Co., Inc.
McDermott International, Inc.*
McGraw-Hill, Inc.
MCL Cafeterias
Merrill Lynch and Co., Inc.
Mid-America Dairymen, Inc.*
Midlands Technical College
Minnesota Mining & Manufacturing Co.*
Monsanto Co.*
Murphy Oil Corp. & Subsidiaries
Nalco Chemical Co.
National City Corp.*
National Service Industries, Inc.
NCR Corp.
Nedlloyd Lines (Rotterdam, Netherlands)
Nestle Enterprises, Inc.*
Nippon Telegraph and Telephone Corp. (Japan)*
NYNEX Corp.
Old Stone Corp.
Oscar Mayer Foods Corp. - Engineering Division
Otter Tail Power Co.
Owens-Corning Fiberglas Corp.
Pacific Telesis Group
Pacificorp
Pacificorp - NERCO, Inc.
Panhandle Eastern Corp.
Parker Hannifin Corp.*
Pfizer Inc.
Philip Morris Co. Inc.
Phillips Petroleum Co.
Pizza Hut - Operations Division
Placer Dome Inc. (Canada)
PPG Industries, Inc.*
Quaker State Corp.
Reed International
Reynolds Metals Co.
Riverside Methodist Hospital - Department of Protective Services
Royal Dutch/Shell Group of Companies (Netherlands)
Royal Dutch/Shell Group of Companies (Netherlands) - Service
Companies
Royal Dutch/Shell Group of Companies (Netherlands) - Shell U.K. Oil
RTKL Associates Inc.
Russell Corp.
Saab-Scania (Sweden)
SAS International Hotels (Belgium)
Scandic Hotel AB
Scottish & Newcastle Breweries PLC (Scotland)
Sears, Roebuck and Co. - Corporate Operations
Sears, Roebuck and Co. - Allstate Insurance Group
Sears, Roebuck and Co. - Coldwell Banker Real Estate Group
Sears, Roebuck and Co. - Dean Witter Financial Services Group
Sears, Roebuck and Co. - Sears Merchandise Group
Seibu Departmemnt Stores (Japan)
Siemens (Germany)
The Singer Co. N.V. (Hong Kong)
Sisters of Saint Joseph (Hamilton, Ont., Canada)
SKF Group (Sweden)
Southwestern Bell Corp.*
Stanhome Inc.

Stelco Inc. (Canada)
Stora Kopparbergs Bergslags AB (Sweden)*
Sulzer (Switzerland)
Summa Group (Indonesia) - Summa International
Summa Group (Indonesia) - Summa Surya
Sunnybrook Medical Centre Cancer Program
Swift Textiles Inc.
Sycamore Girl Scout Council, Inc.
Taisei Corp. (Japan)*
Texas Instruments*
Thomas & Betts Corp.
Toshiba Corp. (Japan)
The Tribune Co.
TRW Systems Federal Credit Union
U.K. Customs and Excise (United Kingdom)
U.S. Air Force - Weapons Laboratory
U.S. National Aero-Space Plane - National Program Office
Universal Foods Corp.
University of Idaho Library
University of Maryland - Professional Schools, Information Resources
    Management Div.
Valero Energy Corp.
VF Corp.*
Volkswagen AG (Germany)
Vulcan Materials Co.*
Warwick & Baker Fiore - Media Department
Waste Management, Inc.
The Webb Companies of Webb/America
The Wharf (Holdings) Ltd. (Hong Kong)
Wheeling-Pittsburgh Steel Corp.
Whirlpool Corp.
Winegardner & Hammons, Inc.
Woodward Governor Co.
World Bank
Yale-New Haven Health Services Corp.
Zenith Electronics Corp.
Sample Product- Line Management Organization Chart
Sample Organization Chart of the Food and Beverage Division of a
    Large Hotel
Sample Organization Chart for a Small Restaurant
Sample Organization Chart of a Marketing and Sales Division in a Large
    Hotel
Sample Organization Chart of the Management of a Large Hotel

Standard Industrial Classification (SIC) Table

The two- and four-digit SIC codes listed in the table provide an overview of the SIC system, which was established and is maintained by the U.S. government's Office of Management and Budget. Use the table to pinpoint industries of interest (represented by four-digit SIC codes), then refer to the SIC Index to locate companies operating in those industries.

AGRICULTURE, FORESTRY, AND FISHING

01   Agricultural Production—Crops

0111	Wheat
0112	Rice
0115	Corn
0116	Soybeans
0119	Cash Grains, Nec.
0131	Cotton
0132	Tobacco
0133	Sugarcane & Sugar Beets
0134	Irish Potatoes
0139	Field Crops Except Cash Grains, Nec.
0161	Vegetables & Melons
0171	Berry Crops
0172	Grapes
0173	Tree Nuts
0174	Citrus Fruits
0175	Deciduous Tree Fruits
0179	Fruits & Tree Nuts, Nec.
0181	Ornamental Nursery Products
0182	Food Crops Grown Under Cover
0191	General Farms—Primarily Crop

02   Agricultural Production—Livestock

0211	Beef Cattle Feedlots
0212	Beef Cattle Except Feedlots
0213	Hogs
0214	Sheep & Goats
0219	General Livestock, Nec.
0241	Dairy Farms
0251	Broiler, Fryer & Roaster Chickens
0252	Chicken Eggs
0253	Turkeys & Turkey Eggs
0254	Poultry Hatcheries
0259	Poultry & Eggs, Nec.
0271	Fur-Bearing Animals & Rabbits
0272	Horses & Other Equines
0273	Animal Aquaculture
0279	Animal Specialties, Nec.
0291	General Farms—Primarily Animal

07   Agricultural Services

0711	Soil Preparation Services
0721	Crop Planting, Cultivating & Protecting
0722	Crop Harvesting
0723	Crop Preparation Services for Market
0724	Cotton Ginning
0741	Veterinary Services—Livestock
0742	Veterinary Services—Specialties
0751	Livestock Services
0752	Animal Specialty Services
0761	Farm Labor Contractors
0762	Farm Management Services
0781	Landscape Counseling & Planning
0782	Lawn & Garden Services
0783	Ornamental Shrub & Tree Services

08   Forestry

0811	Timber Tracts
0831	Forest Products
0851	Forestry Services

09   Fishing, Hunting & Trapping

0912	Finfish
0913	Shellfish
0919	Miscellaneous Marine Products
0921	Fish Hatcheries & Preserves
0971	Hunting, Trapping & Game Propagation

MINING

10   Metal Mining

1011	Iron Ores
1021	Copper Ores
1031	Lead & Zinc Ores
1041	Gold Ores
1044	Silver Ores
1061	Ferroalloy Ores Except Vanadium
1081	Metal Mining Services
1094	Uranium, Radium & Vanadium Ores
1099	Metal Ores, Nec.

12   Coal Mining

1221	Bituminous Coal & Lignite—Surface
1222	Bituminous Coal—Underground
1231	Anthracite Mining
1241	Coal Mining Services

13 Oil & Gas Extraction

1311 Crude Petroleum & Natural Gas
1321 Natural Gas Liquids
1381 Drilling Oil & Gas Wells
1382 Oil & Gas Exploration Services
1389 Oil & Gas Field Services, Nec.

14 Nonmetallic Minerals Except Fuels

1411 Dimension Stone
1422 Crushed & Broken Limestone
1423 Crushed & Broken Granite
1429 Crushed & Broken Stone, Nec.
1442 Construction Sand & Gravel
1446 Industrial Sand
1455 Kaolin & Ball Clay
1459 Clay & Related Minerals, Nec.
1474 Potash, Soda & Borate Minerals
1475 Phosphate Rock
1479 Chemical & Fertilizer Mining, Nec.
1481 Nonmetallic Minerals Services
1499 Miscellaneous Nonmetallic Minerals

CONSTRUCTION

15 General Building Contractors

1521 Single-Family Housing Construction
1522 Residential Construction, Nec.
1531 Operative Builders
1541 Industrial Buildings & Warehouses
1542 Nonresidential Construction, Nec.

16 Heavy Construction Except Building Construction

1611 Highway & Street Construction
1622 Bridge, Tunnel & Elevated Highway
1623 Water, Sewer & Utility Lines
1629 Heavy Construction, Nec.

17 Special Trade Contractors

1711 Plumbing, Heating & Air-Conditioning
1721 Painting & Paper Hanging
1731 Electrical Work
1741 Masonry & Other Stonework
1742 Plastering, Drywall & Insulation
1743 Terrazzo, Tile, Marble & Mosaic Work
1751 Carpentry Work
1752 Floor Laying & Floor Work, Nec.
1761 Roofing, Siding & Sheet Metal Work
1771 Concrete Work
1781 Water Well Drilling
1791 Structural Steel Erection
1793 Glass & Glazing Work
1794 Excavation Work
1795 Wrecking & Demolition Work
1796 Installing Building Equipment, Nec.
1799 Special Trade Contractors, Nec.

MANUFACTURING

20 Food & Kindred Products

2011 Meat Packing Plants
2013 Sausages & Other Prepared Meats
2015 Poultry Slaughtering & Processing
2021 Creamery Butter
2022 Cheese—Natural & Processed
2023 Dry, Condensed & Evaporated Dairy Products
2024 Ice Cream & Frozen Desserts
2026 Fluid Milk

2032 Canned Specialties
2033 Canned Fruits & Vegetables
2034 Dehydrated Fruits, Vegetables & Soups
2035 Pickles, Sauces & Salad Dressings
2037 Frozen Fruits & Vegetables
2038 Frozen Specialties, Nec.
2041 Flour & Other Grain Mill Products
2043 Cereal Breakfast Foods
2044 Rice Milling
2045 Prepared Flour Mixes & Doughs
2046 Wet Corn Milling
2047 Dog & Cat Food
2048 Prepared Feeds, Nec.
2051 Bread, Cake & Related Products
2052 Cookies & Crackers
2053 Frozen Bakery Products Except Bread
2061 Raw Cane Sugar
2062 Cane Sugar Refining
2063 Beet Sugar
2064 Candy & Other Confectionery Products
2066 Chocolate & Cocoa Products
2067 Chewing Gum
2068 Salted & Roasted Nuts & Seeds
2074 Cottonseed Oil Mills
2075 Soybean Oil Mills
2076 Vegetable Oil Mills, Nec.
2077 Animal & Marine Fats & Oils
2079 Edible Fats & Oils, Nec.
2082 Malt Beverages
2083 Malt
2084 Wines, Brandy & Brandy Spirits
2085 Distilled & Blended Liquors
2086 Bottled & Canned Soft Drinks
2087 Flavoring Extracts & Syrups, Nec.
2091 Canned & Cured Fish & Seafoods
2092 Fresh or Frozen Prepared Fish
2095 Roasted Coffee
2096 Potato Chips & Similar Snacks
2097 Manufactured Ice
2098 Macaroni & Spaghetti
2099 Food Preparations, Nec.

21 Tobacco Products

2111 Cigarettes
2121 Cigars
2131 Chewing & Smoking Tobacco
2141 Tobacco Stemming & Redrying

22 Textile Mill Products

2211 Broadwoven Fabric Mills—Cotton
2221 Broadwoven Fabric Mills—Manmade
2231 Broadwoven Fabric Mills—Wool
2241 Narrow Fabric Mills
2251 Women's Hosiery Except Socks
2252 Hosiery, Nec.
2253 Knit Outerwear Mills
2254 Knit Underwear Mills
2257 Weft Knit Fabric Mills
2258 Lace & Warp Knit Fabric Mills
2259 Knitting Mills, Nec.
2261 Finishing Plants—Cotton
2262 Finishing Plants—Manmade
2269 Finishing Plants, Nec.
2273 Carpets & Rugs
2281 Yarn Spinning Mills
2282 Throwing & Winding Mills
2284 Thread Mills
2295 Coated Fabrics—Not Rubberized
2296 Tire Cord & Fabrics
2297 Nonwoven Fabrics
2298 Cordage & Twine

2299	Textile Goods, Nec.

23   Apparel & Other Textile Products

2311	Men's/Boys' Suits & Coats
2321	Men's/Boys' Shirts
2322	Men's/Boys' Underwear & Nightwear
2323	Men's/Boys' Neckwear
2325	Men's/Boys' Trousers & Slacks
2326	Men's/Boys' Work Clothing
2329	Men's/Boys' Clothing, Nec.
2331	Women's/Misses' Blouses & Shirts
2335	Women's/Misses' Dresses
2337	Women's/Misses' Suits & Coats
2339	Women's/Misses' Outerwear, Nec.
2341	Women's/Children's Underwear
2342	Bras, Girdles & Allied Garments
2353	Hats, Caps & Millinery
2361	Girls'/Children's Dresses & Blouses
2369	Girls'/Children's Outerwear, Nec.
2371	Fur Goods
2381	Fabric Dress & Work Gloves
2384	Robes & Dressing Gowns
2385	Waterproof Outerwear
2386	Leather & Sheep-Lined Clothing
2387	Apparel Belts
2389	Apparel & Accessories, Nec.
2391	Curtains & Draperies
2392	Housefurnishings, Nec.
2393	Textile Bags
2394	Canvas & Related Products
2395	Pleating & Stitching
2396	Automotive & Apparel Trimmings
2397	Schiffli Machine Embroideries
2399	Fabricated Textile Products, Nec.

24   Lumber & Wood Products

2411	Logging
2421	Sawmills & Planing Mills—General
2426	Hardwood Dimension & Flooring Mills
2429	Special Product Sawmills, Nec.
2431	Millwork
2434	Wood Kitchen Cabinets
2435	Hardwood Veneer & Plywood
2436	Softwood Veneer & Plywood
2439	Structural Wood Members, Nec.
2441	Nailed Wood Boxes & Shook
2448	Wood Pallets & Skids
2449	Wood Containers, Nec.
2451	Mobile Homes
2452	Prefabricated Wood Buildings
2491	Wood Preserving
2493	Reconstituted Wood Products
2499	Wood Products, Nec.

25   Furniture & Fixtures

2511	Wood Household Furniture
2512	Upholstered Household Furniture
2514	Metal Household Furniture
2515	Mattresses & Bedsprings
2517	Wood T.V. and Radio Cabinets
2519	Household Furniture, Nec.
2521	Wood Office Furniture
2522	Office Furniture Except Wood
2531	Public Building & Related Furniture
2541	Wood Partitions & Fixtures
2542	Partitions & Fixtures Except Wood
2591	Drapery Hardware, Blinds & Shades
2599	Furniture & Fixtures, Nec.

26   Paper & Allied Products

2611	Pulp Mills
2621	Paper Mills
2631	Paperboard Mills
2652	Setup Paperboard Boxes
2653	Corrugated & Solid Fiber Boxes
2655	Fiber Cans, Drums & Similar Products
2656	Sanitary Food Containers
2657	Folding Paperboard Boxes
2671	Coated & Laminated Paper—Packaging
2672	Coated & Laminated Paper, Nec.
2673	Bags—Plastics, Laminated & Coated
2674	Bags—Uncoated Paper & Multiwall
2675	Die-Cut Paper & Board
2676	Sanitary Paper Products
2677	Envelopes
2678	Stationery Products
2679	Converted Paper Products, Nec.

27   Printing & Publishing

2711	Newspapers
2721	Periodicals
2731	Book Publishing
2732	Book Printing
2741	Miscellaneous Publishing
2752	Commercial Printing—Lithographic
2754	Commercial Printing—Gravure
2759	Commercial Printing, Nec.
2761	Manifold Business Forms
2771	Greeting Cards
2782	Blankbooks & Looseleaf Binders
2789	Bookbinding & Related Work
2791	Typesetting
2796	Platemaking Services

28   Chemicals & Allied Products

2812	Alkalies & Chlorine
2813	Industrial Gases
2816	Inorganic Pigments
2819	Industrial Inorganic Chemicals, Nec.
2821	Plastics Materials & Resins
2822	Synthetic Rubber
2823	Cellulosic Manmade Fibers
2824	Organic Fibers—Noncellulosic
2833	Medicinals & Botanicals
2834	Pharmaceutical Preparations
2835	Diagnostic Substances
2836	Biological Products Except Diagnostic
2841	Soap & Other Detergents
2842	Polishes & Sanitation Goods
2843	Surface Active Agents
2844	Toilet Preparations
2851	Paints & Allied Products
2861	Gum & Wood Chemicals
2865	Cyclic Crudes & Intermediates
2869	Industrial Organic Chemicals, Nec.
2873	Nitrogenous Fertilizers
2874	Phosphatic Fertilizers
2875	Fertilizers—Mixing Only
2879	Agricultural Chemicals, Nec.
2891	Adhesives & Sealants
2892	Explosives
2893	Printing Ink
2895	Carbon Black
2899	Chemical Preparations, Nec.

29   Petroleum & Coal Products

2911	Petroleum Refining
2951	Asphalt Paving Mixtures & Blocks
2952	Asphalt Felts & Coatings
2992	Lubricating Oils & Greases

2999	Petroleum & Coal Products, Nec.

30   Rubber & Miscellaneous Plastics Products

3011	Tires & Inner Tubes
3021	Rubber & Plastics Footwear
3052	Rubber & Plastics Hose & Belting
3053	Gaskets, Packing & Sealing Devices
3061	Mechanical Rubber Goods
3069	Fabricated Rubber Products, Nec.
3081	Unsupported Plastics Film & Sheet
3082	Unsupported Plastics Profile Shapes
3083	Laminated Plastics Plate & Sheet
3084	Plastics Pipe
3085	Plastics Bottles
3086	Plastics Foam Products
3087	Custom Compound of Purchased Resins
3088	Plastics Plumbing Fixtures
3089	Plastics Products, Nec.

31   Leather & Leather Products

3111	Leather Tanning & Finishing
3131	Footwear Cut Stock
3142	House Slippers
3143	Men's Footwear Except Athletic
3144	Women's Footwear Except Athletic
3149	Footwear Except Rubber, Nec.
3151	Leather Gloves & Mittens
3161	Luggage
3171	Women's Handbags & Purses
3172	Personal Leather Goods, Nec.
3199	Leather Goods, Nec.

32   Stone, Clay & Glass Products

3211	Flat Glass
3221	Glass Containers
3229	Pressed & Blown Glass, Nec.
3231	Products of Purchased Glass
3241	Cement—Hydraulic
3251	Brick & Structural Clay Tile
3253	Ceramic Wall & Floor Tile
3255	Clay Refractories
3259	Structural Clay Products, Nec.
3261	Vitreous Plumbing Fixtures
3262	Vitreous China Table & Kitchenware
3263	Semivitreous Table & Kitchenware
3264	Porcelain Electrical Supplies
3269	Pottery Products, Nec.
3271	Concrete Block & Brick
3272	Concrete Products, Nec.
3273	Ready-Mixed Concrete
3274	Lime
3275	Gypsum Products
3281	Cut Stone & Stone Products
3291	Abrasive Products
3292	Asbestos Products
3295	Minerals—Ground or Treated
3296	Mineral Wool
3297	Nonclay Refractories
3299	Nonmetallic Mineral Products, Nec.

33   Primary Metal Industries

3312	Blast Furnaces & Steel Mills
3313	Electrometallurgical Products
3315	Steel Wire & Related Products
3316	Cold-Finishing of Steel Shapes
3317	Steel Pipe & Tubes
3321	Gray & Ductile Iron Foundries
3322	Malleable Iron Foundries
3324	Steel Investment Foundries

3325	Steel Foundries, Nec.
3331	Primary Copper
3334	Primary Aluminum
3339	Primary Nonferrous Metals, Nec.
3341	Secondary Nonferrous Metals
3351	Copper Rolling & Drawing
3353	Aluminum Sheet, Plate & Foil
3354	Aluminum Extruded Products
3355	Aluminum Rolling & Drawing, Nec.
3356	Nonferrous Rolling & Drawing, Nec.
3357	Nonferrous Wiredrawing & Insulating
3363	Aluminum Die-Castings
3364	Nonferrous Die-Castings Except Aluminum
3365	Aluminum Foundries
3366	Copper Foundries
3369	Nonferrous Foundries, Nec.
3398	Metal Heat Treating
3399	Primary Metal Products, Nec.

34   Fabricated Metal Products

3411	Metal Cans
3412	Metal Barrels, Drums & Pails
3421	Cutlery
3423	Hand & Edge Tools, Nec.
3425	Saw Blades & Handsaws
3429	Hardware, Nec.
3431	Metal Sanitary Ware
3432	Plumbing Fixtures Fittings & Trim
3433	Heating Equipment Except Electric
3441	Fabricated Structural Metal
3442	Metal Doors, Sash & Trim
3443	Fabricated Plate Work—Boiler Shops
3444	Sheet Metal Work
3446	Architectural Metal Work
3448	Prefabricated Metal Buildings
3449	Miscellaneous Metal Work
3451	Screw Machine Products
3452	Bolts, Nuts, Rivets & Washers
3462	Iron & Steel Forgings
3463	Nonferrous Forgings
3465	Automotive Stampings
3466	Crowns & Closures
3469	Metal Stampings, Nec.
3471	Plating & Polishing
3479	Metal Coating & Allied Services
3482	Small Arms Ammunition
3483	Ammunition Except for Small Arms
3484	Small Arms
3489	Ordnance & Accessories, Nec.
3491	Industrial Valves
3492	Fluid Power Valves & Hose Fittings
3493	Steel Springs Except Wire
3494	Valves & Pipe Fittings, Nec.
3495	Wire Springs
3496	Miscellaneous Fabricated Wire Products
3497	Metal Foil & Leaf
3498	Fabricated Pipe & Fittings
3499	Fabricated Metal Products, Nec.

35   Industrial Machinery & Equipment

3511	Turbines & Turbine Generator Sets
3519	Internal Combustion Engines, Nec.
3523	Farm Machinery & Equipment
3524	Lawn & Garden Equipment
3531	Construction Machinery
3532	Mining Machinery
3533	Oil & Gas Field Machinery
3534	Elevators & Moving Stairways
3535	Conveyors & Conveying Equipment
3536	Hoists, Cranes & Monorails
3537	Industrial Trucks & Tractors

3541	Machine Tools—Metal Cutting Types
3542	Machine Tools—Metal Forming Types
3543	Industrial Patterns
3544	Special Dies, Tools, Jigs & Fixtures
3545	Machine Tool Accessories
3546	Power-Driven Handtools
3547	Rolling Mill Machinery
3548	Welding Apparatus
3549	Metalworking Machinery, Nec.
3552	Textile Machinery
3553	Woodworking Machinery
3554	Paper Industries Machinery
3555	Printing Trades Machinery
3556	Food Products Machinery
3559	Special Industry Machinery, Nec.
3561	Pumps & Pumping Equipment
3562	Ball & Roller Bearings
3563	Air & Gas Compressors
3564	Blowers & Fans
3565	Packaging Machinery
3566	Speed Changers, Drives & Gears
3567	Industrial Furnaces & Ovens
3568	Power Transmission Equipment, Nec.
3569	General Industrial Machinery, Nec.
3571	Electronic Computers
3572	Computer Storage Devices
3575	Computer Terminals
3577	Computer Peripheral Equipment, Nec.
3578	Calculating & Accounting Equipment
3579	Office Machines, Nec.
3581	Automatic Vending Machines
3582	Commercial Laundry Equipment
3585	Refrigeration & Heating Equipment
3586	Measuring & Dispensing Pumps
3589	Service Industry Machinery, Nec.
3592	Carburetors, Pistons, Rings & Valves
3593	Fluid Power Cylinders & Actuators
3594	Fluid Power Pumps & Motors
3596	Scales & Balances Except Laboratory
3599	Industrial Machinery, Nec.

36   Electronic & Other Electrical Equipment

3612	Transformers Except Electronic
3613	Switchgear & Switchboard Apparatus
3621	Motors & Generators
3624	Carbon & Graphite Products
3625	Relays & Industrial Controls
3629	Electrical Industrial Apparatus, Nec.
3631	Household Cooking Equipment
3632	Household Refrigerators & Freezers
3633	Household Laundry Equipment
3634	Electric Housewares & Fans
3635	Household Vacuum Cleaners
3639	Household Appliances, Nec.
3641	Electric Lamps
3643	Current-Carrying Wiring Devices
3644	Noncurrent-Carrying Wiring Devices
3645	Residential Lighting Fixtures
3646	Commercial Lighting Fixtures
3647	Vehicular Lighting Equipment
3648	Lighting Equipment, Nec.
3651	Household Audio & Video Equipment
3652	Prerecorded Records & Tapes
3661	Telephone & Telegraph Apparatus
3663	Radio & T.V. Communications Equipment
3669	Communications Equipment, Nec.
3671	Electron Tubes
3672	Printed Circuit Boards
3674	Semiconductors & Related Devices
3675	Electronic Capacitors
3676	Electronic Resistors
3677	Electronic Coils & Transformers

3678	Electronic Connectors
3679	Electronic Components, Nec.
3691	Storage Batteries
3692	Primary Batteries—Dry & Wet
3694	Engine Electrical Equipment
3695	Magnetic & Optical Recording Media
3699	Electrical Equipment & Supplies, Nec.

37   Transportation Equipment

3711	Motor Vehicles & Car Bodies
3713	Truck & Bus Bodies
3714	Motor Vehicle Parts & Accessories
3715	Truck Trailers
3716	Motor Homes
3721	Aircraft
3724	Aircraft Engines & Engine Parts
3728	Aircraft Parts & Equipment, Nec.
3731	Ship Building & Repairing
3732	Boat Building & Repairing
3743	Railroad Equipment
3751	Motorcycles, Bicycles & Parts
3761	Guided Missiles & Space Vehicles
3764	Space Propulsion Units & Parts
3769	Space Vehicle Equipment, Nec.
3792	Travel Trailers & Campers
3795	Tanks & Tank Components
3799	Transportation Equipment, Nec.

38   Instruments & Related Products

3812	Search & Navigation Equipment
3821	Laboratory Apparatus & Furniture
3822	Environmental Controls
3823	Process Control Instruments
3824	Fluid Meters & Counting Devices
3825	Instruments to Measure Electricity
3826	Analytical Instruments
3827	Optical Instruments & Lenses
3829	Measuring & Controlling Devices, Nec.
3841	Surgical & Medical Instruments
3842	Surgical Appliances & Supplies
3843	Dental Equipment & Supplies
3844	X-Ray Apparatus & Tubes
3845	Electromedical Equipment
3851	Ophthalmic Goods
3861	Photographic Equipment & Supplies
3873	Watches, Clocks, Watchcases & Parts

39   Miscellaneous Manufacturing Industries

3911	Jewelry & Precious Metal
3914	Silverware & Plated Ware
3915	Jewelers' Materials & Lapidary Work
3931	Musical Instruments
3942	Dolls & Stuffed Toys
3944	Games, Toys & Children's Vehicles
3949	Sporting & Athletic Goods, Nec.
3951	Pens & Mechanical Pencils
3952	Lead Pencils & Art Goods
3953	Marking Devices
3955	Carbon Paper & Inked Ribbons
3961	Costume Jewelry
3965	Fasteners, Buttons, Needles & Pins
3991	Brooms & Brushes
3993	Signs & Advertising Displays
3995	Burial Caskets
3996	Hard Surface Floor Coverings, Nec.
3999	Manufacturing Industries, Nec.

TRANSPORTATION AND PUBLIC UTILITIES

40   Railroad Transportation

4011	Railroads—Line-Haul Operating
4013	Switching & Terminal Services

41   Local & Interurban Passenger Transit

4111	Local & Suburban Transit
4119	Local Passenger Transportation, Nec.
4121	Taxicabs
4131	Intercity & Rural Bus Transportation
4141	Local Bus Charter Service
4142	Bus Charter Service Except Local
4151	School Buses
4173	Bus Terminal & Service Facilities

42   Trucking & Warehousing

4212	Local Trucking Without Storage
4213	Trucking Except Local
4214	Local Trucking With Storage
4215	Courier Services Except by Air
4221	Farm Product Warehousing & Storage
4222	Refrigerated Warehousing & Storage
4225	General Warehousing & Storage
4226	Special Warehousing & Storage, Nec.
4231	Trucking Terminal Facilities

43   U.S. Postal Service

4311	U.S. Postal Service

44   Water Transportation

4412	Deep Sea Foreign Transportation of Freight
4424	Deep Sea Domestic Transportation of Freight
4432	Freight Transportation on the Great Lakes
4449	Water Transportation of Freight, Nec.
4481	Deep Sea Passenger Transportation Except Ferry
4482	Ferries
4489	Water Passenger Transportation, Nec.
4491	Marine Cargo Handling
4492	Towing & Tugboat Services
4493	Marinas
4499	Water Transportation Services, Nec.

45   Transportation by Air

4512	Air Transportation—Scheduled
4513	Air Courier Services
4522	Air Transportation—Nonscheduled
4581	Airports, Flying Fields & Services

46   Pipelines Except Natural Gas

4612	Crude Petroleum Pipelines
4613	Refined Petroleum Pipelines
4619	Pipelines, Nec.

47   Transportation Services

4724	Travel Agencies
4725	Tour Operators
4729	Passenger Transportation Arrangement, Nec.
4731	Freight Transportation Arrangement
4741	Rental of Railroad Cars
4783	Packing & Crating
4785	Inspection & Fixed Facilities
4789	Transportation Services, Nec.

48   Communications

4812	Radiotelephone Communications
4813	Telephone Communications Except Radiotelephone
4822	Telegraph & Other Communications
4832	Radio Broadcasting Stations
4833	Television Broadcasting Stations
4841	Cable & Other Pay Television Services
4899	Communications Services, Nec.

49   Electric, Gas & Sanitary Services

4911	Electric Services
4922	Natural Gas Transmission
4923	Gas Transmission & Distribution
4924	Natural Gas Distribution
4925	Gas Production & Distribution, Nec.
4931	Electric & Other Services Combined
4932	Gas & Other Services Combined
4939	Combination Utility, Nec.
4941	Water Supply
4952	Sewerage Systems
4953	Refuse Systems
4959	Sanitary Services, Nec.
4961	Steam & Air-Conditioning Supply
4971	Irrigation Systems

WHOLESALE TRADE

50   Wholesale Trade—Durable Goods

5012	Automobiles & Other Motor Vehicles
5013	Motor Vehicle Supplies & New Parts
5014	Tires & Tubes
5015	Motor Vehicle Parts—Used
5021	Furniture
5023	Homefurnishings
5031	Lumber, Plywood & Millwork
5032	Brick, Stone & Related Materials
5033	Roofing, Siding & Insulation
5039	Construction Materials, Nec.
5043	Photographic Equipment & Supplies
5044	Office Equipment
5045	Computers, Peripherals & Software
5046	Commercial Equipment, Nec.
5047	Medical & Hospital Equipment
5048	Ophthalmic Goods
5049	Professional Equipment, Nec.
5051	Metals Service Centers & Offices
5052	Coal, Other Minerals & Ores
5063	Electrical Apparatus & Equipment
5064	Electrical Appliances—Television & Radio
5065	Electronic Parts & Equipment, Nec.
5072	Hardware
5074	Plumbing & Hydronic Heating Supplies
5075	Warm Air Heating & Air-Conditioning
5078	Refrigeration Equipment & Supplies
5082	Construction & Mining Machinery
5083	Farm & Garden Machinery
5084	Industrial Machinery & Equipment
5085	Industrial Supplies
5087	Service Establishment Equipment
5088	Transportation Equipment & Supplies
5091	Sporting & Recreational Goods
5092	Toys & Hobby Goods & Supplies
5093	Scrap & Waste Materials
5094	Jewelry & Precious Stones
5099	Durable Goods, Nec.

51   Wholesale Trade—Nondurable Goods

5111	Printing & Writing Paper
5112	Stationery & Office Supplies
5113	Industrial & Personal Service Paper
5122	Drugs, Proprietaries & Sundries
5131	Piece Goods & Notions
5136	Men's/Boys' Clothing
5137	Women's/Children's Clothing

5139	Footwear
5141	Groceries—General Line
5142	Packaged Frozen Foods
5143	Dairy Products Except Dried or Canned
5144	Poultry & Poultry Products
5145	Confectionery
5146	Fish & Seafoods
5147	Meats & Meat Products
5148	Fresh Fruits & Vegetables
5149	Groceries & Related Products, Nec.
5153	Grain & Field Beans
5154	Livestock
5159	Farm-Product Raw Materials, Nec.
5162	Plastics Materials & Basic Shapes
5169	Chemicals & Allied Products, Nec.
5171	Petroleum Bulk Stations & Terminals
5172	Petroleum Products, Nec.
5181	Beer & Ale
5182	Wines & Distilled Beverages
5191	Farm Supplies
5192	Books, Periodicals & Newspapers
5193	Flowers & Florists' Supplies
5194	Tobacco & Tobacco Products
5198	Paints, Varnishes & Supplies
5199	Nondurable Goods, Nec.

RETAIL TRADE

52   Building Materials & Garden Supplies

5211	Lumber & Other Building Materials
5231	Paint, Glass & Wallpaper Stores
5251	Hardware Stores
5261	Retail Nurseries & Garden Stores
5271	Mobile Home Dealers

53   General Merchandise Stores

5311	Department Stores
5331	Variety Stores
5399	Miscellaneous General Merchandise Stores

54   Food Stores

5411	Grocery Stores
5421	Meat & Fish Markets
5431	Fruit & Vegetable Markets
5441	Candy, Nut & Confectionery Stores
5451	Dairy Products Stores
5461	Retail Bakeries
5499	Miscellaneous Food Stores

55   Automotive Dealers & Service Stations

5511	New & Used Car Dealers
5521	Used Car Dealers
5531	Automobile & Home Supply Stores
5541	Gasoline Service Stations
5551	Boat Dealers
5561	Recreational Vehicle Dealers
5571	Motorcycle Dealers
5599	Automotive Dealers, Nec.

56   Apparel & Accessory Stores

5611	Men's & Boys' Clothing Stores
5621	Women's Clothing Stores
5632	Women's Accessory & Specialty Stores
5641	Children's & Infants' Wear Stores
5651	Family Clothing Stores
5661	Shoe Stores
5699	Miscellaneous Apparel & Accessory Stores

57   Furniture & Homefurnishings Stores

5712	Furniture Stores
5713	Floor Covering Stores
5714	Drapery & Upholstery Stores
5719	Miscellaneous Home Furnishings Stores
5722	Household Appliance Stores
5731	Radio, Television & Electronics Stores
5734	Computer & Software Stores
5735	Record & Prerecorded Tape Stores
5736	Musical Instruments Stores

58   Eating & Drinking Places

5812	Eating Places
5813	Drinking Places

59   Miscellaneous Retail

5912	Drug Stores & Proprietary Stores
5921	Liquor Stores
5932	Used Merchandise Stores
5941	Sporting Goods & Bicycle Shops
5942	Book Stores
5943	Stationery Stores
5944	Jewelry Stores
5945	Hobby, Toy & Game Shops
5946	Camera & Photographic Supply Stores
5947	Gift, Novelty & Souvenir Shops
5948	Luggage & Leather Goods Stores
5949	Sewing, Needlework & Piece Goods
5961	Catalog & Mail-Order Houses
5962	Merchandising Machine Operators
5963	Direct Selling Establishments
5983	Fuel Oil Dealers
5984	Liquified Petroleum Gas Dealers
5989	Fuel Dealers, Nec.
5992	Florists
5993	Tobacco Stores & Stands
5994	News Dealers & Newsstands
5995	Optical Goods Stores
5999	Miscellaneous Retail Stores, Nec.

FINANCE, INSURANCE, AND REAL ESTATE

60   Depository Institutions

6011	Federal Reserve Banks
6019	Central Reserve Depository, Nec.
6021	National Commercial Banks
6022	State Commercial Banks
6029	Commercial Banks, Nec.
6035	Federal Savings Institutions
6036	Savings Institutions Except Federal
6061	Federal Credit Unions
6062	State Credit Unions
6081	Foreign Banks—Branches & Agencies
6082	Foreign Trade & International Banks
6091	Nondeposit Trust Facilities
6099	Functions Related to Deposit Banking

61   Nondepository Institutions

6111	Federal & Federally-Sponsored Credit
6141	Personal Credit Institutions
6153	Short-Term Business Credit
6159	Miscellaneous Business Credit Institutions
6162	Mortgage Bankers & Correspondents
6163	Loan Brokers

62   Security & Commodity Brokers

6211	Security Brokers & Dealers

6221	Commodity Contracts Brokers & Dealers
6231	Security & Commodity Exchanges
6282	Investment Advice
6289	Security & Commodity Services, Nec.

63   Insurance Carriers

6311	Life Insurance
6321	Accident & Health Insurance
6324	Hospital & Medical Service Plans
6331	Fire, Marine & Casualty Insurance
6351	Surety Insurance
6361	Title Insurance
6371	Pension, Health & Welfare Funds
6399	Insurance Carriers, Nec.

64   Insurance Agents, Brokers & Service

6411	Insurance Agents, Brokers & Service

65   Real Estate

6512	Nonresidential Building Operators
6513	Apartment Building Operators
6514	Dwelling Operators Except Apartments
6515	Mobile Home Site Operators
6517	Railroad Property Lessors
6519	Real Property Lessors, Nec.
6531	Real Estate Agents & Managers
6541	Title Abstract Offices
6552	Subdividers & Developers, Nec.
6553	Cemetery Subdividers & Developers

67   Holding & Other Investment Offices

6712	Bank Holding Companies
6719	Holding Companies, Nec.
6722	Management Investment—Open-End
6726	Investment Offices, Nec.
6732	Educational & Religious Trusts
6733	Trusts, Nec.
6792	Oil Royalty Traders
6794	Patent Owners & Lessors
6798	Real Estate Investment Trusts
6799	Investors, Nec.

SERVICES

70   Hotels & Other Lodging Places

7011	Hotels & Motels
7021	Rooming & Boarding Houses
7032	Sporting & Recreational Camps
7033	Trailer Parks & Campsites
7041	Membership-Basis Organization Hotels

72   Personal Services

7211	Power Laundries—Family & Commercial
7212	Garment Pressing & Cleaners' Agents
7213	Linen Supply
7215	Coin-Operated Laundries & Cleaning
7216	Dry Cleaning Plants Except Rug
7217	Carpet & Upholstery Cleaning
7218	Industrial Launderers
7219	Laundry & Garment Services, Nec.
7221	Photographic Studios—Portrait
7231	Beauty Shops
7241	Barber Shops
7251	Shoe Repair & Shoeshine Parlors
7261	Funeral Services & Crematories
7291	Tax Return Preparation Services
7299	Miscellaneous Personal Services, Nec.

73   Business Services

7311	Advertising Agencies
7312	Outdoor Advertising Services
7313	Radio, T.V. & Publisher Representatives
7319	Advertising, Nec.
7322	Adjustment & Collection Services
7323	Credit Reporting Services
7331	Direct Mail Advertising Services
7334	Photocopying & Duplicating Services
7335	Commercial Photography
7336	Commercial Art & Graphic Design
7338	Secretarial & Court Reporting
7342	Disinfecting & Pest Control Services
7349	Building Maintenance Services, Nec.
7352	Medical Equipment Rental
7353	Heavy Construction Equipment Rental
7359	Equipment Rental & Leasing, Nec.
7361	Employment Agencies
7363	Help Supply Services
7371	Computer Programming Services
7372	Prepackaged Software
7373	Computer Integrated Systems Design
7374	Data Processing & Preparation
7375	Information Retrieval Services
7376	Computer Facilities Management
7377	Computer Rental & Leasing
7378	Computer Maintenance & Repair
7379	Computer Related Services, Nec.
7381	Detective & Armored Car Services
7382	Security Systems Services
7383	News Syndicates
7384	Photofinishing Laboratories
7389	Business Services, Nec.

75   Automobile Repair, Services & Parking

7513	Truck Rental & Leasing Without Drivers
7514	Passenger Car Rental
7515	Passenger Car Leasing
7519	Utility Trailer Rental
7521	Automobile Parking
7532	Top & Body Repair & Paint Shops
7533	Automobile Exhaust System Repair Shops
7534	Tire Retreading & Repair Shops
7536	Automotive Glass Replacement Shops
7537	Automotive Transmission Repair Shops
7538	General Automotive Repair Shops
7539	Automotive Repair Shops, Nec.
7542	Car Washes
7549	Automotive Services, Nec.

76   Miscellaneous Repair Services

7622	Radio & T.V. Repair
7623	Refrigeration Services Repair
7629	Electrical Repair Shops, Nec.
7631	Watch, Clock & Jewelry Repair
7641	Reupholstery & Furniture Repair
7692	Welding Repair
7694	Armature Rewinding Shops
7699	Repair Services, Nec.

78   Motion Pictures

7812	Motion Picture & Video Production
7819	Services Allied to Motion Pictures
7822	Motion Picture & Tape Distribution
7829	Motion Picture Distribution Services
7832	Motion Picture Theaters Except Drive-In
7833	Drive-In Motion Picture Theaters
7841	Video Tape Rental

79   Amusement & Recreation Services

7911	Dance Studios, Schools & Halls
7922	Theatrical Producers & Services
7929	Entertainers & Entertainment Groups
7933	Bowling Centers
7941	Sports Clubs, Managers & Promoters
7948	Racing Including Track Operations
7991	Physical Fitness Facilities
7992	Public Golf Courses
7993	Coin-Operated Amusement Devices
7996	Amusement Parks
7997	Membership Sports & Recreation Clubs
7999	Amusement & Recreation, Nec.

80   Health Services

8011	Offices & Clinics of Medical Doctors
8021	Offices & Clinics of Dentists
8031	Offices of Osteopathic Physicians
8041	Offices & Clinics of Chiropractors
8042	Offices & Clinics of Optometrists
8043	Offices & Clinics of Podiatrists
8049	Offices of Health Practitioners, Nec.
8051	Skilled Nursing Care Facilities
8052	Intermediate Care Facilities
8059	Nursing & Personal Care, Nec.
8062	General Medical & Surgical Hospitals
8063	Psychiatric Hospitals
8069	Specialty Hospitals Except Psychiatric
8071	Medical Laboratories
8072	Dental Laboratories
8082	Home Health Care Services
8092	Kidney Dialysis Centers
8093	Specialty Outpatient Facilities, Nec.
8099	Health & Allied Services, Nec.

81   Legal Services

8111	Legal Services

82   Educational Services

8211	Elementary & Secondary Schools
8221	Colleges & Universities
8222	Junior Colleges
8231	Libraries
8243	Data Processing Schools
8244	Business & Secretarial Schools
8249	Vocational Schools, Nec.
8299	Schools & Educational Services, Nec.

83   Social Services

8322	Individual & Family Services
8331	Job Training & Related Services
8351	Child Day Care Services
8361	Residential Care
8399	Social Services, Nec.

84   Museums, Botanical & Zoological Gardens

8412	Museums & Art Galleries
8422	Botanical & Zoological Gardens

86   Membership Organizations

8611	Business Associations
8621	Professional Organizations
8631	Labor Organizations
8641	Civic & Social Associations
8651	Political Organizations
8661	Religious Organizations

8699	Membership Organizations, Nec.

87   Engineering & Management Services

8711	Engineering Services
8712	Architectural Services
8713	Surveying Services
8721	Accounting, Auditing & Bookkeeping
8731	Commercial Physical Research
8732	Commercial Nonphysical Research
8733	Noncommercial Research Organizations
8734	Testing Laboratories
8741	Management Services
8742	Management Consulting Services
8743	Public Relations Services
8744	Facilities Support Services
8748	Business Consulting Services, Nec.

88   Private Households

8811	Private Households

89   Services Not Elsewhere Classified

8999	Services, Nec.

Standard Industrial Classification (SIC) Index

This index is arranged numerically by four-digit SIC codes. Refer to the table preceding this index for an overview of two- and four-digit SIC codes.

General Index